RECOLLECTIONS OF A
SUSSEX PARSON

REV. EDWARD BOYS ELLMAN
1815 - 1906
RECTOR OF BERWICK, EAST SUSSEX

WITH A MEMOIR BY HIS DAUGHTER
MAUDE WALKER

COUNTRY BOOKS

Published by Country Books
Courtyard Cottage, Little Longstone, Bakewell, Derbyshire DE45 1NN
Te: 01629 640670
e-mail: dickrichardson@country-books.co.uk
www.countrybooks.biz

ISBN 978 1 898941 87 3

© 2004 Country Books
reprinted 2006, 2008, 2009, 2011

*This book was first published in 1912 by Messrs. Skeffington
and subsequently republished with a memoir by Maude Walker by
Combridges of Hove in 1925.*

ACKNOWLEDGEMENT
*I wish to record my thanks to the late Tony Wales for loaning me his copy of the
original book and the postcards of Berwick Church and Drusilla's Tea Cottage.*

A catalogue of titles published by Country Books is available at:
www.countrybooks.biz

Printed and bound in England by 4edge Ltd, Hockley, Essex.

CONTENTS

Short Memoir of the Rev. Edward Boys Ellman by his Daughter, Maude Walker

These selections from recollections of events and people long since passed away were written at different periods by my late Father, the Rev. Edward Boys Ellman, formerly Rector of Berwick, Sussex. I publish them in the hope that a truthful record of Church and country life generally in Sussex, as it was nearly a hundred years ago, will be of interest to the men and women of the present day.

Three months after the Battle of Waterloo, in the quiet little village of West Firle, four miles from the county town of Lewes, on September 7th, 1815, was born Edward Boys Ellman, fourth child and third son of John and Catherine Ellman.

His father, an old Winchester boy, was a county magistrate, gentleman farmer, and a Deputy-Lieutenant of his native county of Sussex.

The old family Bible records that Edward was baptised privately on September 10th, and received into the congregation of Firle Church on December 10th. He was a very delicate baby, but grew into a very quiet sweet-tempered boy. A very keen observer of men and things, he at a very early age took interest in, and remembered in after life, everything connected with the stirring events of the times.

As a proof of this memory – accurate to the smallest detail even – may be mentioned the following fact. Only a few days before his death, in February, 1906, on hearing a favourite clock outside his bedroom door strike midnight, he looked up at me with a smile and remarked, "Eighty-seven years ago tonight was the first time I remember hearing midnight strike. I woke up in the old Firle nursery and heard the nursemaid Philly read aloud to the nurse the account of King George the Third's death, which had taken place that day," and, continued he, "it was not only the same clock that struck midnight but the nursery fire played upon the brass of that same old chest of drawers that the fire is playing on now."

A few hours previously he had been talking over old memories of his childish days, describing the position of the various rooms of this Firle house that he had not entered for more than eighty-six years; recalled the names of the old servants, indoor and outdoor; the walks the nurses took the children; the various old village pensioners they were allowed to go and visit, etc.

It is difficult for us who live in this twentieth century to realise the surroundings of one born in a quiet country village almost a hundred years ago.

He was one of eight children. Money was never plentiful in his home, and when there was any to spare it seems to have been spent on political dinner parties. His father was an ardent politician and in constant touch with all the chief men of the day.

The years of my father's childhood were years of peace for Europe – peace won by the bravery and blood of British men on sea and land.

Waterloo was won. Europe was quiet after so many years of bloodshed, but it was a fearfully hard time for England. During the long war prices of everything had gone up terribly. The country was impoverished. Corn was at almost famine prices. Labour was so cheap and plentiful that even men in full and regular work could hardly support their wives and families upon the poorest of food, and often they starved to death. The disbanding of all the extra soldiers required for so many years during the war threw thousands of extra men upon the unskilled labour market. Men were starving, and this caused much crime which was harshly and cruelly dealt with. To save their children from starvation men stole sheep, field turnips, or anything eatable, and when caught were condemned to death or transportation for life.

The Rev. Edward Boys Ellman aged 88 years

My father's mother was very delicate, and her eight children came so rapidly (the first four within three years and nine months), and some were very delicate, so that she was often for weeks together unable to leave her room. So frequently was this the case, and the exertion of entertaining tired her so much, that she withdrew from almost all society, and my grandfather ended by giving only men's dinner parties to his political and other friends.

In spite of her ill-health she never neglected the religious education of her children, and my father has frequently told me that he could not remember the time when he did not stand up each Sunday with his elder brothers and sister and say the Catechism. Until he went to school she taught my father entirely. He was devoted to his mother, and from his earliest childhood did all he could to save her trouble. As quite a small boy of ten and eleven, during a long illness of her's, he regularly did the house-keeping for her, carrying the storeroom keys in his pocket, giving out the stores for the day with his orders during his breakfast-hour (no light job when he never knew what distinguished guest his father might not bring in to dinner), and everything had to be made and cooked at home.

His father thought him dull and stupid, and his mother, who deferred always to her husband's opinion, thought the same. Yet, curiously enough, it was always "Edward" whom they trusted if there was anything to be done, not either of his elder brothers nor elder sister. If his father was up in town on political business, it was my father who was sent to the bank to draw out money to pay the workpeople, and on one occasion, when some heavy bills had to be paid, he, a boy of eleven, had to draw out £100 in his dinner-time and go and pay the accounts. Neither of his parents seemed to realise that all this work that he cheerfully did hindered him in preparing his school-work, and forced him to work at night. He himself has often told me that not knowing the proper way to prepare his lessons he used to stupefy himself, going on hour after hour trying to commit them to memory, but so tired and worn out that he could hardly keep awake, yet striving his best to learn, and dreading the daily flogging.

Another reason why my grandfather thought my father dull, was that he was so quiet and apparently took little interest in any of the exciting topics of the day. So the young boy was unheeded as he sat in his quiet corner, while eager discussions as to future Bills, etc before Parliament went on. But in his old age he loved to relate how he had seen, and was allowed to be in the room and listen to the Duke of Wellington, Lord John Russell, Arthur Young, and others. He once told me that he was so anxious to hear them that he would take his preparation into a quiet corner of the drawing-room where he thought he would be unnoticed and that he used to get so interested that he had to cover his ears before he could give his mind to his work.

By nature a very quiet, shy boy, he ever shrank from putting himself forward, and would always keep in the background as much as possible. He hated a quarrel, and would never let himself be drawn into one. "It takes two to make a quarrel," he would say, and by gentle answers or silence try to soothe a person's anger. No persuasion could induce him to speak ill of a person even when he knew they were in the wrong. The very fact of anyone doing him an injury or speaking against those he loved, would make him especially gentle and eager to find excuses for them. The *more hurt* he was the *more cheerful* to go out of his way to do the one who had injured him a kindness. In fact he had his temper so well under control that I never in my life saw him give way to it, be cross or speak harshly of anyone. When I was a tiny child an old lady who had known him all his life, on seeing me and being told that I was "Edward's little girl," said: "Little girl, listen to me. I have known Edward Ellman all his life, and I never knew him cross, or say an unkind word or heard of his doing so. Remember that." The same old lady, Mrs. Ingram, then turned to my grandmother and reminded her of the only time my father had ever shown any symptom of vanity.

Some friends were calling just after they had moved to Southover and asked to see the children, who were brought down to the drawing-room. One lady (I think Miss Ingram said Mrs. Newton) remarked on the beauty of the four eldest, and said,

9

"Edward grew handsomer and handsomer every day." The visitors soon departed, and my grandmother went up to her bedroom, where she found her small four-year-old Edward standing on a chair in front of the mirror staring earnestly at his reflection and repeating, "Han-so-mar and han-so-mar every day." Evidently he worked off all his vanity on that occasion, for a man more indifferent to his personal looks could not be found.

When he was thirteen he went to Queen Elizabeth's College, Guernsey, where he remained three years, then followed the headmaster to Brighton. Afterwards he went to Wadham – getting through in as short a time as possible and taking a First Class in mathematics, and doing so well in classics that he was awarded a Fourth – he only having gone in for a Pass. He had offers of mathematical tutorships at Oxford, but he refused them, as he had a great desire to become a Naval Chaplain.

A characteristic incident took place the day the Honours list was out. My father knew it would not be out till after Hall, so directly that was over he walked down to the Schools and met Purday (the School man) coming down the steps with the Honours list in his hand ready to fix up – and my father knew he was a First Class man! He secured his testamur, and quickly walked away down to the river. He was soon seen and recognised, and cheer after cheer went up for the man who had brought honour for Wadham – and the shy man bolted!

As he had to make up terms before he could take his degree, he coached a little – he had been coaching during the last year – when he was up, but spent most of the time at Glynde.

At that time, though born only four miles off, he had never been to Berwick. He told me it was a lovely summer day when he first saw it. He rode over from Glynde and got his first view of the quiet peaceful village, nestling amongst the trees, before he came near. He rode slowly along, turned off the high road across the village green (now enclosed, and trees cut down), past the old forge and up the village street, getting his first sight of Berwick and its people. Past the old thatched cottages – only one remains – saw the men in their smocks, the women in their print sun bonnets, past the pond, the barn, the rick-stettle, gradually ascending and then turning off round the old coach road, and under the shade of the grand old elms, until he reached the church and rectory. He tied up his pony, and having got the key, walked up the churchyard steps and entered the church, with its high pews, tumble-down roof, and bricked-up windows, and general smell of mouldiness from the vaults. It was not an attractive picture – not the work amongst the sailors on the ocean for which he had hoped, but it seemed to him that day that the call had come, and that sometime or other it was to be obeyed. He thought then that he would have a short life, for he fully believed he could not live till thirty. Little did he think then that sixty-nine years later he would be carried up these same churchyard steps, to be laid to rest amongst the people he had learnt to love so well.

A few months later the old Rector of Berwick, who lived at Lewes, urged him to become Curate-in-charge of Berwick, and he consented. For over six years he remained there, "passing rich on forty pounds a year." To get money to support a small Dame's school, a clothing club, and to buy medicines for his flock, and also to eke out his tiny income (on which not only had he to live, but to keep a housekeeper), he grew vegetables in his spare time and sent them to the Lewes market.

At the end of that period he became Vicar of Wartling, a very large, scattered, neglected parish, near Herstmonceux. He found it in a deplorable state of neglect. Few of the people attended church – the vast majority of its scattered population had never been within its walls, and many in the distant parts of the parish had never even seen the outside of the church and only knew vaguely the direction in which it lay.

He got a parish map and began his pastoral visiting, and found it took him thirty-six days hard visiting to go to each cottage once, with the constant sick visiting. Many of the cottages were five miles – some seven miles – from the church. Now two good-sized districts have been taken off, so no house is more than three miles from a church. He established six Dame schools in various parts of the parish, each of which he visited twice weekly to give religious instruction; Bible classes, clothing and other clubs; and by degrees made his way with his parishioners. At first they had held their doors, and when he knocked and said he was their new Vicar, the doors would be held, and he would be asked what he wanted; could he not let poor people alone?

Fortunately for him, soon after he went to Wartling, there was a very great deal of illness – scarlet-fever, measles, smallpox, and low fever. The people could not afford a doctor, and the parish doctor did not trouble himself to look after them much. But their new Vicar had a knowledge of medicine, kept a big medicine chest, doctored them free, and won many hearts by so doing.

He caught low fever himself, but managed to drag himself to church, though for some weeks he had to give up all other work. He worked above his strength, and when, at the end of two years, Berwick became vacant, he was offered and accepted the Rectory.

As soon as his successor was appointed to Wartling, he was instituted as Rector of Berwick. The old Rectory was in a tumble-down state, and the heavy dilapidations enabled him to build a new Rectory on the old site.

He looked forward eagerly for his Rectory to be rebuilt, as he felt that as Rector of Berwick he could at last afford to marry. But before the Rectory was finished he was asked to give a home to his eldest sister and her three children, so he unselfishly put off trying to win the wife he had long wanted.

Time passed on; he quietly worked his parish and did any outside work that turned up, and then in 1853 his sister left him to make a home for herself. Little did she imagine that for years he had been wanting to marry.

In the latter part of his teens, his favourite aunt, Mrs. Barrow, wife of the Rev. Francis Barrow, Vicar of Holy Trinity, Margate, used, when visiting at Glynde, to talk much of her great friends the Plummers, who lived in Bedford Square, London, but who had built a seaside house at Margate, and particularly would she speak of a "Georgie" Plummer, who was tireless in all good works and devoted in nursing her invalid father. "She would be just the wife for you, Edward," she once said, little thinking that her description had made her quiet nephew fix upon the unknown one as his ideal of womanhood. Time passed on and he went to Oxford, and during one vacation went to stay two or three days at Margate with his uncle and aunt. He has often said how it poured with rain each day, and that though he often stood at the window and gazed across the road at "Fort Lodge," he was too shy to ask to be taken there to call, or even to ask for a description of "her" person.

Meanwhile the Ellmans and the Plummers had become great friends, the Miss Plummers came to stay at Glynde, and his sister Emily paid return visits to Margate, but, provokingly, Miss Georgina Plummer always went to Glynde when he was at Oxford. He got to know all her relations; she knew well all his brothers and sisters, and most of his numerous uncles and aunts. Several times they nearly met, but always just missed. So time went on till in 1844 he had a letter mentioning that the Miss Plummers were at Glynde. Now was the long wished for opportunity, but characteristically he did not start at once, but worked extra hard two days to get a few hours free, and then on "Old Hoper" rode from Wartling Vicarage the sixteen miles to Glynde. During the last winter of his life he loved to dwell on the meeting. Walking in unexpectedly he found his ideal alone in the drawing-room. For years he had pictured to himself a tall, handsome, commanding looking woman. For the moment he was taken back, for what he saw was a tiny, slight figure without the slightest pretension to good looks. But it was, as he said, not her looks that he cared about, it was the soul within. He returned to Wartling knowing and feeling that she was the one woman in the world for him, and that directly he could afford to marry he would try and win her for his helpmeet.

In August, 1853, she again came to stay at Glynde, and he resolved to seize the opportunity. He invited his favourite sister to bring her friend over to Berwick. It was a lovely hot August day, and he proposed to walk to show the guests the views. His sister became tired and sat on a stile, whilst the two others walked across a field. In a few quiet words he asked her to be his wife. She was so astonished and startled that she turned off the path and nearly walked into the river.

Never was there an engagement that gave greater satisfaction to both families. It was realised at once how suited the two were to each other.

On December 6th, 1853, Edward Boys Ellman and Georgina Frances Plummer became man and wife. He had waited twenty years for his ideal.

He always held very decided views as to clerical marriages. He said that a clergyman ought to be most particular not only to choose one who was fitted to be a real helpmeet to him, but in choosing to consider his work before his own private wishes. That if he did not meet with a woman whose heart was not in his work and who would not make a good clergyman's wife, then he ought not to marry. He said he had seen and known so many instances of harm done by parsons' wives. Many clergy worked hard and well till they married, and then grew careless and luke-warm. A priest's wife must be either a help or an hindrance in her husband's work. If he could not be certain she would be a help, then let him keep single. Many men have given up work to go where they get better education for their children, or because their wives wanted society; but that if a clergyman married the right woman, then his usefulness was much increased. He held that a woman of influence was needed in each parish, and that the tone of the parish was set by the parson's wife.

He certainly acted up to his convictions and chose one born to be a parson's wife. Her joy and delight was in helping others, and she never cared for pleasure, though she entered into and enjoyed innocent fun. From the first she threw herself into his work.

The things he lacked she supplied; he was too gentle and yielding, and could not scold properly; when he tried he always seemed to end by finding excuses for the wrong-doer. If his gentleness failed she could speak firmly and sharply, but the moment her words had the desired effect was as ready as he was to help the penitent. Small, quick, active, and decided, she was a great contrast to her husband.

They were a strangely undemonstrative couple, often during the first years of their married life, when alone, passing the whole evening without exchanging a single unnecessary word, he writing or reading, she reading or with her charity needlework. Neither cared for society, regarding it as almost waste of time.

During the first year of their marriage they built the school and school house. The site was given and as they thought it right to give the parishioners an opportunity of helping, he called a parish meeting of all the parishioners and told the people what he proposed. He asked the two farmers to assist by carting the materials wanted; this they did, and several of the poor people gave threepence and sixpence to the building fund, but of course almost all the money was found by the Rector and his wife.

Both wore alike in their devotion to all good works: unselfish and self-denying, both eager and willing to help everyone they could, whether within or without the parish. From the very first she insisted upon his giving up the teaching in the Sunday school to her, as she rightly considered that, suffering as much as he did with asthma, the Sunday services were quite enough for him to do. He yielded to her as to not teaching, contenting himself with opening the school and being present.

The site for the school was just at the end of the new road he had made, at the head of the village street, adjoining the Rectory grounds. No better site could have been found: the chief population lay at that time in Upper Berwick, and every house could be reached by a good road, and in the summer the Lower Berwick children had a short cut across the fields.

Until the new school was built, they both taught daily in the small Dame's school that he had started in 1838 in a cottage.

My father always held that it was most important for each parish priest to have a Church school under his own direction, and personally to teach there.

They led a very quiet life, welcoming any friends who looked in, but holding themselves rather aloof from the scattered society of the neighbourhood, and only calling at intervals upon their neighbours.

Their most intimate friends were the Coopers, of Wilmington Vicarage (a charming old couple; he had been a Cambridge don, and the families had been friends for three generations); the Hutchinsons, of Firle, also very old friends; the Fosters, of Selmeston; and the Vidals, of Chiddingly; all four parsons, who could and did appreciate chats and discussions on theological and intellectual subjects.

Another reason why they lived so quietly was that they were anxious to save every penny they could for church restoration and school building. If they had been willing to appeal to outsiders for help towards the church restoration, no doubt they could have done it sooner, but that was not their way.

In the summer of 1854 the school was finished and opened free of debt, and they began saving for the church.

The east chancel wall had at some time been moved inwards, shortening the chancel by several feet; the spire had been burnt down by lightning a hundred years before; the tower damaged; the north aisle had been entirely pulled down in the eighteenth century as it was then in a tumble-down state – the walls were in places almost tumbling down; the roof was literally a rabbit-warren and rotten; the earth came up nearly to the windows in the south aisle; the east window had been blocked up; the flooring was rotten, and altogether the church was in a shocking state.

He thought it right to do as he had done in building the school, give every parishioner an opportunity of giving towards the restoration, so he called a meeting for all the parishioners and laid his plan before them.

He himself would build a vestry, rebuild the spire, practically rebuild the chancel and beautify it, and would give various other things, besides subscribing to the nave and the roofs. His proposal was that the villagers should voluntarily levy a rate for two years upon every inhabitant, so that all would help according to their means, he himself to be rated with the others.

The rate was cheerfully agreed to without a dissentient voice; and moreover was paid regularly by Churchpeople and Dissenters alike for two years.

Of course it did not raise nearly enough money, but it was a great help. A few offerings came from relations and friends, and he made up the rest of the money. My mother sold her jewels to buy a chalice and paten, and to have the ancient church plate regilt. Together they designed and worked the carpet for the altar rails. On St. Thomas' Day, 1856, Church services were once more held in the old church now restored to its old beauty.

It was almost the first church restored in Sussex, and certainly the first in the neighbourhood, and with its new high chancel screen, its reredos, and low open seats excited attention in the neighbourhood.

He started chanting, which, in the fifties, was rarely, if ever, heard in the country churches, and not always in the towns. During the months the church was being restored, the services were held in the newly built school house, which the Bishop especially licensed for the purpose.

Berwick was made a model village. Each house was visited once a week, the school two or three times a day. Every child in the parish regularly attended Sunday and day school. If a child were absent a single time, it was looked up at once, consequently, in after years the inspectors were amazed at the regular attendances. Sick people were visited daily. Night schools for men and lads were held each winter at the Rectory.

As a former parishioner wrote on hearing of his death: "Dear Mr. Ellman – what will the people do without him! How well I remember, if one of us missed being at church, the next morning early we would hear his quick, firm footstep coming up to the door, and as the door was opened to him, hear, "I came to see why so and so was not in church."

He firmly believed that a house-going parson makes a church going people, and certainly the people did attend in those days. Strangers coming to the church almost invariably remarked on the size of the congregation compared with the number of the parishioners, the heartiness of the responses, the behaviour of the children, and the number of men and lads present.

Of course there were Dissenters in the parish, but these had always been Dissenters, or had come into the parish as Dissenters. Many Dissenters became Church people, but never once during his long life did one of his flock leave Church for Dissent.

The parishioners were scattered, and of course in winter the congregations were not as good as in summer.

For the two what may be called winter quarters, Michaelmas to Lady Day, the average morning attendance was eighty-one and the afternoon about ninety. In the summer six months the a.m. congregations averaged ninety-five, and in the p.m. 105. Of course several wet Sundays brought the average down, or the figures would have been higher – out of a population of 170. (At the time of his death the population was 156. The Communicants' roll that year was forty-five).

He was always one to make and keep careful records and statistics of everything. In his church attendance books, look back as many years as you will, you find the number recorded at each service, week-day as well as Sunday. Lists of Parishioners were kept both at Wartling and Berwick, and lines were marked off and marks put against each service. Then there were statistics of the numbers at each service, with the average struck off each quarter, of Sunday and Day school, Clothing Club, and everything else in the parish, so that at a glance he could tell what hour would best suit the majority for any extra service.

He had a mathematical mind, and was always most accurate in accounts and records. Ask what anything had cost, however many years back, he would turn to his right account book at once, and by a peculiar system every separate item could be identified at once.

One thing that he always took great interest in was the working of the Poor Law. He regularly attended the meetings of the Board of Guardians.

He always held decided opinions that the lazy, idle, and drunkards, who through their own faults had come to "the House," should be treated differently from those who by ill-health or misfortune had come to poverty. He was one of the first to suggest that it was bad for children to be brought up entirely in a Union, and advocated sending Union Children to the various parish schools to associate with children not brought up in an institution.

Then he was on the Turnpike Commission, as he thought good

roads did much to help the country and the people. He was on many committees, and always an active member of them.

He was slow of speech and always weighed well the effect of his words, and seemed to have the power of seeing both sides of the question in a dispute.

All his spare time he spent in reading, delighting in ecclesiastical history and law, old church customs, general history, archaeology, science, natural history, travel, etc.; and when very tired he would for rest work out a mathematical problem.

One Winter I remember he was very pleased because some of the night school men and lads learnt equations and logic; to the same lads he gave astronomy lessons.

It was a very peaceful, quiet household. He would still rise early, and get through two or three hours' work before the 8 o'clock breakfast.

Years rolled by without much change, when in November, 1884, after taking a funeral late on a wet afternoon, he was suddenly seized with paralysis. Fortunately, the seizure was a slight one, and he never quite lost consciousness, though it was some little while before the seizure yielded to remedies and he showed faint signs of life. In a few hours, however, he rallied but for some time he remained very weak and shaken, and realised that he must have clerical help for that winter at least; so the Rev. John Walker, who afterwards became his son-in-law, came to live at the Rectory for some months.

My mother had been devoted to him before, always making him her first object of attention, and nursing him untiringly during his frequent attacks of asthma, but now her devotion was redoubled. She could hardly bear him out of her sight, and never let him go anywhere alone, and if he were absent for more than a few minutes would make some excuse to follow him. Night and day her tender watchful care never ceased. By the springtime he was pretty well again, and thought that he could do the work single-handed, but when winter came on again he had to get Sunday help. In 1895 my mother was for a second time struck down with inflammation of the lungs, but got better again though remaining feeble. Still she would insist upon guarding and sparing him all she could, and he hardly realised how nearly he had lost her. Eighteen months later a message came from a dying woman entreating her presence. It was a wet evening but she went nevertheless, caught a chill, inflammation of the lungs set in for the third time, and that day week she died.

We tried to make him realise that there was no hope, but for a time he could not seem to understand, he was so firmly convinced that he would go first, but at last he saw our meaning. He administered her last Communion. Afterwards he tried to speak to her, but he was so deaf and her voice so low that they had to have an interpreter for their last farewell.

A few hours later he knelt by her bed as she passed away from this earth. When he saw that she had indeed left him, he rose from his knees and with outstretched hands blessed her and thanked God for such a wife, such a mother, and for the blessing she had been to the parish.

The next day was Sunday, and he looked very broken and shaken as he sat in his chancel stall, and no one doubted but that he would, as he fully expected, follow her very soon. The thought of the shortness of his time here made him, I think, bear up so calmly. He greatly desired to take the principal part of her funeral himself, as the last thing he could do for her. That seemed his one wish. That week, if asked anything, he said, "You must decide for me, I am past that." He was, as usual, so gentle and quiet, moved when spoken to, but was otherwise perfectly still. The funeral day came and was, fortunately, a bright, mild November day. He went to the special early service quiet and calm.

Later on, quietly and calmly leaning on his long staff, he took the funeral service. He joined in the hymns, and even at the grave managed with broken voice the Committal prayer, but when all was over and he had done what he could for her, he nearly broke down as he stood and gazed into that open grave that held all that remained of her whom he had loved from boyhood. It was a feeble, tottering old man that we half led, half carried down the churchyard steps straight into the Rectory. When after some minutes he revived, he murmured, "It won't be long," and asked for the church register to be brought him to sign. It was the calm resignation of God's will that bent but did not really break the old man.

Sunday came and he went to the early Celebration. Coming out of church he quietly said to the Curate, "I shall preach this morning." And preach he did.

It was Advent Sunday, and when the time came for the sermon his strength seemed to return, as with firm step he left the chancel and mounted the pulpit stairs. And his voice was clear and full, not like that of an old man of eighty-one, as with all his old power he preached on "Behold I come quickly, and My reward is with Me to give to every man according as his work shall be," pointing out how we must all strive to follow the Master's footsteps. Christ is a righteous judge, He knows not only our acts, but the motive by which we have acted. He presses upon his hearers, that now, now, was the time to prepare for eternity. Never shall I forget how, drawing himself up to his full height, with head erect and his clear tones distinct in every part of the church, he exclaimed, "Life here is accompanied with much and many trials, with pain and sorrow, but the life to come for those who have made proper use of their life here, is a life of perfect joy and happiness, freedom from all pain, anxiety, or sorrow. So that we should not grieve for those who have departed hence in God's faith and fear, for they have exchanged for a far better and happier state. Instead of grieving for such, it should be our earnest endeavour to follow them as they followed Christ, that when the time comes that our earthly labours be accomplished, we may be re-united with them in the grave and on the day of the general resurrection be raised with them to glory, to share with them in that happiness promised to all who love the Redeemer, whose hope in is Jesus. "Tis but a little while before Christ shall come again! Death is to the true Christian a peaceful sleep, from which they shall be raised by the trump of God unto a joyful and blessed resurrection!" And for two or three minutes until exhausted he continued urging that the present life was our time for preparation. His clear trumpet-like tones suddenly ceased and there was dead silence for a full minute, then leaning with both hands for support on the pulpit in a low, clear voice he said, "You may naturally perhaps think that I am going to speak of her whom it has pleased the Lord so recently to have removed from among us. I myself have lost a true and loving helpmeet. You all have lost a true and loving friend, who was ever ready to help in affliction, and to comfort in distress, who, like Dorcas, employed her time in making clothes for the poor, who, like our blessed Lord Himself went about doing good. I cannot trust myself to say more. Let it be our earnest endeavour to follow her as she ever humbly followed our blessed Lord. Let us trust in Him as she ever trusted. Let us so live, and watch and pray that whenever the call comes we may be found ready."

As the days passed on he found that the call he expected and so earnestly longed for was not to come yet.

He was as gentle and quiet as ever, but for a time it seemed as if he were utterly crushed by the heavy blow. He would get up early as usual, read the morning service to himself, and then sit in his study for hours, his head buried in his hands, answering in his gentle tones when spoken to, but otherwise still and silent. He wrote, and resigned all the outside work that he had hitherto kept on. He tried to force himself into his old work of school and parish, but his strength was not up to it; try as bravely as he would, he could not work as he had done heretofore.

When I paid him my daily visit, he would often sadly smile and say, "The parish is being neglected. I miss your mother; she was better than any Curate."

The school he managed to visit most days, but the pastoral visiting he could not often manage. He never went by train again, and it was only five or six times in the remaining nine years of his life that I could persuade him to drive outside the parish, and then only to short distances. When he did drive he would go to the more distant cottages.

I think he had never fully realised until my mother had left him the intensity of his love for her, and then it surprised even himself. They had ever been so undemonstrative, so quiet, so silent a couple that somehow he had never realised how strong was their mutual affection. For the last twelve years of her life he had especially leant upon her, at first imperceptibly, even to himself. They were so perfectly one, and she being true wife, true woman, had loved it to be so, to merge herself in him. Ever after her death he had the feeling of incompleteness. He loved to talk of her, and daily, when pretty well, would mount the churchyard steps and go and stand by her grave. Sometimes, when he felt especially lonely, he would go two or three times in the day. But he always tried to make the best of his loneliness. "I don't feel loneliness as much as most people would, you know; I was a bachelor so many years that I am used to being alone. It is not so hard for me," he would say. Still, in spite of all, I used to notice that whenever the weather was fine he would be standing in the churchyard leaning on his long staff, watching down the valley to catch the first distant glimpse of me as I came for my daily visit, and if I was a few minutes later than usual he would come beyond the churchyard so as to see a little further. And he always eagerly laid aside whatever he was doing to tell me any little thing about the parish, to discuss letters he had received, or to talk to his little grandchild.

After my mother's death, her favourite spaniel, "Dash," devoted herself to her master, and followed him about like his shadow. When he went down to the school, or into any cottage, "Dash' would go too, and directly he sat down flop she would go on the floor, ready the instant he rose to rise too. At night she would follow him upstairs and lie under his bed, and in the daytime under his chair or sofa. He was always pleased when former parishioners or their descendants came to see him, and loved talking over old days, remembering perfectly and asking by name after the various members of their families.

Time passed on and the patient, resigned look on his face seemed to deepen and he grew more and more feeble, and it was with greater difficulty that he could go down to school or village, and he confessed that he longed for one of his children to come and live with him. He was anxious, too, about the parish, the congregations had much fallen off, and he thought the people

23

neglected, so he wished to have either his son or son-in-law as Curate.

His son did not wish to come to so small a parish, so his son-in-law consented to throw up the Rectory of Litlington and to come to him. But the Bishop and Archdeacon both advised that Mr. Walker should not resign Litlington, and proposed that he should put a Curate in Litlington Rectory, keeping the oversight himself, and reside at Berwick for as long as my father should live.

And on October 5th, 1899, he quite brightened up as he welcomed us, saying merrily to his little grandchild, who arrived carrying her cat in her arms, "Plenty of room in the Rectory for pussy, too," making room as he spoke for the cat on the sofa beside him; which speech the cat evidently understood, for without a moment's hesitation she jumped out of her mistress's arms, rushed passed the dog and cuddled down happily beside him and went to sleep in the strange room, after the way of all animals that came near him.

All that autumn he seemed better and brighter, and then in December he became very ill with his old enemy asthma. Cardiac dropsy set in, and for weeks the doctors thought each hour must be his last. He himself would gasp, "Can't last – the death struggle." He was always so patient, never murmuring, even when in acute pain. When he could speak, or was the least bit easier he was anxious for Celebrations, or would say, "I don't like being such a trouble; do go and take rest"; or, "Don't overdo yourself," so ever anxious was he for others.

When unconscious he was continually going over the Church Services, and his words and thoughts were constantly of his people. Sometimes he would be praying, at others preaching, but always he imagined himself to be carrying out his priestly office. He would fumble with the bedclothes, turning over the leaves as he thought, here and there the words being distinct, though for minutes at a time coming only as indistinct mutterings. Sometimes he would imagine himself to be translating some Hebrew passage (he had just completed a translation of the Bible, as he was not satisfied wholly with the Revised Edition); sometimes he seemed

24

teaching in the school: a confused jumble of collects, texts, and hymns, never anything else.

Somehow he struggled through, and then came a few days of semi-consciousness, until one day in February he learnt, to his astonishment, that it was no longer December. Afterwards, those weeks of pain ever remained a blank in his memory. One curious fact about his illness was, that previously for some years he had been very deaf, and had also had a peculiar pulse. The pulse entirely altered during his illness, and when he was thought by the doctors to be dying, his hearing became acute, and he heard the slightest sound. Even when he recovered, his deafness seemed gone for a time, and he only gradually became deaf again.

He rose up from the long illness much bent, and ever afterwards his legs remained very weak, so that he was never able to get into the pulpit again, but instead used to preach sitting in the chancel doorway. At last came the Sunday when he was helped into church, and returned thanks for being raised up again to work amongst his people. By degrees he became stronger and took the services again. But he could no longer study Hebrew or work out mathematical problems which he formerly delighted in, and for the first time since early boyhood, he was persuaded to take up lighter reading. When his eyes grew weary in the evening, he played whist or patience, and sometimes netted string handbags to give to charity sales.

He had a great desire to build a Mission Church for the distant part of the parish, as he thought that eventually a population would spring up to the north of the station. But difficulties arose, and he was strongly advised not to build on glebe land, and as Lord Gage, who owned the property round the station, assured him no more houses would be built, he gave up his cherished scheme.

Two more quiet years passed, and then his son-in-law had a long illness and died, and he had to look out for fresh clerical help. He talked of resigning, and said he would if best for the parish; but we all knew it would kill him to leave Berwick, and he himself confessed that he wanted to die in his own home. And as we told him, his very presence amongst the people whom he had loved and worked among so many years, had its influence. In no other parish around was the relationship between Rector and people exactly the same as it was in Berwick. They knew that he loved them, and had their highest interests at heart, whether he could go in and out of their houses or not.

The last death-bed he attended was that of his old servant, Richard Bean, who had been with him forty-three years.

A happy arrangement was in the end arrived at, a neighbouring Vicar taking the week-day work, and the Sunday duty being taken by an Eastbourne cleric; he himself continuing to supervise and to take his full share of the services whenever he possibly could.

It was very rarely that he could then get down the village himself, but he was always ready to see the parishioners.

In the last three years of his life he gradually grew less and less reserved, and to those he loved he would reveal himself more than ever before.

From things he said then, there is little doubt but that he was much influenced by the Oxford Movement, and that if he had been in a larger, or in a town parish, he would have been willing to have had a more elaborate service. But he thought extremes not acceptable or suited to his people, and ever held that though a thing might be lawful it was not always expedient, and that if by a non-essential you placed a stumbling block in any person's way, then you must consider the relative values. He ever pushed onward, but was most careful to go no further than he considered the Rubrics allowed.

The things he considered essential nothing could turn him from, but many things so regarded as non-essentials, and he considered that men, nowadays, sometimes aped Rome and went too far. He had a horror of extremes, and always stuck up for Prayer Book teaching. Most wide and charitable in his views, he condemned no man because he could not agree with him. He himself stated the truth plainly and clearly, and tried to lead (not drive) by his life and example.

He was a Conservative, but never came forward in politics, as he considered that a priest lost his in influence if he was looked upon as a politician, and that he had better leave politics alone unless they interfered with any Church question. Then Church before everything. He keenly felt all such Acts as the Education Bill, Deceased Wife's Sister, P.W.R.A., Church Discipline, etc. When, some years ago, a divorced woman wanted to be married by licence or banns in Berwick Church, he refused to allow it. He told her he could not refuse to put up her banns for the first time but that immediately after publishing them, he should forbid them himself, publicly stating his reason for doing so, and that if she tried to be married by licence he should lock up the church, keep the key in his pocket, only admitting people at service time; that he was fully determined to go to prison sooner than yield and lend his church for the marriage ceremony.

His was a very gradual decline to dissolution. Each summer he seemed better, but fell back again when the winter came, and after every attack of illness he seemed a little weaker. Sometimes his hands would be so swollen and feeble from heart weakness, that he could not write, and hardly use them at all. Then came the last few months. He was ninety on September the 7th, and was much pleased with the heaps of flowers that kept on arriving all the morning, till the room he was sitting in seemed nearly full of them. He liked to see and thank each parishioner himself, and inspected the bunches with great interest, picking out some for the altar and sending some to the churchyard. He made a great effort to get down to the school once more, and managed to walk the three hundred yards with frequent rests, but was more than half an hour in returning, sitting down five or six times on a chair we carried for him.

A week or two later he once more managed for the last time to go round the church and visit his wife's grave, but after that the church door was the farthest walk. Leaning heavily on an arm, and with the aid of his long staff, he would painfully and slowly go up the churchyard steps or sit out in the garden.

The lovely old Rectory garden, full of old trees, was a never ending delight to him. He had planned the borders and planted the shrubbery to give the idea of space and of entering a wood. When too tired and feeble to move about, he loved to sit and gaze, watching the birds, with dog and cat sitting close beside him. Sometimes he would have a visit from the old ponies, who that autumn often managed to undo their field gate, and getting into the garden, would seek him out, going away quite contented when he had patted and spoken to them.

When he sat out in the garden none of the birds were afraid of him – rooks, jackdaws, starlings, robins, thrushes, finches, black-birds wagtails, swallows, sparrows, were all willing to feed on the lawn, and regarded him as their friend. He knew each one apart, and could see differences in them that no one else could see. He would never allow the birds to be disturbed. The rooks knew that they were protected, hence they would feed happily on the lawn, and even come on the window sills or in the porch to be fed. They so loved the Rectory grounds that they built in every available tree; when they had used up the old elms they built in firs, in an acacia, even in a high apple tree, sooner than leave the premises. Their friendly "caw-caw" was heard from morning till night. He loved to watch them building their nests, and was always the first to notice if another nest was begun in another tree, or how far forward the building of any nests were. He often used to say that farmers did not understand the good rooks did them, the vast amount of insects and worms that they destroyed. "People," he would say, "only realised the mischief the rooks did when seeds were first sown, by pulling up the young wheat to get at the grub that is at the root; if they were for a short time frightened off the wheat, the amount of good they do at other seasons would more than pay the expense of keeping them off at sowing time." He always took great interest in natural history, and loved to watch birds, animals, and insects.

He often talked of the peacefulness of his surroundings, and said that he could not understand men in their old age leaving their homes, unless it were better for the parish. "Some people would say I ought to resign," he said, and added, "If I were certain my only son would succeed me, I would, otherwise I think it for the best interests of my people not to do so. I hope they will be properly looked after when I am gone."

28

The winter wore on, and he could often only get to church once each Sunday, but he loved to take part in the service, and always read the prayers or preached.

As in former years, during long sleepless nights when he could not rest for coughing and breathlessness, he would spend the time thinking out his sermons; so now his thoughts were with his parish. Several times he said, "I can't think clearly; my brain seems confused; I forget things." But he did not forget, he only occasionally would get confused over a name. Otherwise his memory was wonderful. He had ever been so methodical and exact in his thoughts that the clearness of thought in former times helped him in his old age.

He was often too weary and exhausted through pain and coughing to do anything. He would half sit, half lie on his sofa, leaning forward, his arms crossed on the table in front of him, and his head on his hands – the only attitude at times in which he could breathe without constant choking. He was always gentle and never complaining, always eager to help or plan for others. No tale of real distress ever came in vain to him. He would investigate, and then help in any way he could. When apparently doing nothing he would often be thinking out cases, and ways and means to help.

Owing to his heart and asthma he could never lie down, and what rest he got was sitting up, supported by pillows, in bed, leaning forward, his head on his hands; so that his back was always aching, and his once tall, erect figure very much bent. If asked whether he was in much pain, he would answer cheerfully "Oh, it will be better by-and-by; I am very lazy."

As he grew daily weaker and less and less able to read or write more than a few minutes at a time, he talked much of old memories and the future of the parish. "Whoever comes after me will make great changes, but he can't love my people more than I have loved them," he several times said.

He would talk over the parishioners individually, rejoicing over one, grieving over another, and especially worrying when any did not come regularly to the Celebrations. He often said, "My work here is done; I can do no more, but I know I must pray for patience to await God's time," or "I feel and know that my work is done; God is keeping me here, and I feel useless; I don't want to be presumptuous, but I can't help wondering why He is keeping me here when I can't work any more."

The mission services that he had so long wanted in the distant part of the parish, were by his wish started that last autumn, the difficulty of a big enough room being overcome by the station master most kindly offering the use of one of the platform sheds between train times. With some benches, a paraffin stove, harmonium, and lamps and big curtains, it was easily fitted up. The services were to be in the evening, and he was very eager about them. He sent messages and wrote to every house in the parish urging people to go, and begging all to pray for blessings on the services. He preached about the mission, and said, "I shall be with you in spirit," and had the mission hymns practised regularly in his presence at the Rectory by a band of lads and girls, who were going to lead the singing at the mission services, and who used to come in directly after afternoon service for the practices.

And how eager he was to hear about the service on my return from the first Wednesday evening. Every little detail was thoroughly gone into, who was present, had this or that person, whom he had especially wanted to get hold of as they did not come to church, gone. And he would recur to the subject again and again. And each Wednesday his interest was as keen as ever. He frequently spoke of the mission services as preparing the way for future mission work under the next Rector.

All the winter he kept saying, "My time here is very short, it can't be much longer; I am getting weaker."

It was a great exertion for him to go to church, but he loved to go, and even when some Sundays he could only sit in his chancel stall, he went; but he loved most to celebrate.

He was so tottering that we dreaded his celebrating, fearing that he might be seized with heart failure whilst so doing, but he used to pray for strength. After each celebration he was utterly done up, and when he got indoors would sink down upon the sofa in a sort of collapse.

He celebrated for the last time on January 14th. It was a surprise to everyone, for he had almost promised not to do so. He was so very weak that we begged of him to stay at home, but it was such a denial to him to stay away from God's House, that when he pleaded, "Let me go while I can," opposition was withdrawn.

He could not go again in the afternoon, but lay on the sofa, utterly exhausted, half dozing, never moving. All the week he was worse, but the next Sunday he so longed to go again that we helped him into church, and he sat in his stall and gave the blessing.

All that winter his legs had been swelling again with dropsy, and by this time he could hardly stand alone. He never left the Rectory again, though the next Sunday he asked to be taken into church, but when the men came to carry him to church in his chair, he felt he could not go. The water got worse and worse, and spread to his body. Each morning he was helped downstairs, and each night half carried up again.

Those last few weeks he talked much and told of early memories, of his hopes and fears, of days and people long since passed away. As he said on February 17th, "I have never talked about myself so much, not even to your mother. I have told you more of my thoughts than I ever told anyone. I can do nothing, so I sit here and think."

The last time he sat in the garden he was sitting on his favourite seat under the verandah, well wrapped up in his big cloak and a rug round his knees. He was very exhausted with the effort of moving, and was leaning forward, his head on his hands. The dog and cat were nestled against his feet, and two small kittens had climbed up and sat one on each shoulder, when the old ponies got out of their field and came marching up looking for him. I patted and petted them, but he took no notice. They would not go away but poked their faces close to his and gazed sadly at him, until he patted them. Then they went quietly back to their field just as if they knew it was good-bye for them.

Animals and children were always attracted to him, something in his gentleness made them know they could trust him. Dogs and cats would bring their young ones, deposit them beside him, and go away happily. Especially that last winter the kittens might be taken out, shut up in the stable or knife-house, but the dog would be on the watch, and no sooner was a door or window opened, than she would rush out and bring in a kitten (generally followed by the cat with another kitten) and deposit them some where about him. When the kittens were very small the would bury them one by one in my father's coat-tails, as he half lay, half sat on the sofa, poking the coat over them, in the way dogs bury their bones. The dog once tried to put a kitten in his pocket, but the kitten objected. Sometimes the dog and cat would each strive to be the one nearest their master, and get on top of one another in their efforts.

He used those last days to talk much of his childhood, of his school troubles, his Oxford life, the people he had met; but he especially loved to talk of my mother – his more than twenty years of waiting for her, the one love of his life, and of the great loss she had been to him and the parish.

He kept baying, "I shall not see the spring," and, "I don't think it possible I shall be here for Lent," and then in broken words he would speak of his anxiety for the parish, of his longing to know that there would be no falling off, but rather an awakening of spiritual life. He said once, "My great failing has been that I have been too easy. It has always been very difficult for me to find fault. I tried to draw my people by showing interest in themselves and their families, and now that I cannot go amongst them they do not come to church as they did."

In the middle of February, when the Lenten services were being settled, he said to the clergyman who was to take them, "You must make what arrangements you think best," and always added, "I shall not be here when Lent comes."

His legs gave him great pain from the huge swelling, and he suffered much from shortness of breath.

Yielding to his son's wish, he let the doctor call in a second opinion, but characteristically fearing to hurt the doctor's feelings, impressed upon us that we must tell the doctor that it was not that we did not trust him, and himself told him so. So the doctors had a consultation on the 17th. He greeted them with, "You have come to see an old man, utterly worn out and done for; you can't cure asthma of seventy years' standing."

The result of the consultation was that the doctors spoke hopefully; with the warm weather they hoped he would gain strength, but he must be content to remain either upstairs or downstairs, as however much he was helped the exertion was too great for his heart, and he must be tapped the next day. He merely smiled and said to the doctors, "I am in your hands, I will submit to anything you think right, but, remember, you can't cure me and make me young again, I am quite worn out." On the doctor repeating that he would get better, he shook his head, "You think so; I don't."

It was arranged that the tapping should take place next day, Sunday. He insisted upon my leaving him for Sunday school and morning service, and sat on the sofa with Bible, Prayer Book, and hymn book, going through the service by degrees, as he, was too weak to read it all at once. In the middle of the day the doctor came. He bore the pain bravely, and afterwards seemed much relieved. Again he insisted upon my leaving him for school and church under the charge of his grandchild, saying, "You know I can't run away, as I can't move off the sofa without you. I think I shall sleep." Service over, by his wish the practising of the hymns for the mission service took place as usual in his presence in the Rectory dining-room, where he was. He could not join in the hymns, but when the practice was over he held up his hand for a moment to attract attention, then spoke feebly a few words to all present in a hardly audible voice on the subject of the mission. Little did the younger ones present realise that it was the last time he would speak to them.

After they were gone he again spoke of the mission, and of his earnest prayers for good to result, but his voice was so feeble that it was difficult to make out what he said, and he soon closed his eyes and dozed off. In the evening he wag too exhausted to speak a word more than absolutely necessary.

As we helped him upstairs to bed – he could only get up two or three steps at a time – he said to me as the maid and I were supporting and half lifting him from step to step, "The last time you will help me upstairs." The next morning he was very restless and had only slept a few minutes all night, and at half past five was eager to get downstairs. It was always a long business dressing him as his breath was so bad, but he got down soon after six. As he left his bedroom he gave a look round, saying he thought he should have died in that room. (His wife had died there.)

As usual that day, when able he spoke of his parish and his people. Once he said when preparing for bed, "I don't know why, but I can't say that I understand people fearing death. I have never feared it, but I pray to be patient waiting for God's call. I sometimes think I have much to be thankful for in having led this quiet life. I have not had the temptations other men have had. Looking back I can't remember ever having wilfully committed sin. My great desire was always to do my duty. No, I cannot have had the temptations of other men."

That night he slept in the study, and urged me to leave him, saying he should not want anything more than he had on his table and that it was better for me to go to bed. To please him I did not sit up, but only came in and out every hour. In the morning he seemed better, and said he had had the best night he had had for weeks. Still he was eager to get up, and by six I had helped him, partly dressed, into the dining-room where he sat all day, very weak, but trying to read at intervals the Daily Service.

Tuesday night he seemed very restless, and did not seem to me to sleep at all. Still he wished to go into the other room. He tried to read the Morning Service, but though he had the Prayer Book open before him all day, he could not read it, and seemed very drowsy. Still the doctor was hopeful. He hardly spoke all day – except once or twice to say he wished help to be sent to two different people. "See to it," he said. As it drew near the time of the mission service he looked up and said, "You will be late." I said I was not going. "But I can be left." A few minutes passed. "You are not ready – you will be late" (he hated unpunctuality). I told him I did not think him well enough to leave. "But I want you to go – you **must** go. There is no one else to take the harmonium, and it is the last mission service. I shall be all right – you can put everything I want by me."

He was so wishful about it that he had to be left. I hurried back as quickly as possible, and he said he had had very sharp pain, but that it had passed off. Eagerly he enquired about the service. We got him to bed, and used medicines, and the pain went away, as he would not let the doctor be sent for. However, the pain came on intensely just before 10.30, and the doctor came and stayed till 2, when the pain seemed to go, and the patient sank into a doze. At 5 he was most anxious to get up and go into the dining-room, but was persuaded to stay until nearly 7. Then, wrapped in his dressing-gown, he was half carried in. Warm milk with brandy was held to his lips, but he pushed it away. "No – prayers first," and, faint as he was, would touch nothing. Five minutes later, after family prayers he could hardly touch it.

The doctor came, and though he did not consider him much worse, consented to telegraph for my brother, who arrived in the middle of the day. At intervals all day the acute pain came on, and he hardly spoke or moved, merely swallowing what we put between his lips. The doctor came again and thought him weaker, and we wished to get him into bed, thinking he would be more comfortable. But he said, "Prefer here," and then later said he would remain up till after prayers. So we had family prayers at 7 and then asked him to go to bed. He shook his head.

At a quarter past 8 he tried to raise his head, looked up smiling, and said, "Ready now," and moved as if trying to rise.

We thought he meant for bed, and lifting him on to the sofa, pushed that into the next room, and lifted him on to the bed. He was so exhausted that I thought I would wait a few minutes before making him comfortable in bed and he swallowed some brandy mechanically. At 8.25 we saw that he was quite unconscious. At first we thought him gone, no heart beat, no breath, and all power of swallowing seemed gone. But after the strongest heart stimulants had been used, of which some must have gone down, there seemed at intervals a faint fluttering of the heart. At 10.30, the doctor arriving, said he had just gone.

And so his gentle loving spirit returned to the God who gave it. Doubtless he heard the summons for which he had been longing for years; he had with patience waited for it, and when the call came for which he was ready and waiting, gladly answered, "Ready now!" in his last fully conscious moment ere he passed into the Valley of the Shadow of Death. And so he fell asleep.

He had, as he expected, gone away before Lent.

On Thursday, March 1st, he was carried to his last resting-place. It was a pouring wet day, and the rain came down in torrents as the long string of clergy filed out of the Rectory in front of the coffin, borne on the shoulders of communicants who had been boys in his Sunday school, up those churchyard steps into the church he loved so well, which on every side showed marks of his work.

And for the last time, as we chanted his Nunc Dimittis, the plain elm coffin, with its long wooden cross, that contained all that could die of Edward Boys Ellman, was borne out of the church and laid to rest beneath the old chestnut trees in the churchyard where he had himself committed to the earth the bodies of so many of his flock.

Maude Walker

BIRTH AND PARENTAGE

Having been repeatedly asked to put on record anecdotes that I have heard in my earlier days, or facts of which I have myself been witness, I have attempted to make a beginning, and in so doing hope that I may be preserved from showing any unkind feeling.

Having at no period of my life mixed much in society, and having been more of a listener than a talker when I have been with others, what I have heard and seen has made a more lasting impression on my memory than is generally the case. These recollections now (written August, 1889) extend over seventy years; and during those seventy years the alterations that have occurred are so great, that I doubt whether any like period of the world's history can show as great changes.

I have seldom read works of fiction; but on meeting with a work professing to describe some event of years long past, and the manners and customs of the times, I have rarely found one which does not commit the writer by bringing into the description something which could not have happened till a much later period, I must confess that in reading such a work I have read as a critic, rather than for mere enjoyment. It has ever been my desire to profit and gain knowledge by what I have read.

I was born at Firle, and there resided for the first four years of my life, in the house opposite the pathway, made a few years since, direct to the west door of the church. It is a curious fact that during my long life I have always lived close to the church without any other residence intervening.

In our house at Firle (but before my birth) workmen, in repairing the roof, discovered a hiding-place formed of rushes, and

In Firle Village

within the same tiny room were two common hen's eggs, supposed to have been deposited there towards the support of some person concealed therein. I have mentioned this in S.A.C. vol. xix. (Sussex Archaelogical Collections), page 210, and there suggested that the person concealed was the Marquis of Ormond, and the house the residence of Sackville Graves Esq. I recollect perfectly the way by which one might ascend into the roof. Leading out of the room which we occupied as our nursery there was a closet, in which we kept our play things. There was a kind of shelf in this closet, and the partition at the shelf end was not carried up beyond the shelf, it being open (I believe) to the space around the chimney. I distinctly remember many things that happened at Firle the summer before I was four. How the nurses took us into a hayfield, and how hard I worked at making little rows of hay, and how indignant I felt because the haymakers pushed into a heap all the little rows I had made.

One Sunday a stranger occupied the pulpit at Firle Church, and when he ascended the huge three-decker and emerged to view clad in a black gown, instead of the white surplice to which I had been accustomed, I called out in astonishment to my mother, "Look at that black man!" As a punishment for speaking in church I was kept at home for several Sundays.

I used to like to watch the men making the new turnpike road, and I fancy our nurses also must have been rather fond of seeing the men at work. But their favourite walk was to take us into the park; every day we went there and met the Gage's nurses, and the nurses gossipped while we children all played together. As our

Glynde village

39

head nurse soon after married one of Lord Gage's grooms I have since thought that he was also an attraction for her.

My grandfather lived at Glynde, in the house close to Glynde Place; in fact, part of what is now the Glynde Park was then the pleasure grounds attached to his house, and it was a great delight to us children when the nurses took us to see him. There were no perambulators then, but we had what was called a "child's carriage" – a sort of big basket on wheels – in which two children could sit, and which was drawn by a handle in front. An elder cousin, who was playing with us once in turning a corner in the garden, upset this child's carriage and I was thrown out so violently that the result was a deep cut on my eyebrows, the mark of which I shall never lose. About this time my second sister, Emily, was born, and I was sent to stay at Glynde to be out of the way for two or three days. On my return home Dr. Raynes, the vicar, came to baptize Emily privately. While the service was going on I was industriously occupied in sewing some bits of stuff on to my mother's bedroom curtains, and had fastened two or three "rosettes," as I called them, before I was stopped.

My father was at this time very much from home. I have learnt since that he was much up in London on political business, and also busy about various county matters. Both my grandfather, John Ellman, of Glynde, and my father, John Ellman, the younger, were Deputy Lieutenants of the county, and in those times this involved a good deal of work. In 1809, when the Militia was formed, every man was summoned to attend at the various towns to ballot. My father's was one of the names drawn. But instead of serving as a private, the Lord-Lieutenant offered him a commission, and after serving a short time as lieutenant, he was promoted to a captaincy. The headquarters of the regiment being at that time in Lewes, he had frequent opportunities of going backwards and forwards to Glynde. The following year, 1810, the battalion to which he belonged was sent to Brighton, an inconvenient distance, both from Glynde (where his services to his father were a great help), and also from Firle, where he was to enter upon a farm from Michaelmas, 1810, previous to his marriage, which was to take

John Ellman of Glynde 1753-1832.
Edward's grandfather, who perfected the Southdown sheep breed.

A Southdown ram in the time of John Ellman of Glynde.

place in 1811. This led him to try and effect an exchange into another battalion, which was stationed at Lewes, commanded by Colonel Thomas. This battalion was short of officers and Colonel Thomas and Lord Chichester (I cannot quite understand Lord Chichester's position with regard to the battalion) were anxious he should, providing that Colonel Graham, under whom my father was serving, consented. But Colonel Graham withheld his consent, whereupon my father wrote to Colonel Graham, requesting him to forward his application to resign his commission. It afterwards appeared that in so doing Colonel Graham appended a request to the Lord-Lieutenant, the Duke of Norfolk, that he would not accept the resignation. The Duke was at that time in the West of England, and being uncertain how he ought to act, deferred writing to my father. In the meantime the day appointed for the assembling of the Militia at Brighton arrived, and my father did not attend, expecting every day to receive the formal document accepting his resignation of his commission. This led to his being tried by court-martial, and the sentence was that he should be dismissed the service and be incapable of serving His Majesty for the future. He was detained at Brighton, where the court-martial was held, for some time, waiting for the confirmation of the sentence, owing to the King's mental ailment and the delay in appointing the Prince of Wales Regent, who at last confirmed the first part of the sentence but not the latter. *

A few years later, at the first vacancy, the Lord Lieutenant appointed my father Deputy-Lieutenant (my grandfather was already one), and in this capacity, when the active duties of the Militia were revived many years since, my father, as Deputy-Lieutenant, with Sir Henry Shiffner, was especially selected by the Lord-Lieutenant (the Duke of Richmond) to assist him in making the requisite preparations and regulations, the Duke at the time being fully cognisant of the fact of the court-martial trial and his mind refreshed on the subject by a printed copy of the trial that my father insisted on giving him.

My father was intended for a barrister, and my grandfather meant him to go on from Winchester to Oxford. For some reason my father suddenly took a dislike to the law and persuaded his father to promise that when he became captain of the school he might leave. He was a clever boy and had a splendid memory, and by hard work became head of Winchester before his sixteenth birthday, and immediately claimed his father's rash promise. Having made the promise, his father reluctantly yielded, though the headmaster pointed out what a pity it was for the boy to throw up all his prospects and not to go on to the University. In my father's time at Winchester places were won and rapid advance

* I have several letters in my possession written to my great-grandfather directly after the court-martial (as well as the printed court-martial trial) by the Prince Regent, Duke of Sussex, Earl of Egremont, Earl of Chichester, and others, condemning the court-martial and Colonel Graham's behaviour. The Duke of Sussex was especially warm in his expressions of sympathy, and concluded his long letter by stating that it was well-known how energetic both the father and son had been in raising Militia in Sussex, and that he utterly condemned the verdict. –

was made by the boys who took up the greatest number of lines. On one occasion he took up and repeated 1,200 lines of Virgil (I think). The head form then consulted and decided that no boy was to take up more than six hundred lines at a time.

My mother was a Boys of Betshanger in Kent. After her marriage she was frequently in delicate health, and sometimes had to keep her room for weeks at a time. But in spite of her ill-health I cannot remember her ever neglecting our religious education.

EARLY SCHOOL LIFE

At Michaelmas, 1819, my father gave up the "Home Farm" at Firle, retaining farms at Beddingham and Rype, and we moved to the Manor, Southover – a suburb of Lewes – so that my elder brothers could be day boys at the Grammar School. The new turn-pike road was then in process of making, and as soon as it was completed my father was able to ride over to Beddingham daily to attend to his farming concerns. This he constantly did, returning at 5 or 6 p.m., or later, to dinner and then, after reading his paper or magazine, took a nap on the sofa. Hence I always considered that my mother had much more to do in forming my character than he had, as I saw so little of him.

On Sundays my father always used to attend the service at Beddingham Church, which enabled him to see that his workmen also attended; and as soon as I was old enough I generally used to accompany him, walking in the summer, but in the winter frequently going over in the old hooded gig. At that time and for many years afterwards there was but one service on the Sunday, alternately morning and afternoon, in any church – almost every clergyman having to serve two churches. Even in Lewes this was the case, Mr. Scobell being Rector of Southover and All Saints, Mr. (afterwards Sir) George Shiffner, Rector of St. Anne's and Hamsey; Mr. Crofts, Rector of St. John's and Malling; Mr. Lupton, Rector of the Cliffe and Curate of Ringmer, where he resided.

After I was sent to school it was my religious education only

Southover Grange.

that I received from my mother, and for that I have the strongest reason to the thankful. No secular books were allowed to be read on a Sunday; but it was never a dull day with us. We always attended service A.M. and P.M. But should the weather be such as to prevent us children from going to church, my mother read the service with us at home. It must be recollected that there was only one service in Southover Church, morning and afternoon, on alternate Sundays. From the time I was eleven or twelve I generally read the service, so I am one of the few still spared who as a reader have conducted it, reading the prayers "for his gracious Majesty King George." As I have previously mentioned, my father used always to attend service at Beddingham in the p.m. when the Southover service was in the a.m.; or in the a.m. when the Southover service was in the p.m.; thus he never missed the service at his parish church, save occasionally, when after morning service at Beddingham he would go on and dine at my grandfather's at Glynde and attend the service there. At Sunday evening prayers he would read a sermon. So we had our father's example to supplement our mother's more direct religious training. In earliest childhood, before we could ourselves read, we were taught the Church Catechism and various hymns which I have accurately remembered ever since, and which I have always valued as groundwork for teaching.

I first went to the Grammar School at Lewes in the spring of 1822. My first admittance to school was on a Wednesday in Lent, my mother taking me there on her way to St. Michael's Church, where the Rector had started a Wednesday morning service in Lent. I was for a long time the youngest boy in the school, though no one knew the words of the Catechism or the multiplication table better than myself, thanks to my mother's instruction. I recollect when I was five years old, on my birthday, my godfather and uncle, Captain Edward Boys, R.N., tried to puzzle me with the multiplication table, and he only did so at last when he asked me what was eight times naught. He was pleased and gave me half a crown to buy a Prayer Book. Delighted at his gift I went with my mother the same day to an old shop (long since pulled down) at the top of Keere Hill, and directly I got home, sat down and learnt the next Sunday's Collect – overjoyed to learn it from my own book.

At school we used to stand round in class, say the tables and take places, which I did not understand doing, and was just as ready to rush down the class as up, to take any boy's place whom I had corrected.

I was tried with the Latin Grammar directly I went to school, but Mr. Proctor (the master) soon saw it was advisable to wait a few months. I am convinced that it would have been wiser had I waited for years. (Written in 1893).

Looking back after a long life, I see that a great part of my school life was misspent. Not that I was ever accused of being idle, but I had the greatest difficulty in learning by heart, and ciphering I could not understand. My handwriting was never good, the canings and floggings that I daily received on my hands and arms I think accounted for that. I often misunderstood the directions given me. The consequence was that I was always at the bottom of my class, and rarely a day passed but what I received punishment. Proctor and the other masters were fond of the cane, and it was in constant use. I recollect on one occasion to my amazement seeing a boy not flogged but given an extra lesson as punishment for an ill-learnt lesson, reasoning with myself that surely that must be a mistake. There might be some virtue in the cane which I did not understand, but when a boy failed in saying a lesson to have to say twice as much must be wrong.

Being a day boy Proctor had no idea how much time I spent on my lessons. When ten years of age I was generally up till 10 or even 11 o'clock trying to learn them, and then frequently begin again by 4 A.M.

We had to be in school at 7 A.M. in the summer and 7.30 in the winter. We were allowed from 8.30 to 9.30 for breakfast, and from 12.30 till 2 for dinner, and then came out of school at half-past 4. Much time was taken up in going backwards and forwards to Southover. I rarely joined in a game of play, and when I have had an offer of going to an evening's entertainment I have positively refused, saying I must learn my lessons. Competition certainly never answered in my case, and it was only when I was released from working in class and allowed to go my own pace that I got on. I leave on record this account of my own school days as a warning against making mistakes in the instruction of children, from the teacher not understanding the child, or the child not understanding the teacher. Idleness obstinacy, or some other fault is ascribed to a child, and the child feels it keenly in after years.

My eldest brother, Spencer, soon after we moved to Southover, was sent to school at a Mr. Sergeant's at Brighton. There the boys had to drink half a pint of salt water every Saturday morning. I remember being taken over to Brighton to see him in the summer of 1822, and seeing him bury the rod, which he had somehow managed to get hold of, in the garden. On that occasion I had left Southover soon after 5 o'clock, being driven to Brighton by the groom, who had to carry some butter to the market. I remember one visit to Brighton of earlier date. When only about four, my grandfather took me to Brighton, and we went on the old pier, my cap blew off into the sea and my grandfather bought me another.

My father, who was a clever man and a brilliant scholar, always regarded me as a very dull and stupid boy, and could not understand why I was always at the bottom of my class. I was never fluent or ready of speech, and though I often possessed the information had not the ready words to express my meaning when suddenly asked a question.

My second brother, Frederic, was my father's favourite, as he regarded him as the cleverest. He would help him with his lessons, and afterwards sent him to Winchester, his own old school. Spencer was regarded as the mischievous one, so was sent away very early, before he was four, to a boarding-school, and was only home in the holidays. On one occasion he was at home when my father was giving a large dinner party. It was a grander one than usual, and one of the Royal Dukes was present, so there were some hired waiters to assist the footman. The maids had to carry every dish as far as the dining-room door, and to take away the empty dishes, so that the waiters had only to come just outside the dining-room door. A table stood in the hall, on which the dishes were placed. We children were watching from the top of the stairs to see the guests arrive, and it occurred to Spencer that he might have some fun. He had some very young rabbits; these he fetched indoors and watched for an opportunity. By-and-by the door was opened and a waiter put down an empty dish on the table outside the door. Quickly Spencer placed his baby rabbits on the dish and popped a cover over them. A moment later another waiter came out, seized up the dish, and placed it in front of the host. To our delight, through the open door, we saw him remove the cover with a flourish, and the rabbits were exposed to view. A laugh went round the table as my father angrily ordered the dish to be removed.

The first fifth of November after I went to school, on coming out I saw some street lamps lighted, and thinking it was very late, tried to run down "Care Hill," as we always called Keere Hill – the steepest of all the steep streets of Lewes, and which I believe is still paved with cobble stones to make a better foothold – I fell and cut my forehead badly. Bleeding and unconscious, I was picked up and carried home by a butcher who fortunately saw the accident. My forehead and eyebrow were sewn up by the doctor for the third time in my short life. Bandaged up and only able to see out of one eye, I was sent to school next day.

Writing of cobble stones, the streets of Lewes were all paved with them at the time I can first remember. I think it was later in 1824 that the side walks were first laid with paving stones, the cobbles being still left in the roadways. Lewes was very badly lighted with oil lamps, and I recollect the time when even these lamps did not extend to Southover. It was in the late autumn in 1822 that the extension was first made, and November 5th was the first day I had seen them lighted.

DRESS OF THE PERIOD

From the pictorial papers of the present day the dress of the period will be known hereafter, but in the reign of George IV. wood-engraving was very poor and seldom employed. It is to the first eight of the ten years (1820 to 1830) that my remarks on dress especially apply.

Men generally wore knee-breeches; long trousers were quite the exception. My father never wore long trousers except on Sundays; on other days he wore top boots, but when he went shooting half-boots and gaiters. The earliest trousers I remember him wearing were of nankeen – a material I never see now, a kind of jean, in colour something between yellow and brick-dust. This material, which was especially used for little boys' trousers and jackets, I wore myself. There were no waistcoats for boys, but the jackets buttoned closely, with the trousers buttoned over the jacket. A frill was worn round the neck. Turn-down collars for boys were introduced about 1825, but I never saw them worn at school. Of course, our under-clothes were of linen; we wore low shoes and stockings. It was not warm clothing then. My father always wore a blue cloth coat with brass buttons, a light-coloured waistcoat and a loosely folded white necktie; indeed, frequently two of these large neckties made of squares of lawn. These neckties were so big that they almost hid the shirt collar, which was very stiff and came up each side of the chin. The shirts had large frills over the bosom. A huge thick watch chain, with the owner's seal attached, hung down from the fob over the knee-breeches. Out of the other pocket would protrude a coloured silk handkerchief For outdoor wear in cold weather a huge tight-fitting overcoat, double-breasted with high turn-up collar, in brown, blue or green. (It must be remembered that at that time no black dye had been invented, the so-called black dyes being really only very dark browns or green.) A hard, high-crowned hat, and a large warm shawl of merino or some such material wrapped round the neck, completed the costume. For evening wear men always had black silk stockings, shoes with buckles, lace ruffles to their shirts, and elaborately worked waistcoats.

The linen for men and boys was of the finest quality. Pocket handkerchiefs were always of silk.

The pigtail had gone out of fashion, save for soldiers or sailors, though old gentlemen sometimes still clung to the custom.

Boys wore a high-peaked cap, and in winter overcoats like men.

Old gentlemen, and amongst them my grandfather's old friend, Mr. Hoper, sometimes wore over their coat a short jacket called a "Spencer." Swallow-tail coats were the usual dress, even of the clergy. Single-breasted coats with upright collars, and the usual clerical white collar, were then unknown.

Ladies' dresses were made with what has been called "leg of mutton" sleeves, or the sleeves were very much puffed out if they wore short ones. When my mother went out of an evening she wore a "turban," which she twisted up for the occasion out of a coloured silk handkerchief and a piece of net or muslin. The dresses were worn short and rather narrow, with the waist high up under the arms. Long mittens were worn, and in winter-time a little shawl over the shoulders. Sandled slippers indoors. Outdoors, large coal-scuttle bonnets with caps and flowers inside, and big veils, low shoes, and a thin tippet of silk in summer, when they carried dainty parasols. In winter a warm cloth or velvet cape, to which a boa and huge muff would be added. Girls would be dressed like women, with the exception that they always wore short sleeves and wore no cap. A married woman from the day of her marriage always wore a large cap tied under the chin; an unmarried spinster of twenty-five would be looked upon as an old maid, and would dress in an elderly fashion and wear a cap. The only hats known were tall chimney pots, or straws with a high crown. Maid-servants would never think of having anything but the plainest of gowns, short sleeves, and large caps tied under the chin.

The lower classes did not wear linen underclothes, but calico. The men wore thick breeches of some strong material and smocked frocks. Even forty years ago the labourers always came to church in clean smocks, and it was only the general use of machinery that drove out the smock frock. At first its place was taken by the "slop," but for years now for Sunday wear the men wear coats.

Other things besides dress are changed also. In the early part of this century, when a servant left, the mistress would try to keep the fact from being known to save herself being worried by the number of anxious applicants. There were any amount of good servants to be had, who stayed years in their situations and only left to be married. Wages were low, some female servants £6 or £8 the year; a very good cook £10. Holidays were rarely given, and servants seldom went out save to church. Charwomen got 9d. a day. Men going out to work, 1s. a day. Of course, there were bad masters and mistresses, but these were the exception, not the rule. The usual thing was for the servants to look upon their master and mistress as their friends to whom they could turn for help, not only while in their service, but after they had married, and to regard the whole family with affection. The employers seldom lost sight of their old servants.

For my early days housekeeping was not such a simple affair as it is now. Every middle-class household had its still-room, and if there was no housekeeper the mistress superintended her maid in the making of pickles, jams, wines, sauces, sweets, etc. Home-made medicines were in common use, and every mistress of a household would produce them as a matter of course. All the needlework was done at home by hand, not machine, and the ladies of the family would work elaborate pieces of dainty needlework.

My uncle, Edward Boys, once presented us with a macaw which he had brought home on one of his voyages. This bird was generally kept in the children's sitting room, a room given up to us for lessons, etc. The room was really intended for a housekeeper's room and had a door of communication leading into the kitchen. We children were very fond of playing "hide and seek" with the bird. One of us would go in and hide something in the room, then another would come in and ask where such and such a thing was hidden. The bird would immediately answer, "Under the chair," "Look behind the coal scuttle," "Look under the rug," as the case might be. It knew the names of all the objects in the room and never told us wrong. One evening the bird was alone in the sitting-room when my mother entered, and wishing to give some order to a servant summoned the maid. As the kitchen door opened the macaw cried out, " Look behind the door! Look behind the door!" and continued to shriek this out so that my mother could hardly hear what the maid said. To quiet the bird she moved across the room and found a man trying to hide himself between two doors on the kitchen side of the room. This turned out to be a persevering admirer of our cook. His usual approach to the house was through the stable-yard, so that he might not be seen from the front windows. Our groom had frequently threatened what he would do to him if he persevered in coming, but the man continued to haunt the house in the evening, so the groom got the assistance of the butcher's man one evening and dug a deep hole in a very moist manure heap outside the stable. The men then hid themselves and waited for their victim. As he opened the door they seized him and pinioned his arms (and well they did so, as he had a pistol in his hand) and deposited him in the manure heap hole. Then they ran away across the meadow behind (the meadow that the railway now comes by). In the meadow were two horses. My father, on hearing the horses gallop wildly about the field, took his gun and went into the garden. There he found a man with a pistol creeping along the other side of the hedge, which apparently confirmed his suspicion that a party of horse stealers were trying to catch one of the horses. Indeed, one of these horses, a pony, had been thrice stolen, but each time recovered. It appeared that the groom and butcher had frightened the horses by running across the field, whilst the unsavoury lover was watching to take vengeance on them.

Once on returning from school by Rotten Row (Lewes), on arriving at the bridge which crosses the Winterbourne Stream, I saw a rush of water, and was just in time to see a man scramble out of a well which he had been digging when the water rose so fast as to carry him to the surface and to overflow. Of course, he lost his tools, which are still, probably, after the lapse of nearly eighty years, at the bottom of the well.

In the earlier part of these reminiscences I have mentioned the trouble of my school days. I wish now to add that we always had a holiday task given us, which made the holidays miserable. I was always glad to return to the regular steady work of school life, though rarely a day passed but what I felt the cane for my stupidity and dullness.

I always had the greatest difficulty in committing to memory and recollect on one occasion spending three or four hours in trying to commit to memory four lines of Greek and failing. One task required of us at the Grammar School was, each Thursday afternoon, to repeat a piece of English poetry. I invariably got punished. One day I had to learn from the Eton grammar a long rule of syntax. I stopped up till 11 the night before trying to master it, when my mother would not let me stay up any longer, but I was down by 4 o'clock the next morning and went on poring over it till it was time to start for school. Whilst I was getting ready my brother Frederic took up my school-bag in mistake for his own and started without me. As soon as I was ready I missed my bag and went hunting about after it, and said I could not go to school without it. I was still searching when Frederic came home for breakfast and explained his mistake. When I went to school after breakfast Proctor evidently thought I had stopped away to escape the lesson, so he tried me, and finding I did not know it, told me to stop in school till the afternoon and threatened to flog me severely if I did not say it correctly then. I was so frightened by the threat and his manner that I did not even notice that I was not to go home, and felt confident that I must submit to the flogging, for I felt sure I could never say it perfectly. So I did not stop in, and on going back to school in the afternoon got a most severe flogging, Mr. Proctor supposing I had wilfully disobeyed him. Occasionally Proctor used to come to our house for a rubber of whist. On those evenings, as I remained in the room poring over my lessons all the time, he could see that I was not idle, and the following morning I always found that I escaped punishment for not knowing my lesson. I was, therefore, always glad when he spent the evening at the Manor.

My father would frequently begin a Latin or Greek quotation, and then say to me, "How does it go on?" and finding that I could not continue, he would go on himself repeating several lines. He was also a very good French scholar, and it seemed to be no more difficult for him to joke in French than in English. He was a fluent speaker and I never knew him to hesitate for a word in either language. He was also a very ready versifier. I have in my possession long letters written to my mother in his courting days, describing the incidents of various long journeys that he took on horseback and the people he met, all being in rhyme. Also a MS. book in which he copied numerous political *jeux d'esprits*, and some very lengthy poetical pieces, some of them tales of lovers of the milk and watery type that he had written during his Winchester days. He clearly, even as a schoolboy, entered into the politics of the day, for while still in his teens he wrote two or three political fables relating to the Ministers of the day – Pitt, Fox and Addington, the French War, Buonaparte, etc., which were published at the time.

AMUSING VISITORS

In the holidays we often went over to Glynde to spend the day with our grandparents. My father's mother never recovered from the birth of her only child. My grandfather's second wife had been his ward and was the eldest daughter of his old friend and neighbour, the Vicar of Glynde. The second wife (unlike many cases of second marriage) soon won the deep affection of her stepson, and in after life was much beloved, not only by my father and mother, but by his children. We very much enjoyed going there, and were never allowed to return home without going to Glynde Place to see old Lady Hampden, who was very fond of us children. She had no children of her own, and was always most kind to us, taking us about the house and garden and making a fuss over us. If we went to Glynde in her absence the old housekeeper, Dame Cornwall, had orders to entertain us.

Glynde was one of the very earliest parishes to have a Sunday School. Amongst other papers I have in my possession, is one in my grandfather's handwriting, "Rules for a Sunday School in the Parish of Glynde." It is not dated, but as amongst the list of managers is named Rev. Mr. Davies, Vicar of Glynde, who died in 1789, it must have been prior to that date. The list of managers seems to include all the leading men in the parish, save my great-grandfather, Richard Ellman, who died May 22nd, 1780, so we

The entrance to Glynde Place.

Glynde Place.

know it must have been established between those dates. Now it is said that the first Sunday School was founded by Richard Raikes in 1780; so the small village of Glynde is thus shown to have been one of the earliest country villages to have a Sunday School.

About 1826 my half-uncle George had staying with him at Beddingham, as an agricultural pupil, a son of one of the firm of Enderby, South Sea merchants. Young Enderby related that one of their ships had brought home a New Zealand chief, who, whilst in England, stayed with his father, and that on the occasion of an evening party this chief excited great interest. In the course of conversation a lady asked him whether he was married. The chief replied that he had had several wives, but he had not one then. This led to further inquiries about the wives. What had become of them? He replied that when he got tired of them he ate them. One gentleman asked if he had ever eaten white people. He acknowledged that he had, but said he did not like them as they were so salt. Soon afterwards the chief went back to New Zealand. Nothing was heard of him for some time, but a year or two afterwards we asked young Enderby if he had heard anything more of the chief. In reply he said the chief was dead. He had heard that on the chief's return to New Zealand he told so many wonderful things about England that he himself had been eaten as an inveterate liar!

A very constant visitor of my father's was Monsieur Alexandre Bille. I rather think my father first made his acquaintance when he visited France in 1824. At any rate, in the autumn of that year M. Bille visited us at Southover in company with Mr. Chapman, our Vice Consul at Dieppe, and from that time for upwards of forty years he rarely missed a year without coming to us on a visit. His great desire was to carry out improvements in agriculture in France, and for this purpose he first came over to England to purchase sheep, seeds and agricultural implements. He was quite a character We could never persuade him to attempt to speak English. Though his position in Normandy was decidedly above the bourgeois class, his spelling of his own language was decidedly faulty, as evidenced by his letters, which were written in a flourishing hand. We used to leave a French-English dictionary out for his use.

On one occasion he wanted a brush to brush his coat when we were all out of the way. He looked in the dictionary and turned to "broche" instead of "brosse," and then went to the kitchen door and asked the astonished cook for a "spit."

He used to get into various scrapes, at which he would laugh, as well as produce laughter in others. He always seemed full of fun, and his temper was so good that I never knew him to be offended at the jokes that were frequently played upon him. He had a great desire to marry an English wife; and on three different occasions did he by letter request my father to make the proposal for him. But not one of the three ladies, though they were amused at his oddities, would consent to become Madame Bille. One of the ladies, as my half-aunt, Catharine Ellman, who afterwards married F. P. Walesby, her brother's college friend. Another was Miss George, my sister's governess, who was very tall and dark. My father, in joke, told him she was a Jewess, whereupon he wrote back that if she would marry him as he was a Roman Catholic and she a Jewess, their children would be Protestants! The third lady was a Miss Hick, of Lewes, who afterwards married Dr. Haire. Miss Hick was an only child, watched over very closely by her father and mother, and it was said that even when turned thirty she occupied the same bedroom as her parents so that they could watch over her! The truth of this statement, of course, I cannot vouch for. I believe Mr. Hick was a retired merchant. Once when they were spending the evening with us, my eldest brother, Spencer, who had only recently begun the Latin grammar, went up to my mother and said: "Mr. and Mrs. Hick do not agree," – a most unfortunate speech as it had been reported shortly before that there was some little difference between them. My mother tried to stop him, but he repeated his observation, adding that it ought to be Mr. Hic and Mrs. Hoc.

But to return to M. Alexandre Bille. As he failed to get any of the three ladies he wanted, I believe he remained unmarried. What has become of him now I know not. If alive he must be a very old man, for he was about twenty-five when I first knew him in 1824.

I last saw him in Lewes about 1878.

Mr. Hick had a very good opinion of himself, and amongst other things he considered himself to be a first rate judge of wine. One of my uncles who was staying with us determined to play him a trick. It happened that in 1811, my mother had made a cask of sloe wine. I recollect even seventeen or eighteen years afterwards it was still a full-bodied and rather luscious wine, and no one would ever have supposed that it was made out of sloes. Of this wine my uncle filled a pint bottle and sealed it, and after dinner (at which Mr. Hick had formed one of the guests) produced this bottle, saying that his brother Richard, who was a chaplain in St. Helena, had sent some wine to his family and that this bottle fell to my mother's share; that as there were such good judges of wine at the table it was produced for the occasion. One after another tasted it and condemned it, for probably it had not then got sufficiently mellowed; but when it came round to Mr. Hick he said: "Gentle men, you are all mistaken. This is a very scarce and valuable wine, and it is always put in pint bottles. It is called 'Pexaretta'."

JOHN HOPER, SENIOR

In our estimation as children, the most delightful person in Southover (Lewes) was Miss Ingram. She frequently gave children's parties, at which we played some round games of cards, such as "Commerce," or "Pope Joan." She lived close to us, in a delightful old house. There was a terraced walk in her garden overlooking our meadow, in which we used to play, and many were the times that she gave us over the wall oranges from her conservatory, or something equally nice. She was a great friend of my mother's, and we saw a good deal of her. Miss Sarah Ingram, when a girl or very young woman, had saved the life of a young man named Bostock, from drowning. He had somehow fallen into the Pells (water in some brooks close to St. John's Church). She jumped in after him and pulled him safely out. In gratitude he fell

59

in love with her and proposed. In refusing him she strongly urged him to transfer his affections to her sister (who, she evidently knew, cared for him). After a short time he took her advice – proposed, and was accepted. I have always had the idea that Miss Sarah cared for Mr. Bostock, but that she valued her sister's happiness more than her own. Anyhow, she never married.

Not far from her house, on the other side of the street, was an old porched house. In this house lived an old woman named Dame Harman, whom we were allowed to visit when we were children. We always saw her in one room. In this room hung a portrait of a female, blackened with dirt and age. This picture was said to be a portrait of one of the wives of King Henry VIII. I did not then, as a small child, know that tradition said that the house was the residence of Anne of Cleves, after her divorce. I suppose it would be very difficult now to trace what has become of the portrait. To the best of my recollection the size of the picture was about sixteen inches by twelve inches. It was my impression at the time that the picture belonged to the house, and that no one had a right to remove it. I never heard any mention made of the portrait after Dame Harman's death in 1823 or 1824. Her grandson was for many years a carpenter and builder, residing at Lewes. I hardly think the picture can have been retained in the family.

About this time I remember my uncle, the Rev. James Boys, coming to stay with us before going out to India. On the Sunday he was very much surprised to learn that there was no evening service in any Lewes church. My father told him there was an evening service at a place called the "Tabernacle." My uncle thought he would like to attend, and that being a stranger in Lewes, if he disguised himself he might find out what kind of service there was at a dissenting chapel. So my uncle put on a brown great coat of my father's with a bright-coloured shawl round his neck, and attended the service. He afterwards said he certainly was not edified thereby, and when the sermon, which was very long and prosy, began, he felt inclined to doze off to sleep, but was aroused by the words, "The light of the gospel is a very good thing," which he said was the only sensible thing in the sermon, "but as we cannot have the light of the gospel without the light of candles, there will be a collection after service," continued the preacher, so my uncle slipped out.

When my father first married, in February, 1811, the country was in a disturbed state, and people had to be on the alert to prevent horse stealing, etc. For several weeks he was disturbed each Friday at midnight by a noise as if someone had got into the house. At first he thought a thief had got in the house – but it was several weeks before he could find out the cause. At last, one night as he was sitting up to watch, he found it was only the weight of an eight-day clock that stood in the passage. He always wound up the clock when he came down on Sunday morning, and on Friday night the weight caught on a narrow ledge inside the clock and bounded off as it struck midnight.

From my earliest years I was very fond of watching any work that was going on. I frequently visited the carpenter's or the black-smith's. I was always interested in the way the blacksmith obtained a light, which he always did by hammering a piece of iron till it was sufficiently hot to set alight to a match.

At that time there were various manufactures carried on at Lewes and in the neighbourhood. Thus, there was a pipemaker's factory on Keere Hill, a paper mill near St. John's Church, and a soap house on the river bank below Southerham, etc. Even since I have been in Berwick, yellow sheep-skin leggings and tanned gloves were manufactured at Alfriston; and the building which is now converted into a racing stable was a malt-house – the last of these malt-houses which in the last century existed at Alfriston.

I remember a very amusing Lewes character, Cooley, the hair-dresser, who, when he came to cut our hair, used to amuse us by his fund of anecdotes. His shop was in the High Street, and over the shop a huge sign hung out on which was painted a picture of Absalom hanging by his long hair to a bough of a tree, while his ass was galloping away. Under the picture were the words –

> "Oh! Absalom, unlucky prig!
> Had'st thou but worn a periwig!

For had thy luckless head been shaved,
Thy life most surely had been saved."

Under this again was the barber's name, formed of brushes, combs and razors, placed together to form the name "Cooley." He himself always wore a wig.

My brother Frederic was very fond of angling. I have been fishing with him in the early summer morning before school in the Southover Pells, the striking of six by the St. Michael's clock being the signal for us to take up our lines and prepare for being in school by seven. We occasionally, during the summer holidays, used to fish up the river between Hamsey and Barcombe; but the best place for fishing was the old part of the river at Southease, which was strictly preserved. At the beginning of each season, Mr. Hoper, the owner, used to give us boys six blank forms of permission to fish there, leaving us to fill up the dates. After two or three times Mr. Hoper's men did not ask to see our "permit." Therefore we merely carried a blank form with us ready to give up if requested; and did not limit ourselves to the six times during the summer.

To show the power of sound in certain states of the atmosphere, I may mention that on one occasion while fishing there, we distinctly heard the ringing of the handbell at Southover, which was used to call us in, though rung four miles distant.

Mr. John Hoper, senior, was a great friend of my grandfather, and his two sons, John and George, were my father's life-long friends, and had been at Winchester with him. Mr. Hoper was ever kind and generous, but not unfrequently taken in. When he built Asham House on his property at Beddingham, he did not put the building into the hands of a regular builder, but looked after the workmen himself. Though he constantly visited the work, he was surprised at its slow progress. He said he always found the men steadily at work, though they never knew when to expect him. He purposely some times went to Beddingham by the road, sometimes by the river bank, and sometimes over the Downs, he never found a single man idle, and yet the building did not progress properly. The fact was the workmen passed a great part of their time at cricket. A boy was set to watch on the high ground behind, who had to make a signal whenever Mr. Hoper was seen approaching.

He maintained a Sunday School at Beddingham at his own expense, at which his managing clerk used constantly to teach; and he himself walked over regularly from Lewes to attend the Sunday service. During a thunderstorm he would, with his silk umbrella, walk up the Cliffe Hill to see the grand spectacle of the storm. Mr. Hoper had a pony which he used to ride. One day the pony stumbled and fell with him. He accordingly ordered the pony to be sold the next market day, Plummer Verrall, the Lewes auctioneer, as usual, holding an auction sale in front of the Star Inn, Lewes. On the evening of the sale day, Plummer Verrall sent him the money for which the pony was sold – a much larger sum than Mr. Hoper expected. Whereupon he asked the man who brought him the money if his master had said at the auction why it was sold, as he had especially desired him to do. The man said "Yes." Mr. Hoper was not satisfied, and asked exactly what his master had said. The man hesitated. Mr. Hoper insisted upon knowing exactly what Mr. Plummer Verrall had said. "Master said Mr. Hoper had desired him to say that the pony had been down, and that that was the reason it was sold; but that everybody knew what a bad rider Mr. Hoper was, and that he would throw down the best horse in the world."

It was my father who had bought the pony, and a very valuable animal it proved. I myself had it here at Berwick for some years. Once when I timed its pace trotting from the fourth to the fifth milestone on the Lewes road, it trotted the mile within five minutes. I have ridden it from Berwick to Brighton and back in the day; from Berwick to Battle without a rest on the way on more than one occasion. Once returning from Battle I rode round by Crowhurst, a distance of considerably over twenty miles, and in 1844, when I went from Berwick to Wartling twice a week, "Old Hoper," as we always called him, was most valuable.

Quaint Ladies

In the early part of the nineteenth century there was very good society in Lewes. Many of the county families had houses there, and Lewes, the county town, was a far more important town than it is now.

Brighton had only of recent years come into fashion. Eastbourne was only a small town, Bourne as it was then commonly called in the neighbourhood. Hastings, another small town; St. Leonards and Bexhill, more like big villages; Seaford, quite a small seafaring town. Lewes was the place were each winter the good old families had their winter "town houses." Up many of its steep streets, in out of the way lanes, are many most comfortable family mansions; unpretentious looking from the street, but running far back into the high walled-in gardens, and containing large rooms well suited for entertaining. Southover is a part of Lewes, and our house, Southover Manor, was there. A big white house. its front supported on a row of white pillars abutting on the street, with a large old garden and meadow behind sloping down to the Priory grounds.

The chief house in Southover was "Southover Grange," a delightful old house. Its mistress, Mrs. Newton, was a well-known character, and looked upon herself, and was looked upon, as the leader of the Southover society. (There was the Lewes society and the Southover society in those days.)

It happened at the time I was a child that almost all the better class of houses in Southover were occupied by widows or un-married ladies, and tea-parties were a great institution. Mrs. Newton was looked up to almost as a queen by many of these good ladies, but she seldom consented to attend at these evening tea-parties. On one occasion one of the Southover ladies invited and managed to get Mrs. Newton's acceptance to tea for a certain evening. Delighted at securing her, she immediately issued invitations to other ladies to meet Mrs. Newton. When the evening arrived, instead of Mrs. Newton herself came a note, briefly stating that she could not come to tea, "as she had got a better thing, an invitation to dinner."

On Twelfth Night she always gave a party herself the large cake being adorned with Twelfth Night characters, for which the company drew, so that every one was assigned a partner by lot, the numbers being in pairs, ladies and gentlemen, number one being always king and queen. I believe that this custom of drawing for king and queen on Twelfth Night has long gone out of fashion. I attended the yearly parties as long as I remained in Southover. In January, 1828 and 1829, we younger ones went on January 7th, as she increased the number of her invitations, and so had to divide the party, having the grown-up people on the 6th and children on the next night.

I remember, as a small boy of about six, drawing for my partner the grown-up Miss Catharine Smith daughter of the Vicar of Newhaven, who afterwards became Mrs. Cooper, of Wilmington, and in some game that followed I was told that I must kiss her, which to the company's amusement, I refused to do, as I thought it improper.

The usual conveyance for women to go about in to the evening parties were Sedan chairs. These chairs were very convenient for ladies when dressed for a party. The chair was brought into the hall, into it the lady stepped, and got out in the hall of the hostess. In many of the narrow, steep, dark streets, any other conveyance would have been most awkward. Mrs. Newton and the Miss Shelleys, of St. Anne's, each owned a private one. The last time I saw a Sedan chair in use was in Bath in 1837. They are now quite superseded by Bath chairs, which in those times had not been invented.

The Miss Shelleys, of Lewes, were amongst the Lewes notabilities. They prided themselves on their state of spinsterhood, and were very indignant at their sister for having married a Mr. Dalbiac, saying, "That it was an unheard of thing that a lady of the Shelley family should marry."

At the census of 1841, when the collector called for the paper, on looking at it to see whether it was filled up correctly, he noticed that the ages of the two surviving Miss Shelleys and of their three

65

domestic were all stated to be twenty-five years. Whereupon the collector told the maid he should like to see her mistress. On being shown into her presence he said he thought there must be some little mistake as to the ages entered on the schedule, whereupon Miss Shelley indignantly said that she "had never in her life met with such impudence as to ask the age of a lady! In that house they were all unmarried females, and that she could not think of putting each one down as more than twenty five." How it ended I do not know; but I do know that a fortnight earlier, on a visitor complaining before my mother the difficulty she had in keeping servants, one of the Miss Shelleys had remarked that they were very fortunate as they had not changed a servant for upwards of thirty years!

But to return to Mrs. Newton's peculiarities. She always had a load of wood brought every year and spread out in the meadow opposite her house for the use of the rooks who occupied a rookery there, in order to prevent them breaking branches or twigs off the trees. She always liked to go to the butcher's herself to choose her meat, and I have frequently seen her there with her basket of keys on her arm, which in the morning she always carried about with her.

Later on in her old age she always had a chop at 2 o'clock, being waited upon by her old butler, who had been in her service upwards of thirty years. One day, just as the time approached for the chop to be carried in, the old man suddenly dropped down dead. While the other servants were hastily considering how to break the information to their mistress, the bell was violently rung. On a servant appearing, the old lady demanded why the butler did not bring in her chop. On being told of his sudden death she merely said, "That is no reason why I should be kept waiting. Is there not anyone else who can bring in my chop?"

In my young days one of the families we were most intimate with were the Tourles of Landport; there were three sons and six daughters, all about our own age. On one occasion they had a cousin staying with them named Greene, who was a monitor at Midhurst School. Whilst the young people were talking together in

66

one room, Mrs. Tourle was entertaining some early visitors in the next room, who stayed so long that it was evidently their intention to stay on and join the Tourles in their early one o'clock dinner. Just before one o'clock Mrs. Tourle came hastily into the room, saying she did not know what to do as she had only a small shoulder of mutton for dinner and a little cold meat. As she was speaking a big party of the Stamfords from Brighton unexpectedly arrived. Greene said that as a monitor at school he had learnt to carve and to make meat go a long way, and if his aunt would let him show his proficiency therein he would do his best. To the amusement of the girls, who related the story, he covered plate after plate with slices not thicker than a wafer for all the twenty odd people, who most of them had a second helping.

Guy Fawkes Day is always a great day in Lewes, and the town on that night used to be given up to rioting. I recollect a rocket coming through the window and falling on the bed where I lay in the night nursery. Fortunately it was soon put out; but many cases of fires through lighted fireworks being thrown through windows occurred and much damage was done. Some years later a Lewes butcher named Morris lost the sight of one of his eyes through a rocket being fired into a house. About fifty or sixty years since the magistrates tried to stop fireworks being let off in the streets of Lewes on bonfire night and wanton damage being done, and some of the rioters were prosecuted. But instead of the fireworks being suppressed it led to an organised opposition to the magistrates and police, and to large processions with lighted tar-barrels, etc., being dragged through the streets. In the old days of which I write all business had to be stopped during the day, and by the afternoon the inhabitants of the chief street had to barricade their windows and doors with thick boards to protect the glass and prevent windows and doors being smashed by the rioters. Strange as it may seem, this 5th of November observance is supported by subscriptions from many of the inhabitants. Hundreds of young men used to come over from Brighton and other places, many of them dressed up and masked, and take part in the procession. At one time it was not safe for anyone to be seen in the street, as the rioters would seize him and often fill his pockets with fireworks which they would proceed to light, and bad accidents have occurred. But for many years now the proceedings have been kept in some sort of order by the leaders of the procession; the huge bonfire, which has always been made in the middle of High Street, near the top of St. Mary's Lane (or Station Street as it is now called) being extinguished punctually at mid-night. But the houses are still barricaded.

Another thing I remember at Southover was seeing a man in the stocks being supplied with beer by his friends! The stocks were close by Southover Church, and I have often seen men with their feet therein. I believe it was the punishment for drunkenness. Speaking of Southover Church, I well remember that Mr. Scobell who was a very tiny man) had placed a large hassock in the pulpit to stand upon, his predecessor, who come back to preach one Sunday, was a tall man, and on mounting to the pulpit somehow stepped on the big hassock and knocked his head against the sounding board. He opened the pulpit door hastily and gave the hassock a kick, and I saw it rolling down the pulpit stairs. Another time during service there was a storm and the wall adjoining the church to the east was struck by lightning and split asunder in the middle, but though I was in church at the time I knew nothing about the damage done by the lightning till the next day, when I saw several cartloads of flints and mortar lying on the ground.

LEWES PEOPLE

Amongst the well-known Lewes characters was the worthy auctioneer, Plummer Verrall. He was quite a character, and was so well known for his amusing and at times witty remarks at his weekly auctions that he thereby attracted a large attendance to his sales.

Once, at a furniture sale at East Hoathly, one of the principal bidders for some nursery furniture was a lady. On putting up a swing cot, he called especial attention to the fact that it was utterly different from the old-fashioned kind of cradle, and said everything he could in its favour. But immediately he had knocked it down he turned to the unfortunate lady who had secured it, and said he did not like these new-fashioned things, that there was nothing like the old-fashioned cradles, which were always safe. "Whereas, ma'am, if the child attempts to raise himself in this swinging cot, he will easily fall out." His remarks evidently made the lady uncomfortable. She, however, was not prevented from bidding eagerly and becoming the possessor of a nursery fire-guard. On putting it up Plummer Verrall had especially drawn attention to a bar to strengthen it across the middle. The hammer fell, the guard was bought. "Madam," said he, "that bar is a great mistake! The little boy will try and climb up on it to reach something off the mantel-piece and pitch over into the fire."

At another sale at Firle, I noticed that he was a long time before he knocked down an old carpet whose praises he had been extolling, evidently trying to get another bid, by saying he always recommended putting an old carpet under a new one, as it made the new carpet warmer to the feet and also wear much longer. At last he knocked it down and turning suddenly to his wife who was sitting at the table, and to whom the carpet had gone, exclaimed: "You fool! What did you buy that for? You know we have lots of carpets at home that we don't know what to do with." She pleaded: "But you said it was so cheap." "You ought to have known me long enough not to believe everything I say," he rejoined, amidst roars of laughter.

Another time he gave great offence to a Mr. Edward Cane, farmer at Berwick Court, by saying he supposed he should soon have to sell him up as it was a long time since he had a sale there.

There were several families of Verralls at Lewes when we moved there in 1819. George Verrall, who lived at "The Friars," an old house that was afterwards pulled down when the railway was made, was the father of Plummer, the auctioneer, and George. Then there was Edward Verrall, a solicitor and clerk to the Commissioners of Taxes, being succeeded in his business by John Lewis, only son of the Incumbent of Bishopstone and

Blatchington, who married one of his daughters.

William Verrall was another. He was a brewer at Southover. When he married, the post-chaise in which his bride was going to church was upset, and the bride had some teeth knocked out, but this nothwithstanding, she went through the ceremony with a bleeding mouth, as I have heard. Curiously enough, an accident also happened when their son William was married about 1825. I recollect on my way home from school seeing the wedding party returning from church, and saw the bride nearly knocked down by a boy swinging a pair of dead fowls he was carrying. William Verrall took up his residence in the house on the east side, at the bottom of Keere Street, but he afterwards purchased the house (Southover Manor) in which we lived for ten years. It was, when he bought it, occupied by the Rev. Harry West, the non-resident Rector of Berwick. Mr. West was so indignant at receiving notice from his new landlord to quit, that he added to his new landlord's name either on a cheque or some official paper, "small beer brewer."

One member of the family, Harry Verrall, when an old man, was so fond of a chat with his medical attendant, Dr. Doyle, that he was quite put out at his not calling every day; and on Doyle telling him that there was no real occasion for a doctor's daily visit, offered him £100 a year to make one. A daughter of the last mentioned William Verrall married Rigden, another Lewes doctor.

On one occasion meeting Richard Turner, another Lewes medical man, who had married Miss Crockford, sister of my old school-fellow, George Crockford, children of yet another Lewes doctor), I asked him what he thought would be the result of the then highly electrical state of the atmosphere, the heat being excessive. Turner's answer was the one word, "Sweat."

In writing of the Lewes doctors, I must not leave out Mr. Hodson, who was one of the chief Lewes doctors in the first quarter of the century. Mr. Hodson was a skilful surgeon, and delighted in an operation. It was his boast that he was ready to use the knife under the bedclothes and so save exposure to a lady. I never heard whether he was allowed to do so, but remember as a

Keere Street, Lewes.

71

boy thinking that if an operation were really necessary any lady would prefer the exposure on such an occasion to the doctor cutting in the dark.

Hodson was a great gourmand, and would go anywhere for a good dinner. On one occasion, while dining at Southover Grange, Mrs. Newton mentioned that she had intended to have some grouse for the dinner party. She had had some sent all the way from Scotland, but they had arrived in such a state that she had ordered them to be buried at once; whereupon, next day, Mr. Hodson bribed Mrs. Newton's groom to dig them up and bring them to him. A week later they were served up at his table. On one occasion, not feeling well, he consulted his old friend Dr. Blair, and said that he had lost his appetite. Dr. Blair rejoined "That he was very sorry for the poor man who had found it."

The Blakers – descendants of an old county family – were brought up at Tilton, in Selmeston parish; one son became a linen draper at Lewes. He left two sons, John and Edgar, who became solicitors there. Another son, Harry, became a medical man at Brighton, and was a clever, well-known surgeon. Being able to use his left hand equally as well as his right, he performed an operation the more speedily, which was a decided advantage at the time chloroform was unknown.

I was always sorry for Dr. Taylor, of Brighton. He was attending a case of typhoid at Worthing and returning to Brighton after seeing the case, it being a very cold, windy day, he buttoned his overcoat up close as he was driving in his gig. Upon reaching Brighton, before returning home, he made a few professional calls, amongst others, upon two ladies who had recently been confined. One was his own daughter; both caught the fever and died. It is supposed that in coming into their warm rooms he unbuttoned his coat and let out the infection from which the ten miles' windy drive had not purified him.

To go from doctors to chemists. The chemist's shop up on School Hill, Lewes, was in my earliest recollection occupied by a Mr. Pitt. "Pitt's Sauce," "Pitt's Ginger Beer," etc., were well known in the neighbourhood for many years afterwards, the celebrity of the ginger beer being enhanced by the fact that the cork from one of the bottles which was being opened in the shop destroyed the sight of one of Pitt's eyes.

Another chemist was an Austrian named Pam, who had for some reason set up a shop in Lewes. As he was an oddity several people would go to his shop for the express purpose of having some conversation with him. Till late years the Cattle Market used always to be held every other Tuesday in High-street, and there were always some pens of sheep immediately in front of his shop, and consequently on market days he had an unusual number of customers, and some visitors. To one of the latter he once said, "You are always coming in, but you never buy anything," and pressed him to any rate buy a bottle of ginger beer, to which the man consented. But when old Pam proceeded to open the bottle the cork flew out and broke the window, whereupon poor Pam exclaimed, "I wish you had never come in! It will cost me 3s. 6d. for a new pane."

He had some very good lodgings to let over his shop, which on one occasion were occupied by a Miss Law, whose house at Brighton was being repainted. At the end of the time for which she had taken rooms, finding that her own house was not quite ready, she stayed on for two or three days and then tendered payment for half a week, at which payment the old man demurred and spoke his mind freely, whereupon Miss Law said, "Do you know that you are speaking to the Honourable Miss Law?" His answer was, "The dishonourable Miss Law to cheat a poor tradesman so."

A little lower down School Hill was the confectioner's shop kept by the Miss Hills. For three generations the Hills had kept the shop, universally respected by everyone. Mr. John Hoper, junior, had rooms at Miss Hill's for use when he was in Lewes. Wishing to give old Miss Sarah Hill a great treat in the 'forties, when the South Coast Railway had been made, he invited her to go and stay with him at Shermanbury. With great difficulty he persuaded Sarah Hill to accept. She had great fear of the railway and had never entered a train. On her arrival Mr. Hoper pointed out that after all her fears she had arrived quite safely, whereupon she replied that she herself had, but that fourteen people had been killed on the way. It appeared that someone had told her whenever a man was killed the engine was made to scream. So she sat trembling and counting each time the engine whistled. In the early days of railroads, before the block system was invented, engines were made to whistle at frequent intervals.

Old Sarah Hill's grandmother once told me that she had lived in the reign of the four Georges. I was a small child at the time and she a very old woman.

Anecdotes of Assizes, etc

My father was always very fond of attending the assizes, and during my summer holiday frequently took me with him. Holidays in those days were much shorter than they are now – generally four weeks in June, a week or fortnight at Christmas, and sometimes a week at Easter.

The judge I remember best was, I think, Judge Graham – about 1825. I always thought he wore a moustache; but one morning when I was present at the opening of the Court he appeared as if he had been shaved. But within an hour his upper lip was as black as usual. The fact was that every few minutes he took a large pinch of snuff from an enormous snuff-box, which was lying by his side. I believe that he himself took down every word of the evidence, as he kept on writing as fast as his pen could move, and while doing so, would frequently exclaim, "Stay! stay! stay! stay!"

I have frequently heard sentence of death passed for horse or sheep stealing, and to the death sentence was generally appended a rider that the condemned's body should be given up to the doctors for dissection, which latter, it was said, the convict dreaded more than the hanging.

During the assizes my father always had a party of barristers to dinner. In fact, they came in most evenings and thus I became acquainted with several of them. Amongst others I got to know well was George Darby, of Markly, who afterwards became our member for East Sussex. Mr. George Darby was not very particular as to his personal appearance. Once when he was canvassing he came to stay for a few days at Lewes with my brother-in-law, Thomas Scutt. Scutt, followed by his servant to take the luggage of the future M.P., went down to the White Hart to meet the coach. On being asked about his luggage, Darby pulled a tooth brush out of his pocket, saying, "Here it is."

Once I had him for a parishioner for about a fortnight, he having been thrown from his horse on Berwick Common and broken his leg, and been carried into the Fullers Arms. After a day or two Mrs. Darby came to nurse him, and of her I formed a very high estimation. I met one of the daughters afterwards when she was staying at my mother's house at Glynde, and was at once struck with her simple dressing and the way she had evidently been brought up. She was very pleasant, intelligent and sensible, with no nonsense.

Once I heard a prisoner, on being sentenced to a long term of transportation say, "Thank you, my lord, and I hope that you may sit there till I come back again."

I have often been present when the leading counsel were Thessiger and Platt. Thessiger, in his examination of witnesses, seemed to me *sauviter in modo*, whereas I considered Platt a gruff and very unpleasant examiner. He used to frighten the witnesses, and I have seen a women faint under his cross-examination. I much preferred Thessiger, but I believe that Platt is generally acknowledged to have been the sounder lawyer.

It was not at all uncommon at that time for the chief offenders to turn King's evidence. In the riots of 1830 a half-witted lad was tried and hung for burning the barn at Milton Court. When I took charge of Lullington in the summer of 1839, I found there residing the man who had turned King's evidence against him, and who, I understood, had first decoyed the poor imbecile to join him in the crime, and then, to save his own neck, had given him up to the gallows.

In those days, in the early part of this century, several of the magistrates and sheriffs were certainly not refined, and many of them were very deficient in education.

On one occasion my father saw at Lewes sheep fair four ex-sheriffs of the county all drink brandy and water out of the same glass.

At that period it was usual for certain of the magistrates to hold a court at the Ram Inn, at Firle. On one occasion there were three of them there on the bench when a message was brought to one of the trio that there was someone waiting below who particularly desired a word with him. So he went down, and immediately had a writ served upon him, and was informed that he must consider himself under arrest. He asked what he was to do, and was told that he had better send for one of his fellow magistrates to come down and be his bail. So he sent up a message to one asking him to come down at once without giving any reason. The magistrate came down and he, too, was served with a writ. The third magistrate was then summoned by the two first, and he likewise was served with his writ. After the three had become bail for each other they were suffered to return to their magisterial duties. Serving all three writs together was a clever stroke.

At that time many of the men placed in authority wasted their means on their own pleasure and left their just debts unpaid.

One of the three magistrates was Sir Thomas Carr, of Beddingham. He was knighted on the occasion of carrying up an address of congratulation to the King on his providential escape, when fired upon in the theatre. After being knighted, Sir Thomas did not at all understand the extent of his honour. On one occasion, on his being contradicted in something, it was related that he said, "Be-ant I a noble man then?"

The woman who fired the shot at the King was arrested by a glazier named Holroyd. Holroyd refused money when offered him as a reward for what he had done, but instead requested that he might be employed as a glazier to the palace. He was thus brought into notice, entered upon a large business, and amassed wealth, with which he purchased some land at Barcombe, and built Barcombe Place, now the residence of Sir William Grantham. After his death his son squandered his property and the estate and sold it to Sir William's father.

I remember when Queen Victoria came to the throne the Clerk of the Peace made a *lapsus linguae* in swearing in the magistrates. It had been so long since we had had a female sovereign, that the only form that the Clerk of the Peace had to go by was that for a king, and consequently he had to change "his" into "her." "Our most gracious Lord the King" into "Our most gracious Lady the Queen," etc. This he carefully did, and got on all right in reading the formal document until he came to the date in the year of our Lord, when to the astonishment of all he altered that also into "in the year of our Lady," and that in Protestant Lewes!

ANECDOTES, DISCONNECTED AND VARIOUS, AND OLD MEMORIES

When I first went to the Grammar School, in February, 1822, the headmaster, Mr. (afterwards Doctor) Proctor, had been appointed about nine months previously. Under Dr. Merriman, his predecessor, it had been a very good school. Dr. Merriman fell downstairs and injured his back so badly that, after lingering for five or six months, he died. The work of the school had, in the meantime, and until a successor was appointed, been carried on by the assistant master, Robert Airey. Directly a new headmaster was appointed, Airey set up a school in Brighton, taking many of the Grammar School boys with him. So when I first went to school the number of boys was only about thirty; but this was soon increased to about fifty (principally by the boarders Proctor took). The number of the boys on the Foundation was twelve. The class of boys, with I think only two exceptions, consisted of the sons of the clergy, retired officers, solicitors, bankers, doctors, etc. One of the exceptions was a remarkably clever lad named Saxby, son of a saddler living in Lewes, who promised well, and whose father Proctor urged to allow the boy to go on to the University. But the father objected to raise his son above the position to which he was born, and would not consent. It is hardly to be expected that he would have risen as high as the present Bishop of Gloucester, who was a saddler's son from Gloucester. But it seemed a great pity that one who as a boy far excelled his companions in Greek and Latin, should afterwards be seen stitching saddles in his father's shop, as I often saw him doing when on my way home from school.

In several cases the widows of officers and clergymen moved to Lewes on purpose for their sons to have the advantage of the Grammar School. I was one of the boys on the Foundation. The trustees of the school each had in turn to nominate a boy, and when Lord Hampden's turn arrived, in 1822, he offered my father the presentation for me, knowing that my two elder brothers were already at the school. When Proctor left, in 1829, the numbers were again much reduced by those who accompanied him to Guernsey. His successor was the Rev. C. H. Williams, but he kept such a poor table, nearly starving the boys, that he had but few boarders. My younger brother, Harvey, was one who had to be removed very ill with a sort of low fever, brought on by want of sufficient food.

Williams' successor was Dr. Carey. In his time the school premises were rebuilt, sufficient a subscription being raised for the purpose – to which I was very sorry not to be able to contribute, but as I was at the time rebuilding Berwick Rectory, I had not a guinea to spare. Dr. Carey was succeeded by Mr. Green, who was starved to death by ossification of the throat, which, gradually closing, prevented his taking food. Green was succeeded by Wooley. In his time the numbers at the school gradually dwindled till his only pupil was his own son. On Wooley's death the school was shut up for a time. Meetings were held to try and revive the school, but without effect.

At last a Mr. White, who had a good commercial school in the Cliffe, made an offer for the use of the premises, which was accepted, and he has since carried on a school there, with the assistance of a University man to teach classics.

The cause of the dwindling of the school was (in my estimation) principally the First Reform Bill, which made Parliamentary voters of every £10 householder, and consequently boys were appointed on the Foundation to secure their father's votes; and a class of boys were admitted which lowered the whole stamp of the old Grammar School. Consequently the upper classes of the Lewes residents sent their boys elsewhere.

Looking back to my boyhood, I often think that people nowadays hardly realise that many things we now regard as almost indispensable, were not invented then.

There were no cheap books, no cheap newspapers – the very cheapest paper was one single small "news sheet" for sevenpence. Then, and for long afterwards, there was a duty of threepence to be paid on each newspaper sold.

No steel pens, so each person had to use quills and to know how to mend them. Blotting paper was in use, but sand was much more generally used, and always kept in its proper place, in a thing like a pepper castor, in each inkstand. Wafers were used to fasten papers together, and every gentleman carried his own seal. Of course envelopes were unknown. There was no penny post, the postage of a letter from London to Lewes was eightpence, and if the smallest scrap of paper was put inside the folded sheet double postage was charged. Letters from a distant part of England often cost three or four shillings.

The letter was a sheet of paper, folded so as to leave a blank space for the direction, and fastened by being sealed down. Inside, the paper was often covered every square inch with writing, crossed and sometimes re-crossed. Letters were not prepaid, but the postman collected the postage on delivery.

Poor people could not afford to have letters, and so it was often years before they heard even of the death of a relative living at a distance.

One common device to get to know if a friend or relation was still alive, was to get a sheet of paper, direct, seal and post it to the absent one. The person whose name was on the letter would know the writing, and refuse to take it in, saying he or she could not afford the postage. Then the person whose name was on the letter would get another blank sheet and direct it to the sender of the first sheet, who also would refuse to take in the letter. Other devices were to have pre-arranged signals: for instance, if a letter came addressed to Mrs. W. White, Mrs. White would know that the sender was well – Mrs. I. White that the sender was ill – Mrs. B. White better, and so on.

My father told me of some kind-hearted old gentleman who in passing heard a poor old woman tell the post man that she had no money so she could not take her soldier son's letter in. The gentleman stopped and paid three or four shillings for the letter from a distant land, so that the poor mother might have it. She thanked him gratefully, but as soon as the postman was gone opened the sheet which was a perfect blank. Poor old thing, she could not read, but her son had arranged to send the letter to let her know he was alive.

A member of Parliament had the right to "frank" three or four letters every day, and then they were delivered free. To "frank" a letter the member would write his name on the lower left-hand corner. Franks were often asked for and given especially for letters going a long distance when the postage was very heavy.

Lucifer matches were not invented till 1827 or 1828, and at first were half a crown a box, but very soon got down to a shilling. Before that, flint, steel, and the tinder box were used to light the matches, which were strips of cardboard dipped in brimstone. As a boy, getting up early on dark winter mornings to learn my lessons, I always had to strike a light by this slow process. On very cold mornings, instead of sitting in the special children's sitting-room, I used to go quietly into the kitchen and light the kitchen fire, knowing that the maids would never betray me, being only too pleased to find their fire lighted.

Trains, electric telegraphs, telephones, and steam vessels were not thought of in my young days, any more than bicycles or sewing machines.

Eighty years ago, before the establishment of the present system of police, shrewd artifices were resorted to collect money, which would now be immediately stopped. I have repeatedly seen men with a box of cigars and a handful of straws, about seven to eight inches long, and heard them cry, "Who will buy a straw? Only a penny each"; and on receiving the penny, give a cigar in addition to the straw.

Once a man came round with little packets, which he declared to be flea powder, and promised to give full directions for use to anyone who would buy a packet. The directions were as follows: "Catch the flea first, then squeeze the flea between your finger and thumb, so as to make it open its mouth, and then put a small quantity of the powder on its tongue." This he said in the most good-humoured way and had ready some mild answer to all that was said to his nonsense. Thus if a person told him that if he could catch a flea he would not want the powder to kill it, he could civilly say, "Of course, sir, you can kill it what way you like"; or if told that the powder was no use, he would say, "How could you expect the powder to have any effect unless you made the flea take it?"

There was once a notice stuck up outside a stable in Brighton, that within was to be seen a horse with his tail where his head ought to have been. Charge two pence only for the exhibition. On entering, a horse was seen tied up by his tail to the manger. Some young men who had been themselves taken in, induced several others to go in and see the wonderful sight for themselves, declaring the fact to be perfectly true.

CARELESS CLERGY, AND CHURCH CUSTOMS
AT THE BEGINNING OF THE CENTURY

In my young days the reading of "briefs" in churches frequently occurred, but the collections (I think) were generally very small – but I myself remember nothing about the collections.

A "brief" was a sort of letter giving official orders for collections to be made. These collections were for various objects, generally for things people knew and cared little about; but occasionally they were for local objects.

At Beddingham the Ante-Communion Service was always read from the desk. Immediately we came out of church we found the clerk, who had already hastened out with bills of sales in his hand, reading the same in the churchyard for the edification of the congregation as they were leaving the church. In this way news of sales or markets was circulated.

I recollect being present once at a funeral at Beddingham. Mr. Nott, who had walked over from Lewes to take it, appearing in yellow sheep-skin gaiters which were very visible, especially when his surplice was blown aside.

The Holy Communion was celebrated only once a quarter in any church, as far as I know.

Some clergy used constantly to hunt; the Rev. Doctor Hooker and Rev. P. G. Crofts always appearing in a regular hunting cap. On one occasion the Rev. W. Harison, Vicar of Alfriston and Malling, passed me on his way back to Lewes with his scarlet hunting coat besmeared with mud from a fall he had evidently had, and my judgement at the time was that it served him right.

At that time very few of the clergy were resident in their parishes – most of them were pluralists – and Lewes was spoken of as "The Rookery," from the number that rode out of Lewes in black coats to their various duties each Sunday.

At the time the new turnpike road from Lewes to Eastbourne was made (1819), along the whole distance the only resident clergyman was Capper of Wilmington. *A propos* of him I may mention an anecdote which I had from his grandson, Bishop Vidal, who had it from his grandfather's old coachman. It is as follows: The coachman said that years before, when a young man, he drove his master on a Sunday after morning service at Wilmington to Hurstmonceux Rectory, where four clergymen met to dine together between services. It turned out to be a wet afternoon, and so the four clergymen instead of turning out to their various services, spent the whole afternoon in card playing. Mr. Capper's servant said he saw them himself. Mr. Hare's servant had invited him to follow him to the door of the room where they were playing and to peep in, telling him he would see such a sight as he probably had never seen before, four parsons playing cards on a Sunday afternoon. The four were Robert Haire, Vicar of Hurstmonceux; Edward Raynes, Vicar of Firle (afterwards Archdeacon);

Harry West, Vicar of Wartling; and Capper, Vicar of Wilmington. Raynes, whilst he was Archdeacon, was head of a whist club in Lewes. His house was in St. Anne's parish, just at the eastern entrance to Rotten Row.

I recollect that while he was Archdeacon he gave a dinner party on Ash Wednesday, quite forgetting the day, and when he did recollect it, he merely ordered pancakes as an extra dish.

Ever since I have been in Orders, I know that a clergyman living in Lewes, who was looked up to as an eloquent preacher, played whist on a Saturday night and did not leave off till daylight on Sunday morning.

Seventy or eighty years since the clergy generally largely indulged in good wine. One man, especially, used to take his place next the Archdeacon at the Visitation dinners that he might seize the opportunity of filling his glass before the bottle was passed round, and again when it returned to the chairman.

There were some, however, who were too poor to indulge in wine. Poor Mr. Jenkins, Curate of Isfield, for instance, of whom it was reported that he washed his own shirt and mangled it by putting it between the leaves of his big Bible and sitting upon it.

I have been told that Mr. Williams, a Welshman, once in Alfriston pulpit gave out his text from the 111th chapter of Colossians!

While I am writing of the clergy, I think I might mention that in 1827 I remember witnessing the building of the new church of St. Peter's, at Brighton, which is now the Parish Church. At the Lewes end of the church was the Brighton cricket ground, which I think was a frequent cause of my being taken to Brighton, as my father was always fond of watching a game of cricket.

The rating of tithes has always been a source of dispute. Before the new Poor Law all the holdings were rated far below their value, and the consequence was that the total amount of the Poor Rate, though very high, was not really so high as it appeared. In many parishes the rates were more than twenty shillings in the pound. At Bexhill they were twenty-seven shillings.

Bexhill was always considered the richest living in the diocese, and on its becoming vacant during the Episcopacy of Bishop Maltby, he presented thereto his brother-in-law, Baker. The farmers, instead of making a regular rate upon him, when they paid their tithes deducted a fixed sum for rates, which Baker objected to, saying that he would much rather be rated, and pay the rates himself. So they rated him on the full amount of the tithes paid, and as rates were twenty-seven shillings in the pound, demanded a larger sum than he had received for tithes. The consequence was that he was only too glad to revert to the old plan of leaving the farmers to manage it.

The new turnpike road was of the greatest benefit to Beddingham, for previously the only road from Lewes to Beddingham went round by Glynde, which almost doubled the distance. There used to be a plank across the river for foot passengers, but no regular track. On one occasion a clergyman from Lewes, who had engaged to take the service at Beddingham, wishing to make a short cut, came that way. He got across the river all right, but on attempting to jump a brook jumped in. After the congregation had been kept waiting for half an hour, the clerk, who had frequently been out to see whether he could see the parson coming made this announcement: "There will be no service to-day, for the parson has fallen into a dick." Even some years later the Beddingham clerk would refuse to begin to ring the bell till the clergyman came in sight, for, he said, "How could he tell whether he would get there."

CHEAP METHODS OF ENTERTAINING

When Buonaparte with his army was at Boulogne and threatened to invade England, every preparation was made, not only to resist his landing, but also to ensure the safety of the people. Every farmer had to register the number and size of all his valuable wagons and carts. Beacon fires were built in readiness to be lighted the moment his fleet was seen to be approaching. These beacon fires would flash the news all over England long before messages could be sent any other way.

Directly the beacon fires were lighted all the helpless old men, women and children were to go to the particular vehicle to which they had been allotted. Drivers had been appointed to each wagon, with full instructions as to how they were to reach the refuge inland to which they were to go. The fair land of Sussex was to be made as bare as possible if the enemy appeared, and flocks and herds driven up country. Fortunately, the invasion did not take place. A man named Borrer had a contract with the Government for horsing the different vehicles. How far he had been instrumental in arranging matters with the farmers I cannot say, but as the threatened invasion came to nought Borrer pocketed a large sum of money by his contract.

He, for a long time, partook of other people's hospitality, but was very slow in making any return of the same. At length, having received a present of a haunch of venison, he asked a large party of men of whose hospitality he had partaken, to dine with him at the Old Ship Inn at Brighton – a noted house then, and since, for such entertainments. The day arrived, and the guests assembled. Borrer told them to call for what they liked, and the guests, knowing that Borrer was very wealthy but usually very penurious, seized the opportunity of calling for the best wines, bottle after bottle. Now the Old Ship Inn was also noted for its wines. Dinner over, at length Borrer asked for his bill, which, after receiving, he handed to the guest sitting next him, saying that as he was a good accountant he should ask him to estimate how much ahead the feast cost. Then he left each guest to pay his share – about three guineas. First one paid, then another, and the rest, being taken by surprise, also did so. It came out afterwards that he had made an agreement with the landlord that the venison was to pay for his own share.

I remember having the following anecdote from George Simcox, the Lewes stage-coach driver. Mrs. Davies Gilbert, of Eastbourne, was quite a character. She was the only daughter and heiress of Mr. Gilbert, solicitor, of Lewes, and predecessor of Mr. Hoper, my grandfather's great friend, and married the celebrated and learned Mr. Davies Giddy, of Cornwall, who took his wife's name of Gilbert. One evening someone called on Mrs. Gilbert to ask for a subscription. She refused, but to show it was not the money she grudged she burnt a ten pound note in a candle which stood on the table.

Once a visitor, who was staying at Eastbourne with the Gilberts, said to Mr. Gilbert at breakfast that he had been up early, and occupied in doing him a great service by destroying in the garden some enormous snails. Mr. Gilbert received the information with horror, for these were some rare kind of snail that had been sent him from South America, and he was making observations on their habits.

After her husband's death, at her request, my father acted for a time as her adviser and steward for her landed property, but she was so peculiar that he soon threw it up. She had great ideas of economy and wanted cows as well as oxen to work and draw a plough, and had a team of four donkeys to draw a small wagon. Once she found out that one of her tenants was using bone manure; she forbade it at once, saying "for all she knew they might be her grandmother's bones."

My grandfather's old friend, Mr. Hoper, senior (father of my father's two school-fellows, John and George Hoper), as his first wife had married the daughter of a celebrated London wine merchant, who probably would not have prospered as he did had it not been for Sheridan. When Sheridan was made Under-Secretary of State, he thought it necessary to give a dinner to his colleagues, who, knowing Sheridan's mode of life and his poverty, were, when they sat down to dinner, especially astonished at the excellency of the wines. The port, sherry, madeira, champagne, hock, claret, etc., were all of the best. Sheridan was asked where he got them, and how he chose such excellent wine. The only answer he gave was that he left it to his wine merchant, who was So and So, to choose for him. All the guests thought that as Sheridan was so lax in paying his debts, no wine merchant would have trusted him with any decent wine. The fact was, that when he had decided on giving this dinner party, Sheridan himself went to this wine merchant and told him his difficulty in procuring any decent wine to set before the Ministers, who included Buckingham, Fox, etc., and gave the wine merchant a very broad hint that if he served him well he would recommend him as the supplier of the wines, but acknowledging candidly at the same time that the merchant must not look to him for any payment. The result was that the wine merchant sent a dozen each of the very best of each sort of wine on the understanding that the payment was to be the recommendation. His rapid increase in business soon repaid him his expensive advertisement.

Sheridan was utterly unprincipled. On one occasion his son Tom expressed a desire to go down a coal pit. His father asked what he could want to do that for. Tom answered, "To say that I have been down." The father then said, "Why could he not say so without going down?"

An extraordinary character was the Rev. Harry West, who lived in Lewes, though he was first Vicar of Wartling and then Rector of Berwick. When my father gave up Southover Manor in 1829, Mr. West took the house. Previously he had lived in lodgings over Huggett's, the shoemaker, on School Hill, for many years. As a young man he had been very fond of society, and often imagined himself in love.

Once he went to Mr. Hoper, who was his legal adviser, and gave him instructions about drawing up a marriage settlement. Mr. Hoper said he did not believe Mr. West was going to be married, as so many of his previous proposals had come to nothing! West declared that the marriage was sure to come off this time, where upon Mr. Hoper took a five pound note out of his pocket and, laying it on the table, said that he would give Mr. West that note on condition that he repaid him one guinea each first of January, till he was married. The little man took up and pocketed the note, and on each succeeding first of January till he married, for fifteen years, Mr. Hoper made a point of calling upon Mr. West and demanding his guinea. He eventually married twice, the first time in 1816. The first wife made her appearance at Berwick wrapped up in a blanket, as she was very delicate, and it was for her sake that the old mortar walk was made round the front garden. Mr. West never had any family, and his second wife was dead before I came to Berwick in 1838. When Mr. West left Huggett's lodgings he refused to pay for breakages, whereupon an action was brought against him at the assizes. The claim was made for breaking twelve dozen decanters, twelve dozen rummers, twelve dozen wine glasses, etc. When the case was brought forward, the counsel explained that this was a point of law to cover the whole amount of breakages, and it was for the jury to decide what portion, if any, the defendant was to pay for. He added that they must not think the little reverend gentleman was so uproarious as to commit so great an amount of damage, which they might be sure of when they saw him sitting by his side. Whereupon up jumped Mr. West, who was not much more than five feet high, very indignant against the counsel for describing him as small.

At another assizes he was summoned for refusing to pay for a second-hand pair of leather breeches. In those days riding was the principal means of locomotion. Elphick, tailor, of School Hill, Lewes (the predecessor of Hother), had obtained the appointment of Breeches Maker to H.R.H. the Prince of Wales, who was then very much at Brighton. The consequence was that Elphick was much patronized by the nobility and all who wished to be in the fashion.

Mr. West had gone to Elphick and asked him his charge for making him a pair of leather riding breeches. His answer was ten guineas. Whereupon West tried to beat him down and said "That it might be all very well to charge his Royal Highness, and his noble friends such a price; but that he ought not to think of charging the same amount to a poor country clergyman." At length Elphick said, "You know Lord Leslie. He is much about your size and figure. A short time since I made for him a pair, which he declared did not fit, so they were returned on my hands, and I made him another pair. If you like to have the pair that has been returned to me, you shall have them at half price." West was pleased and ordered the breeches to be sent to his lodgings for him to try on. The result was that he agreed to take them. When the bill was sent in it was made out "For a second-hand pair of leather breeches." West refused to pay unless the bill was made out differently. At the trial the counsel said that if Mr. West was able to show by a receipted bill that he had purchased a new pair of leather breeches at so much less than the usual price, it would be a great injury to Elphick, and that therefore it was necessary to state on the bill why they had been supplied at less than the usual price. Of course Mr. West lost his case – as he invariably did.

He was at times threatened with several actions, for which he paid "smart money" to prevent their being brought into court.

Even at the time of his death he was under threat in an action for the offence of writing to the postmaster of some town, desiring him to post up one of the inhabitants of the same place, who had somehow displeased him, "as a rogue and a vagabond."

Mr. Hoper, his solicitor, was the means of stopping several actions and arranging what smart money was to be paid. Somehow he seemed to live in perpetual state of quarrel, and to take a delight therein.

CELEBRATED MEN I HAVE MET

At one time or another I think I saw most of the celebrated men of the day, either at my grandfather's or my father's house. Most of them were Tories, but a few were Whigs. Amongst the most interesting from a boy's point of view was the Duke of Wellington; he dined at my grandfather's both before and after he was Prime Minister, and I remember seeing him over at Glynde on two or three occasions. George Canning, who afterwards became Prime Minister, also used to come. I remember the news of his appointment being brought from the Post Office by our groom William, who had been sent to meet the London coach one evening on purpose to hear who was appointed. The message was brought in, "Please, sir, Mr. Saxby (the postmaster) says I am to tell you that Mr. Canning is a very good minister." Thus was the appointment announced, the word "Prime" being altered to "very good." As far as my recollection goes he was Prime Minister in 1827 and died three or four months later.

Lord John Russell (only it was long before he was Prime Minister), I also remember, was a very clever man, a most able speaker and very much interested in the Reform Act which eventually he got passed in 1832. I think he was first brought to Glynde by his father, the Duke of Bedford, who was an intimate friend of both my grandfather and father, and who kept up frequent correspondence with them as long as he lived.

Arthur Young, who by his writings and travelling about the country studying the various states of agriculture in the different parts, was doing good service to his country, was frequently our guest. A very keen observer, what he had to say was always worth listening to.

At one time or another, I have seen all the Royal Dukes at my grandfather's, with the exception of the Duke of Kent – whom I cannot recall having seen there. It must be remembered that Glynde and Southover were both within riding distance of Brighton, and that the Court was often there. I think the Duke of Sussex must at one time have ridden over at least once a week. He was most pleasant and friendly, not only to his host but to all the family. The first time he came over unexpectedly with the evident intention of being invited to luncheon, my grandmother was rather overwhelmed and retreated to hastily supervise her maids in preparing additions for the repast. While they were hard at work, she turned up her sleeves and putting on an apron began before an open window in the pantry to make some fancy dish. Suddenly a voice exclaimed, "If every farmer's wife would look after her household things as well as you do, Mrs. Ellman, it would be better for their husbands." It was the Duke of Sussex, whom her husband was taking by a short cut across the garden to Glynde Place. After that he frequently came over, was most cordial in manner, and would drop in at meal-times and seemed to enjoy getting away from the Court.

He was very intimate with the Earl of Egremont, and I believe it was the Earl who first brought him to Glynde.

Neither my grandfather nor father were courtiers but treated Royalty respectfully and naturally, which I fancy was appreciated. I remember some years later being told that my in formant had the previous day seen four men walking together on the Brighton race-course, engaged in eager, animated conversation – that three of them were Dukes and the fourth my father, and that no one would have guessed from their manner that one was of so much lower rank than the other three.

I never met with the following anecdote of George II in print, so I will give it here. Printing was in those days a much slower process than it is now. People were for some reason especially anxious that year to see the King's speech on opening Parliament, and whoever could first get the speech printed off would command a good sale. So a certain person had printed off what he supposed would be the King's speech and issued it before there was time for the real speech to be put in print whereupon Sir Robert Walpole proceeded to prosecute the man for so doing. The King on hearing of the proposed prosecution directed that the man should be released, saying that he considered it very clever of the man. He had read the speech and liked it much better than his own.

William Pitt died before my time; but the last time I saw my eldest aunt, Mrs. Sankey (I think about 1863). I found her reading the life of Pitt, and she then told me that as a girl on one occasion she had to entertain Pitt for two or three hours at her home in Betshanger. Her father was out and her mother ill. She said that my Grandfather Boys acted as steward for some of Pitt's property. William Cobbett I remember well, and his political skits. He was getting an old man when I saw him, but had lost none of his vigour of mind or speech.

Richard Cobden was a Sussex man, son, I think, of a farmer. He was very ardent in his views about the Corn Laws, and at the time I saw him had not got into Parliament.

There was an article in the Quarterly Review (about 1830), on Rat Hunting, evidently written with an underlying political meaning. It was generally ascribed to William Cobbett, being in his style; but Cobbett's son, the barrister, acknowledged to my father that he himself was the author.

There is an entrance to the house at Glynde, opposite the stable, which leads past various offices, baking room etc., and thence into the house. By this passage, which made a short cut, old Lord Hampden, who was on the most friendly terms with my grandfather, frequently entered the house unannounced. On one occasion he suddenly appeared with the Duke of Cambridge, whom he was bringing to get some agricultural information or to see the celebrated flock of sheep. Finding in the house another Royal Duke and the Earl of Egremont, he said my grandfather must give an impromptu dinner that evening, adding, "I shall invite myself." Making some excuse he went hastily back to Glynde Place, told the housekeeper to go over at once and see what dishes she could hastily make, and returned in a very few minutes. The consequence was that between the two kitchens everything was cooked in time. After that, whenever my grandfather was giving a big dinner party, or even a small one to celebrities, Lord Hampden would come in as a matter of course, and often at the last moment one or two dainty dishes would appear from Glynde Place.

I only remember Lord Hampden as a very old man; he died childless and was succeeded by his brother, who also left no children. The Trevors. who were distant cousins, then inherited the Glynde property, and through them it came in the end to the Brands. Mr., afterwards Sir Henry Brand, being raised to the peerage, took the old title of Hampden, which was associated with Glynde.

BANK FAILURES

At the Grammar School at Lewes, when we broke up for the Christmas holidays, we always had an evening of theatricals in the schoolroom. A regular stage was fitted up, with drop-scene, etc. The scenery was made of sheets of brown paper pasted together and painted. Of course, the scenes did duty in various plays, but there was always at least one new scene painted every year. One of the boys was chief artist.

Our drop-scene was a very good representation of the front of the Black Horse Inn in St. Anne's (Lewes). One scene I recollect was very elaborate, the deck of a ship, masts, etc., being made separate. I think I may say it was quite up to the theatrical scenery of the times. Prologues and epilogues were always written for the occasion. Our poet was Arthur Lee, an uncle of one of the boys who was one of our principal actors. Mr. Lee was no mean poet, as various rhymes that were published testified. As a specimen of one of the things he wrote for our breaking up, I will give the concluding lines of one of the prologues that I still remember: –

"A stout yew bow, if strung for many hours,
Loses its virtues, and elastic powers –

Unstring the classic bow a little while
With temper'd play relieve the scholar's toil
He'll turn to labour with a keener zeal,
And study be with him a welcome guest."

Old Lee, the original proprietor of the Sussex Advertiser, was always glad to get anecdotes for his paper, and was frequently imposed upon by some of my schoolfellows sending him wonderful tales. One anecdote amongst many others sent him was that a wild duck had a nest in Miss Shelley's rookery, and had hatched out there. This was repeated for two or three years in the paper.

Old Lee had very long grey hair, which after a time he dyed, with the result that it became all the colours of the rainbow.

My cousin, Fanny Sankey (afterwards Mrs. Ottaway) learnt miniature painting on ivory from a Miss Biffin, who had neither arms nor legs. Miss Biffin came to Brighton in 1829 for the purpose of giving lessons.

As my eldest sister, Catharine, was always fond of drawing, in which she was successful in various styles she thought she would like to have lessons in miniatures. Knowing that Fanny Sankey had formerly been Miss Biffin's pupil, she thought it well to take advantage of her coming only eight miles away. The first portrait she painted under Miss Biffin's instruction was that of myself. Miss Biffin was a heavy-looking woman; she wore a turban, and was always seated on a sofa. Her paint brush was pinned to a large puff sleeve, which covered the short stump of the upper part of the arm. She fixed and removed the paint brush with her teeth when it was necessary to wash the brush. When painting she leant her right shoulder forward, almost touching the table. She declared that she considered that for painting she had the advantage of those who had arms, for surely it was easier to paint with a short brush than with a long stick.

Once I was asked by her to ring the bell, when her man-servant appeared, who took up and carried his unwieldy mistress out of the room. In a few minutes he brought her back and deposited her on the sofa.

If I recollect right, after a few weeks she suddenly disappeared from Brighton, greatly in debt.

Strange to relate, she was married to a Lieutenant Wright, R.N., who, it was said, had eloped with her!

About 1824 Cook's circus came to Southover and performed in an open field, there being no tent. After the performance there was a collection, as being in an open field it was impossible to exclude anyone.

I perfectly well remember the great number of banks failing in 1825, though of course I was too young at that time to know the cause of the great monetary crisis. Almost everyone who had money in a bank was for drawing it out, fearing that the bank would, like so many others, come to a smash.

To give confidence to the Old Bank, Lewes, I recollect a long printed list of men each stating for what amount they would be answerable, the sums varying up to thousands of pounds. Notwithstanding this, the crisis led to the suicide of Dicker, the junior partner of the bank. One of the customers had given notice that on a certain day he would require, and must draw out, a large sum. When the day arrived, Dicker saw the customer on his way to the bank, and knowing that owing to the large number of small customers drawing out all their money, the cash in the bank was at a very low ebb, and the large sum could not be paid, went out hastily to the back of the bank and shot himself, little guessing that the man was coming to say that after all he could give them longer time before drawing his money.

Post chaises were employed in all parts of the country to bring down cash from London to the various banks, many of which were obliged to close business, though perfectly safe, through not having the cash in hand.

All kinds of schemes were made use of to protract payment. Frequently it would happen that the bank was hourly expecting a fresh supply of gold from London; gold being the only medium which the customers would accept.

One very common device was for a clerk to go into an inner room, and after a time come out with a bag of guineas, and to be most deliberate in his counting them. He would then purposely hand over the money one or two guineas short, asking the payee to count it, which, when he did, of course he found short. The clerk would express astonishment, and re-count, again make a mistake, or say he feared he had, and the money would be slowly counted again by each in turn.

Another not uncommon dodge was to retreat into a back room, and putting a pile of gold pieces into a shovel, hold it over the fire till the shovel itself was red hot, then tilt the money into something else and hastily empty that on the counter in front of the customer. The unfortunate person would burn his fingers in trying to take up and count the gold; and several times a rush on the bank was prevented by the person, as soon as he could pick up the money and was let out of the bank, telling the crowd outside that there was no cause for alarm at that bank, for they were coining the money so fast that there was not time for it even to cool! For some time during the bank failures, and the consequent rush of people to the banks, it was found necessary to barricade the doors, and only let one person in at a time.

One banker tried the expedient of when a large number of smaller customers were drawing out their entire deposits, to, after paying one or two, detain them in the bank while the next person was let in. Then, after apparently ending the conversation with the people already paid off, he would loudly order two bank clerks to bring in another sack of gold from the strong room. With every appearance of tremendous exertion, two clerks would drag in a heavy sack, carefully tied up and sealed. Other clerks would go to their assistance, and the sack would be pushed or carried near enough to the inside of the counter for the onlookers to see it opened. The seals broken, the cords cut, and the sack opened, it was apparently full of sovereigns. From the gold that was seen the small clients would be paid, and return to the crowd outside with the news of the sackfuls of money still in the bank. Of course, only the bank officials knew that the sack was filled with stones, on top of which rested, first sawdust, and then a thin layer of coins.

ELIZABETH COLLEGE, GUERNSEY

When I was confirmed, in 1829, the Confirmation service was held in St. Anne's Church, Lewes. And on that occasion, some of the confirmees were brought all the way from Seaford in wagons – a distance of eleven or twelve miles, great boys and girls riding together, and all feasted before they returned home. The day was looked upon by most of the young people as a regular outing, the greater part of the day being spent on the road, going backwards and forwards. It is easy to imagine how little they came prepared for the solemn rite.

At that period a bishop would frequently only repeat the prayer, "Defend, O Lord, this, Thy child," once for a whole railful, and then pass along the rail laying his hand on the head of each. Even in much later years I have known incumbents to communicate a whole railful with one repetition only to each railful. Needless to say, they were very careless churchmen.

At that time, and for many years after, in the Chichester Diocese, as well as in other dioceses, confirmations were held only once in every three years, and then only in the towns, so that all the villages around had to send their candidates to the nearest town. I was only thirteen when I was confirmed, which was rather an early age at that date; but I was anxious to be confirmed, and my parents also wished my confirmation to take place before I left home. Mr. Proctor, in the spring of 1829, had accepted the post of head-master to Queen Elizabeth's College, in Guernsey, which was being rebuilt, and at my request my parents consented to my being one of the boys who were to accompany him to his new school in the summer.

As we were only to come home for the midsummer holidays once a year, I had to take with me quite an outfit, and for the first time was given some pocket money. Before that I had only had money given me very occasionally, and never much at a time. I remember how pleased I was to have some pocket money, and spending the first month's instalment on a birthday gift for my mother – a small seal, set in silver, which she ever after carried in her pocket.

The first time I went to Guernsey all the principal luggage of the boys was sent with Proctor's furniture, he having chartered a small vessel to carry his goods from Newhaven to Guernsey.

Then the morning we started, either the Southampton or the Portsmouth coach (I forget which) came from Brighton to Lewes to pick us up, so that we all might start together, Proctor taking several of his old pupils with him besides several new ones, Proctor himself, with his family and some of the boys, going by another coach to Portsmouth, intending to proceed to Southampton by boat.

But when it was time for us to proceed from Southampton to Guernsey, the Portsmouth portion of our party had not turned up. The captain, saying we were sure to meet the Portsmouth steamer, started, and so we did a few miles down the Southampton Water, and transferred Proctor and his party to our small vessel.

On reaching Guernsey we all stopped at an hotel for three days, and fared sumptuously, which hotel was, whilst I was still in Guernsey, burnt down.

The new college (Queen Elizabeth College was being rebuilt)

was not quite completed. They were hurrying forward the finishing of the schoolrooms, and about three weeks after our arrival in Guernsey Queen Elizabeth College was re-opened; but the residential portion was not completed until the following Christmas. So in the meantime Proctor had hired the corner house in New Street, into which we moved three days after landing, as soon as he could get his furniture, which arrived when we did, unpacked, and put into the house.

As we were very much pressed for room, directly the first bed-room could be got finished off enough to sleep in, five or six of us went in there to sleep, of whom I was one. We had the top room in the north-east tower.

Proctor had upwards of thirty boarders; Davies, the vice-principal, whose house adjoined the north-east corner of the college ground, also had several pupils; and so had Taylor, who was another of the masters.

The total number of the college pupils whilst I was there was just over two hundred. We each had our own number, which number commenced when Elizabeth College was revived about 1825. My number was 219. Our numbers were marked in our books, on our clothes, cap, etc. We all wore college caps; the sixth form with tassels, the others without them.

The college cap was a most dangerous missile, and I know of some most awkward accidents, such as a head cut open badly with them.

These caps were at Elizabeth College commonly called "congers," being considered by the boys to resemble the shape of soup bowls, and conger soup being a common dish in Guernsey. By the wearing of these, boys were known to belong to the college, and in the outskirts of the town and in the country the boys were not in good repute. Unless we had a special permit, we were limited to certain bounds, about a mile and a half on two roads, and a less distance on some others. We were especially forbidden to go down the town. But I myself was frequently sent by Dr. Proctor there to do various things for him. After a time a roll-call was instituted, fixed at such times as to prevent our being absent above an hour and a half at a time. This I found very annoying, and it led me to ask for a watch, which my father accordingly sent me. I frequently took a book, and after getting into the country, got over into a field and sat down to read. The watch enabled me to know how long I might stay.

We had about twelve fixed holidays in the year, of which Queen Elizabeth's birthday, which was the same as my own, September 7th, was one. On these holidays I generally used to get permission for a walk to a distant part of the island. My usual companion was George Crockford, the orphan son of a former Lewes doctor. His only sister married Richard Turner, another Lewes medical man, and father of the present Lewes doctor of that name.

In the basement floor of the college were three or four large rooms, not finished off in my time. Here I spent much time in quiet study, for I could never study with any profit except when alone. I never cared to join in a game of play. Indeed, I grudged the time. My favourite relaxation was a walk, and I soon became acquainted with all parts of the island, my walks extending to Totteval Common and Librou inland, a distance of seven or eight miles from the college. There are some very pretty bays to the south, to which I was very fond of going, such as Fermain, Saints, and Petit Bot bays. In these the bathing was particularly good and retired.

At the college we bathed frequently, usually before breakfast. We generally went in one or more boats to some suitable point, according to the tide. Our most usual bathing-place was a small bay just under Fort George. Here we were frequently joined by some of officers from the barracks just above, who came down in their dressing-gowns, and afterwards ascended to their own quarters to dress. While at Guernsey I have frequently seen a horse accompanying his master when he went to bathe, swimming by his side a long way out to sea. Sometimes, when far away from land, his master (Mr. Le Fevre) would climb on his back for a short rest.

Having weekly pocket money at Guernsey, I indulged myself by subscribing to a Guernsey newspaper, as I was anxious to learn all the information I could about the new discoveries in science, which were then being made. I also was particularly anxious to hear tidings of Sir John's Franklin's explorations in the Polar regions, in which I had always been much interested.

At St. Pierre-Porte, Guernsey, gas was first used soon after I went there in 1829. A short time previously a Russian vessel having been wrecked off the coast, the sailors climbed the lamp posts and drank the oil.

GUERNSEY

It was not till I went with Dr. Proctor to Guernsey in 1829 that he understood me. I at once asked to be allowed to sit up later than the other boys, in order to learn my lessons, and from that time his manner was completely changed towards me, and I escaped all punishment.

During the three years I was at Guernsey I was each year awarded the fifth form prize for good conduct, but I always remained at the bottom of my class. However hard I worked it seemed as if I could not do well in the competition of a class. Competition certainly did not answer in my case, and it was only when I was released from working in class, and allowed to go my own pace that I got on. I leave on record this account of my school days as a warning against making mistakes in the instruction of children. I have written it before, and write it again. Over and over again I have gone over their lessons with boys in my own class and helped them to prepare – often giving them the information which enabled them to keep above me – but I never could bring out in time what I knew when an answer was required.

Two or three times during the three years I was in Guernsey Proctor took us over in boats to the island of Herm. For about a mile on the north and north-west of Herm, and again in a small bay on the south-east, the whole beach is composed of minute shells, some of which are very elegant; but mixed up with these were still larger quantities of broken shells. The usual mode of collecting the shells was to fill a small bag with a handful or two which could be picked over at leisure.

One common shell at Guernsey was the Auris Marina, or Sea Ear, commonly called "Aurmers." I have myself at low tide picked them off the rocks. Now they are strictly preserved, as mother of pearl ornaments are made from this lovely shell. In size they vary from an inch to five or six inches long, the usual size being about four and a half inches. This fish, when cooked, was a favourite dish, and said to taste like a veal cutlet.

Whilst I was there the new Fish Market was built, and it was said to be the finest fish market in the world at the time. There were forty-five large marble slabs, which were usually plentifully supplied with fish. A very common fish there was the "Gar" fish. John Doreys were fairly plentiful; large conger eels very plentiful; these the salesmen had frequently to prevent from wandering too far from their stalls. Crabs and rock crabs and very large crawfish were also abundant, also lobsters, not all of which, however, are caught on the Guernsey coast, for once I went on board a lobster vessel just arrived from Norway and saw the large well (which was open with pierced holes to let in the sea water) full of lobsters.

There appeared to be a great deal of trade done by the Guernsey shipping with most parts of the world. The harbour at that time was only a tidal harbour, but it has since been very much enlarged. The mail packets, when weather permitted, came from Weymouth three times a week. Occasionally they were very much delayed, and I recollect on one occasion our being a whole week without letters. Whenever the mail arrived there was soon a crowd collected round the post office, waiting for the letters to be sorted, which usually took an hour.

While at Guernsey I was surprised to see the number of animals attached to one plough. On one occasion I saw five yoke oxen and six horses pulling a plough. The field that was being ploughed was one probably of about three acres, on a steep slope, in the parish of Catel, and studded with large pieces of rock. The large number of animals attached to the plough seemed to encumber rather than assist each other.

I afterwards learnt that as the farm holdings were very small, twenty acres being considered a very large occupation, each small farmer seldom had a sufficiently strong team for ploughing, therefore they used to combine teams, and the occupiers of the land, instead of paying for the use of the animals, feasted their owners, expecting the like treatment from them when their own land needed ploughing.

The carts were very low and heavy and were usually drawn by an ox in the shafts, with a horse as leader, the harness being composed entirely of rope and matting. The women used to ride to market sitting between a pair of panniers, with one leg on either side of the horse's neck. My observations only relate from 1829 to 1832.

The money used at Guernsey was usually old French coins, so worn that it was difficult to make out the inscription. One peculiar coin was the "double," of which eight went to a penny. At first old centimes and metal buttons with the strig off were used as such, but in 1830 there came out a new copper coinage of pennies, half-pennies, and doubles, and then it required very careful calculation to add up a sum of money. The largest silver coin that was commonly used was a two and-threepence-halfpenny.

Though French monies were used accounts were reckoned in pounds, shillings and pence. Directly I went to Guernsey I tried to keep money accounts, but when it was suddenly enacted that a tenpenny piece for the future would only pass as ninepence, and a fivepenny piece as fourpence, I gave up in despair. The two-and threepence-halfpenny piece had at one time, I heard, been of much larger value, but the value had gradually been reduced. What coin it had originally been I never could make out. No French names were ever applied to the coins. One pound notes were in common use, and I recollect on one occasion on going to the bank for change for a note, receiving exchange in "doubles," or actually 1920 coins for a pound note. But fortunately I had not to count these doubles, for they were delivered in rolls of a shilling and sixpence, as they came from the Mint, and these rolls used to pass from hand to hand without being opened. The size of the roll and the very feel, with the paper they were rolled in, was quite sufficient to show the value.

I learnt to swim at Guernsey by deliberately walking out of my depth when bathing. I then kept on treading water, which kept me from sinking. Then I paddled with my hands and swam like a dog with alternate motion of the arms; and thus gained in my floating powers before I learnt the proper swimming stroke. I soon learnt progression in the water with any two of my limbs, and by throwing myself on my back could swim backwards by using my legs, and at the same time carry something in my hands clear of the water.

While we bathed there was generally a man near in a boat in case of accident. On one occasion, when I was close by, a boy had climbed into the boat, and to my surprise the boatman began a quotation from Horace. I found he was equally at home with other authors, but he would not tell us what made him turn boatman, or where he was educated. I was convinced that he was a gentleman when he forgot himself and spoke in his evidently natural voice.

Soon after I went to Guernsey, in the summer of 1829, my grandfather gave up the Glynde house to my father and retired to Lewes for rest and quiet. So when I returned home after a year I found Southover no longer my home. Though my grandfather had given up the house he came and stayed with us for part of the holidays, and I spent a good deal of time driving him about the country lanes, or often slowly in the grounds of the house, which have now been turned into enlarging Glynde Park. I took advantage of getting him quietly to myself to question him about old customs, places, and people, and particularly on family history. He had become very feeble in body, and was slowly dying of ossification of the heart, but he still took great interest in everything.

I heard of George the Fourth's death as we came into Southampton Water; it must have taken place the previous day, near the end of June, but William the Fourth's Coronation did not take place for fourteen months.

On June 28th, 1830, the day of King William's proclamation, I dined in the midshipmen's mess on board H.M.S. "Hyperion," my brother Spencer being at that time attached to that ship. My father had been invited (with my uncle, Rev. Francis Barrow, who was staying at Glynde) to dinner with the captain, and he took me with him to see my brother, whom I had not seen for some years, he having been absent on foreign service ever since he had joined the Navy. It was amusing to hear at mess the frequent exclamation, "Who would not be a middy now? A middy is a King."

We did not get back till very late that night, and I remember falling asleep between my father and uncle during the long drive home from Newhaven, where the ship was stationed.

I think that the glass of grog that one of the mates insisted upon my drinking the Sailor King's health in, helped to send me to sleep.

MY SAILOR BROTHER

I think it was not till about 1835 that the present Coastguard Service was organised as a special department, though special naval officers and sailors were stationed on different parts of the coast to prevent smuggling.

About 1827, H.M.S. "Hyperion" was stationed at Newhaven for that purpose and remained there for several years. Before the "Hyperion" arrived to look after the coast, my cousin, Lieutenant Henry Sankey, was despatched on Preventive Service (as it was then called) and stationed at Seaford. He was a married man, so very glad of some shore work. The house he occupied with his wife and family was a corner house on the sea-front. In December, 1824, one rough day, whilst he was sitting upstairs with his wife, hearing a noise below, he went down, and found a cask, which had been in the cellar, floating about in the hall. The sea had broken through the shingle bank and flooded the lower part of the town. As the water was rapidly rising he lost no time in wading through the water with his wife and children and taking refuge on the higher ground near the church. It was stated publicly that on this occasion of the sea breaking in some fish were drowned, also some ducks, though some fowls in the same yard as the ducks and fish escaped.

The fact was the fish were fresh-water fish and had their home in a pond. The salt water breaking into the yard killed the fresh-water fish. The ducks went swimming about the salt-water flood in the yard quite happily until the water, continuing to rise, they got pent up under a roof and had not the sense to dive under the roof and escape; whilst the frightened fowls, on the water coming in, flew on to the top of a haystack which floated.

About 1860 the sea again broke into Seaford, shortly after it had been arranged to build terraces and stray houses on the shingle. The water remained for a long time, and it was amusing to see a large board in the middle of the water announcing "This desirable building land – To be Let or Sold." However, the water was by some means after some months drained off, and the houses are now built. It is hoped the sea will not break through again.

My eldest brother Spencer, before entering the Navy, was sent by my father for four or five months to a school near Yvetot, in Normandy, to learn French, the knowledge of which language he afterwards found most useful to him. Even as a youngster he was often taken ashore by the Captain to act as interpreter. He was first appointed to the "Aurora" frigate, Captain Maxwell, on March 25, 1825, and went in her to Lisbon. In 1826 the "Aurcra" returned to England and was at once ordered to the West Indies. While they were weighing anchor at Spithead the Captain died. At that time Captain Austen was living at Anglesea Terrace, Gosport, and with his glass was watching the "Aurora" preparing to sail, when he suddenly saw the anchor, which was being weighed, drop, and the Captain's flag' half-masted. He immediately hired a small boat and hasted to the frigate, where he heard of Captain Maxwell's death. Hastening on shore again, he immediately posted up to London to the Admiralty, carrying the news of Captain Maxwell's sudden decease, and asked for the appointment. On being asked how soon he could be ready he said, "To-morrow." As it was desired that the "Aurora" should proceed to her destination without delay he got the appointment. He hastened back to Gosport, at once joined the frigate and sailed within four days of the former Captain's sudden death.

Under Captain Maxwell there had been amongst the crew much insurbordination and drunkenness; and it was said that the late Captain's illness under which he sank was attributable to excessive drinking.

Under Captain Austen matters were soon altered. He was firm in his discipline, but kind. At that time the West Indies was considered to be a most pestilential climate, and the mortality amongst the sailors was very great. Captain Austen, in consultation with the Doctor, was convinced that this arose in great measure from getting chilled after excessive heat. So it was agreed between them that whenever a man came under the Surgeon's hand, the Doctor should prescribe flannel to be worn, of which they took care to have a sufficient supply in store. The result was only one death – and that out of a crew of about three hundred – in all the three years the "Aurora" remained in the West Indian station, to the great astonishment of the Admiralty; and moreover the man who died was suffering from liver disease before he left England.

When Spencer was in the "Galatea," Captain Sir Charles Napier undertook to rig the ship in twelve hours with his own crew alone, and did so. He invented paddles for the ship to be worked by hand, and with these he brought the ship out from the harbour to Spithead, my father and mother being witnesses thereof from a boat. They had gone down to Spithead to see my brother, who had not been home since he joined the Navy, but had been transferred from ship to ship without any loss of time. When their boat neared the vessel, Spencer appeared at a port-hole to tell them that he would ask for permission for them to come on board, but stepping on the scuttle, which was not securely fastened, he fell overboard, and was picked up by the boat before he was missed on board. Thus my father and mother got on board sooner than they otherwise might have done, and received especial attention from the officers. Spencer was not long on the "Galatea," but was transferred to the "Hyperion" at Newhaven for a short time. Thirty years later, when he was in command of the "Salamander," he was at the capture of Martaban and Rangoon in 1852, and having obtained permission from the Admiral "to open the ball," he him self fired the first shot. Seeing the Admiral's boat between the "Salamander" and the city, he pointed a gun at a large pagoda with a very conspicuous cupola about two miles off, and then waiting till the Admiral was in the direct line of fire, sent the shot over the Admiral's head, and fortunately struck the cupola; whereupon the Admiral remarked: "The man who fired that shot is looking for promotion."

It was Admiral Austen, his old Captain when he was in the "Aurora," who had always shown him great kindness, who made this remark.

As Captain of the "Aurora," he himself always looked after the instruction of the midshipmen, taking them into his cabin for the purpose. One day Spencer, wanting to mend his pen and having no knife with him, took the Captain's razor, for doing which Captain Austen threatened to disrate him, at which threat he was greatly alarmed. In after years a warm friendship sprang up between them, and he continued the good friend of the former middy to the last. The Austens always showed my brother marked kindness, and for years they saw a great deal of him, as Mrs. and Miss Austen went out to the East to be near the Admiral. Just before the commencement of the war Admiral Austen sent his wife and daughter in Spencer's charge to Pulo Penang in safety that they might be out of the way of coming hostilities.

The Admiral died very shortly after, on 7th of October, 1852, greatly respected and regretted, but the friendship with the family continued. On more than one occasion Miss Austen insisted upon personally seeing to the fitting up of Spencer's cabin.

Unfortunately for him his deafness increased so much – deafness caused by a practical joke when a middy. He was asleep on a gun, and for a joke (when the gun was going to be fired off for some reason) he was not roused; this broke the drum of his ear, and he was obliged to retire in 1856.

I never smoked, nor did my grandfather, or any of my brothers. I once saw an article in the "United Service Gazette" about my brother when in command, checking all the youngsters from smoking, and not allowing them to smoke on board. I know, however, that he kept a supply of tobacco to give to the men, but he did not approve of young officers wasting their own and their parents' money in smoke.

VISITS TO LONDON

In 1831 my eyes, which had always been weak, became so much worse that for three months I was not able to look at a book, and for some weeks had them bandaged, and the glare of the sun on the sea or on a road was most painful. There had been much whooping cough about in Guernsey, and I got a very bad cough, though I did not whoop. Years before I had had a similar cough, and not many years ago when the whooping-cough was bad in the village, I had it again, but to this day I cannot say whether I have had the complaint. The Guernsey doctor – Hoskins – physicked me with some most disagreeable medicine (the odour of it alone annoyed the others), and the other boys declared that he was experimenting on me in a way he would not have dared to do on a Guernsey man. I became weak, whether as a result of the medicine or not I cannot say.

At all events that summer I returned from Guernsey sooner than the regular time. My father had written to say that if the doctor would give me leave to travel, he would himself meet me at Southampton on a certain day, on his way home from Wiltshire, where he had been shooting. Of this I was kept in ignorance till the day before starting.

The passage usually took about fourteen hours, leaving Guernsey at 2 p.m. On this occasion there was a little sea on, which so frightened most of the passengers, who had come from Jersey, that instead of proceeding to Southampton they landed at Guernsey, and others from Guernsey deferred their intended crossing till the next boat, two or three days later. I thought the passage all the pleasanter from not having the cabin crowded; for it was not thought prudent for me to pass the night on deck, as I should have liked.

On reaching home I was attended by a Lewes doctor, Armstrong, who, with one of his lotions, stained the whites of my eyes. Afterwards I twice went up to London to see the great oculist, Alexander, before returning to Guernsey.

On my first visit to London I stayed the night at Mr. Robert Proctor's, in Northampton Square, as I could not return the same day after being with Dr. Alexander. Mr. Robert Proctor kept a large dairy. I went to see his cowhouse, which was but a short distance from his residence. I there saw two hundred cows tied up on the ground floor, and two hundred on the floor above. I was told that he kept six hundred cows, but the other two hundred were on a farm in Hertfordshire, some of the cows being sent down as they failed in milk, whilst others were sent up to take their places in the cowhouse.

At that time neither cabs nor omnibuses had been introduced. In the morning the only conveyance I could secure to take me and my carpet bag to meet the coach at Charing Cross was an old lumbering hackney coach. Even that the servant was so long gone after that I was kept waiting a quarter of an hour or twenty minutes. Then, on reaching Charing Cross, the coach had started, so we followed it to the Elephant and Castle, where it waited for a branch coach, which brought passengers from the City. So I had to pay for the hackney coach about seven shillings. These hackney coaches were generally the old private carriages of the nobility.

At that time extensive stabling was required in London for the number of horses required for the various coaches starting from London to all parts of the country.

Of the old-fashioned inn yards I especially call to mind The Bolt-in-Tun, Fleet Street, and the Blue Boar, in Holborn, which is so well described in "Pickwick." I have inspected the stables in the interior triangle at the Golden Cross, Charing Cross, where there are (or were) three floors of stabling, one over the other, the upper and lower ones being entered from the yard by inclined planes. The entrance from the yard into the street used to be under an archway, which entrance, being no longer required, is (as elsewhere in various parts of England and at the Paris Hotel, Rouen) now built up, and so gives greater accommodation to the hotel.

In the yard at Charing Cross a spare coach for the Lewes traffic was always kept. On one occasion, when the coach drew up at the door of the Golden Cross, a female got in. She was told that all the inside places were taken, and was requested to get out, but she would not move, whereupon George Simcock, the driver, ordered the coach to be backed into the yard, and the horses taken out and put into the spare coach. This was done, and the spare coach taken for that day's journey. The woman, ignorant of the existence of the other coach, was left sitting in possession of the usual Lewes coach, probably wondering why the coach was so long in starting.

On my second visit to London that summer to see Dr. Alexander, I went and inspected the building of New London Bridge, the arches being sufficiently completed for me to cross the river over them, which, boylike, I did, and returned the same way, not being hindered by the workmen.

My eyes getting better by the end of the holidays, I was able to return to school. But ever since, when there has been a strong glare on the roads, as there frequently is in summer, I have avoided the high roads as much as possible and kept to the fields. When at Oxford, at such times, my favourite walk was by the Cherwell. It was at this time (1831) that I began studying Hebrew under Davies, the Vice-Principal of the Elizabeth College; but the class was soon broken up by his illness, which lasted some months, and some years passed before I found the time to take it up again.

At Guernsey there was a race for ponies – catch weight – consequently a very small boy was put up to ride. Before the end of the race he fell off, but the pony came in first – without a rider. The judges decided that the pony won the race as it was especially stated to be "catch weights."

Races never had any attraction for me, but as a lad I have been to some, being interested in watching the thimble-riggers and other sharpers of that class. I never felt the slightest inclination to stake a penny, my only object being to try and find out how the thing was done.

Once at Lewes races, as the horses were approaching the

winning post, the jockey who was foremost lost his balance, the saddle slipping; he, however, held on with his left arm, using his whip vigorously with his right, till the post was passed, and then fell to the ground. His winning the race was disputed, but the judges decided in his favour.

The first thing that brought my mathematical tastes forward was an article in The Comet – a Guernsey news paper – finding fault with the Elizabeth College examinations, and asserting that questions were given that it was impossible to answer. The article in question mentioned, as an instance, a geometrical problem at a recent examination. This excited my curiosity. So I tried the problem, and did it. Some of the great boys insisted upon my writing a letter to The Comet in answer to the article, which I did, but destroyed it before reaching the office.

That I, a fifth form boy, had solved the problem, somehow came to the ears of the masters, who gave me the amount of three shillings' worth of tickets, which were very acceptable as my number of tickets was always very low.

Proctor was no mathematician himself, and his assistants at Lewes were not very efficient. Rev. Charles Taylor, the mathematic master at Guernsey, was fairly good, but the trammels of school were a hindrance to my progress.

Queen Elizabeth's College was governed by a body of fourteen directors, who held fortnightly meetings. They would not allow Proctor, as Principal, to have any authority over the other masters, and the consequence was that there was an amount of insubordination, which it was almost impossible to restrain. For instance, more than once when an under master had seen me down the town – which was out of bounds – he has turned his head away, or downright told me he would not report me to Proctor, being somewhat taken aback when told that I was on an errand for the Doctor or Mrs. Proctor, who used frequently to ask me to do things for her. Therefore, in 1832, Dr. Proctor resigned. The directors found out their mistake, and gave the Doctor's successor the authority they had refused to him.

Of my schoolfellows but few have risen to eminence. One lad

at Guernsey. named Kennedy, was a clever fellow. Unfortunately, he had no roof to his mouth, and it was most difficult for anyone to understand what he said. He tried for an open scholarship at one of the Universities. At the conclusion of the examination the poor fellow was told that the examiners found his paper work superior to that of all the other candidates, but that owing to his unfortunate impediment he would never be able to pass the University examinations, and therefore, instead of admitting him as a scholar, the College requested his acceptance of twenty guineas' worth of books.

I always consider that my three winters at Guernsey saved my life. Previously, every winter I had had a bad cough for months at a time, and not being strong the going backwards and forwards to school at Lewes three times a day in all weathers, racing up and down Keere Hill to be in time before and after my hasty meals, was not good for a boy.

After my illness at Guernsey I grew rapidly and was over six feet by my fifteenth birthday.

BRIGHTON

When Dr. Proctor left Guernsey in 1832 he settled at Kemp Town, Brighton. I found that he had made a special request to my father that I should accompany him there, instead of remaining at Queen Elizabeth's College.

I was now sixteen and a half, so I was one of the elder boys, and was expected to assert my authority in his new school. I was given a cane, but I never used it. I think the chief use I made of my position was to put a stop to all bullying.

Dr. (as he was then – having taken his doctor's degree in 1830) Proctor was always successful in getting pupils, and very soon had as many as he could take, amongst others Henry Gage and George Shiffner, both of whom were put by their fathers under my protection, in the same way that Henry Gage's father, Lord Gage, had been under my father's. Shiffner was a little fellow, and a favourite amusement of these two was to get me to let Henry Gage stand on my shoulders with Shiffner standing on his, while I jumped over a low form. Of course, they had to stand very steady.

Once when bathing at Brighton the waves were breaking in such a manner that I found it most difficult to get to land through the breakers, and was getting very much exhausted. In the end I, when a breaker came, hastily turned and dashed through the wave, allowing it to break over me. I then rose on the back of the wave and was carried some distance further in, repeating this till at last I was enabled to rush up the beach clear of the water.

Some three years later I was once bathing at Dover, and I thought I was swimming famously, when I heard a voice called out, "Shameful to swim past the ladies' machines!" Whereupon I immediately turned to swim back, and then found that I had been carried on by a very strong under current, against which in going back I found it most difficult to make progress. I was perfectly unaware that I had been carried past the ladies' machines. I battled with all my might against the current, but found the greatest difficulty in even slowly swimming in the right direction. If it had not been for those same machines I should have come nearer the shore, or even run along the beach in shallow water to my own machine. When I did get back I was utterly exhausted.

Once when I was on the Brighton beach at 5 a.m., watching the boats coming in with fish, a gentleman present wished to buy a fine turbot straight out of the boat. He was told that he could not, but that if he very much wished to buy it, he could attach his card to the turbot and it would then be sent to him in a few hours. The men stated that they were under contract to send the whole catch to London, so his fish must go there first. A four-horse van was waiting by the beach to take the fish to London without delay. This was in 1833.

At this time, 1832-1834, while I was with Dr. Proctor at Brighton, I used frequently to meet King William driving along the front of the sea, and used to delight in the King returning my bow. It must have been very troublesome to the old King to be continually doing so when out for a drive. Once on seeing the King calling at a house in Brunswick Terrace, my schoolfellow with whom I was walking, remarked that he did not know the King lived there.

King William was always very amiable. Once my father sent him a haunch of a prize sheep. The King, in acknowledging the same, requested to see him, as he said he perfectly remembered going to Glynde in my grandfather's time, when he inspected the Glynde flock of Southdowns.

My father, of course, immediately obeyed the summons, and presented himself at the Pavilion at the appointed hour. After he had been kept waiting for a long time he was told that as the time for the King to receive visitors was expired he must come another day. My father said that he had come by His Majesty's express command, he therefore requested before he left that the King might be informed that he was there, whereupon King William (who had not known that he had obeyed the summons) in a few minutes sent for him, and then kept him for half an hour or more, chatting in a most kind manner.

I always heard that the Queen was very domestic in her habits, fond of needlework; and by her desire her ladies in attendance had always to have some needle work when they sat with her of an evening. King William and Queen Adelaide were both evidently very fond of Brighton, and were much there.

A poor man near Brighton grew a huge turnip and sent it to the King. The King graciously accepted it and sent the man a guinea. Hearing this an individual (whose descendants are living, so I leave out the name) bought and sent King William a beautiful valuable horse. The King accepted, and immediately sent the huge turnip in return, saying the horse was so fine that he must give something in return that was equally fine of its kind. The man, who had expected a valuable gift, was not pleased.

When Queen Victoria came to the throne she was so much annoyed by the inhabitants thronging her, that she ceased to come down, and the Pavilion was sold to the town for £53,000. I have only once seen *Queen* Victoria, and that was at Victoria Station. On arriving there to start by a train, I saw policemen keeping back the crowds, and immediately after the Queen and Princess Beatrice drove out, having just arrived by train.

But when she was a girl I have often seen her riding on a pony through Lewes. At that time she very often stayed at Buxted, the Miss Jenkinsons, daughters of the Earl of Liverpool, seeming to be her favourite companions.

My father had a mare from which he had bred several colts and fillies. At that time there were spring races at Lewes, called "Hunt Races," and professional jockeys were not allowed to ride. Also the distances run and the weights carried excluded regular race horses. My father, wanting to sell one of the horses that he had bred, was strongly advised to let it run in one of these races. His horse won the race.

The Princess Victoria was on the Lewes racecourse with her mother, the Duchess of Kent. in a carriage, and someone prevailed upon her to present the prize, which was a silver bowl.

So my father was called up to the side of the carriage, and I, finding what was going to happen, stood close to the other side. Princess Victoria was evidently very nervous and wanted to escape doing it, but I heard the Duchess of Kent say that she must. In handing my father the bowl, she said: "Mr. Ellman, I have great pleasure in presenting you this," and if I recollect rightly did not say much more. My father, on receiving the bowl, seeing the Princess's nervousness and being always ready to talk, in order to put her at her ease, framed his answer in a way in which she has never been addressed before or since, and which evidently amused and took away her nervousness.

After the presentation was over she turned to her mother and I heard her say, "What a funny man Mr. Ellman is."

LOVE OF READING

As a child, till I went to Guernsey in 1829, I had never had money, except it was occasionally a penny or, on very rare occasions, a sixpence. This I always spent on books such as "Jack the Giant

Killer" or "The Seven Champions of Christendom."

Children's books were very scarce. My brother Frederic, who was the most highly indulged of us, possessed Miss Edgworth's "Parent's Assistant," in five volumes, and "Sandford and Merton," which books I devoured eagerly; and some of the tales made a great impression upon me, especially "Waste Not, Want Not." There was in the house "The Arabian Nights," which I surreptitiously read, but which my mother, when I had nearly finished, found me reading and took from me, as she considered it improper reading for a boy.

I would also read books from the library when they were in the house, especially tales in magazines; and I could even now give a very good outline of those tales, or the parts of them that I read, for often I only got hold of the magazines or book for a few minutes.

When I went to Guernsey, besides being entrusted with two or three sovereigns, I had a weekly allowance. So I indulged myself by taking in a bi-weekly paper, the Guernsey Star, at twopence a number.

Newspapers at that time were of much less size than they are now. In England sevenpence was the usual price of a paper, of which fourpence was for the Government stamp. There was also a duty of one shilling and sixpence on each advertisement and three-halfpence a pound on the paper itself. I think that such a tax is little known at the present day.

For many years afterwards, at Oxford and since, I have been very fond of picking up cheap books at a bookstall. At auctions I have picked up various books (which were at the time considered standard works) at a very cheap price.

At Guernsey, after a vain attempt to balance them, I gave up keeping accounts, owing to the vagaries in the currency to which I have before alluded. The result was that I was not so careful with money, but spent pence at a tuck shop, just outside the college gates. Another thing that contributed to this waste of money was that the town was out of bounds, therefore the boys could not go to where there were other shops without a special permit. In the last year I was at Guernsey I was frequently sent into the town, either by the Doctor or by Mrs. Proctor, and thus had the opportunity of spending money in a reasonable manner.

After I left Guernsey I recommenced keeping accounts, and have ever since continued to do so. I still have in my possession my account books from January, 1833. My method has always been to enter every penny received or paid, and to balance the accounts once a week. Such a system has very great advantages. It shows not only one's income and expenditure, but how the money has been spent; also when a bill has been paid and the date thereof. For two or three years I analyzed my accounts, how much spent in travelling, in books, etc.

But the principal advantage of keeping accurate accounts is the check it is upon spending money foolishly. One does not like that there should be a record of money so spent, and yet if the smallest item were not entered the accounts would not balance at the end of the week.

Until I went to Guernsey I can only remember being away from home twice: the first time when I stayed at Glynde at three years old for two or three days, when my sister Emily was born, and later at Beechland, when my youngest brother arrived on the scene. On that last occasion our groom, William, rode over from Southover with the news to my aunt, who immediately drove off to Southover to see her sister and her new nephew. It was a very hot day and the haymakers were hard at work trying to make and get some hay carried from a field close by. I went into the field and helped, working till the field was cleared at 10 o'clock that night, just before a thunderstorm, that had been theatening all day, burst I remember on that occasion our dog "Daphne," who had come over with the groom, was so delighted to see me that she could hardly be induced to return home.

I used to spend a good deal of time during the holidays with my two younger sisters, Emily and Elizabeth. They were both very delicate and always ailing one way or another. To amuse them I used to cut out and help make dolls' garments, make up queer medicines and pretend to doctor their dolls, etc. On one occasion, to please Emily, I got a strip of canvas and worked a whole farm-

117

yard of animals all along. When completed it was made into a waist-band and given to a cousin, who, I believe, wore it.

I never myself get excited over politics, but well recollect the intense excitement there was in 1831 and 1832, before the passing of the First Reform Bill, and, of course, remember all the different changes in the Ministry.

My father always entered warmly into politics, especially so far as they concerned agriculture. My grandfather was very decided in his opinion upon certain points, but though he wrote and spoke on any bills that he considered of importance to the country, he did not by any means enter as publicly into any political question as my father did. For one thing, my father was a much more fluent speaker, and did not care how often and how publicly he spoke. My grandfather saw the necessity for a new arrangement about tithes. He said that under the law as it then was, there was no encourage-ment to a farmer to strive to improve his land; that if, for instance, by expending £100 he could raise £110 in extra produce, the tithe owner would take £11 as his share, and thus leave him worse off than before.

He was very desirous to see the Malt Tax removed, and when, instead of taking the duty off malt, it was taken off beer, and at the same time beer-shops were established, he was very disappointed, and publicly pointed out the mischief of such legislation. He always encouraged the labourers to brew at home and thus supply themselves with wholesome beer; whereas the new law led to the discouragement of home-brewing. Instead, it led to the establish-ment of a custom amongst the labourers of drinking at public-houses and beer shops, which those who brewed at home had no temptation to do. He said, moreover, that men would not be tempted or inclined to drink so strong a beer, or to drink in such large quantities, when it was brewed at home.

He also saw the evil of the Poor Law System then in vogue. Wages were then largely paid out of the rates. It was a very common thing to allow a man who had more than three children a gallon of flour weekly for each child over three in number. And the magistrates were much too easy in ordering relief. There was one exception on the Lewes Bench, and that was Mr. Hoper, who would publicly refuse to sanction an unreasonable allowance being made, and then meet the man outside, and if he thought it a hard case, would out of his own pocket give him five shillings.

Glynde, Beddingham and Firle were under a private act for Poor Law management, which, when the "General Act" came in force in 1835, they refused to give up, unless they were allowed to choose their own Union of Parishes. As Ringmer and Alfriston bore a bad name for Poor Law management, they refused to admit them, and consequently the West Firle Poor Law Union was made of only eight parishes, being the smallest Union in the kingdom.

My father, who had been a leading member in the management under the Private Act, became the first Chairman of the West Firle Union under the new Act, and retained that position till he left Glynde in 1846. I little thought that I should ever be appointed to the post, but I was elected Guardian for Berwick more than forty years ago, was first Vice and then Chairman, ever since the retirement of Doctor Skinner about thirty-five years ago. (Written in 1888).

I don't think my grandfather entered as much into public business as my father did, except in things that specially concerned practical agriculture. One exception, however, was that as Commissioner of Taxes, he regularly attended all the meetings. My father was also a Commissioner, and I have been Commissioner for upwards of forty years.

MATRICULATION

I remained with Dr. Proctor at Kemp Town, Brighton, till after my matriculation in February, 1834. When I went up to matriculation at Wadham I passed so bad an examination that I should probably have been rejected had not my uncle, the Rev. Francis Barrow, taken me up, he being a member of the college, and a great friend of one of the tutors (Rev. John Griffiths, afterwards warden).

I was asked what I had read, and I mentioned among others

Aeschylus and Sophocles. The conclusion arrived at, after the examination, was that I was very badly grounded, and that Proctor's system (under which I had been for twelve years) must have been decidedly wrong.

Therefore, by my Uncle Barrow's advice, I was sent for the intervening time – till I could go into residence at Wadham – to my cousin, the Rev. Richard Sankey, then living at Farnham, who had taken a classical first. At this time he had four other private pupils, of whom, as I soon found out, the only decidedly reading man was John Stephen Hodson (son of the Archdeacon), who be came a postmaster of Merton, took a classical first and afterwards became headmaster of Bradford for a time. My cousins did not receive me very cordially; probably the way I reached their house had something to do with it.

I had travelled by coach as far as Guildford, and my father had told me on reaching that place, I should be sure to find some return vehicle going back to Farnham. So on getting down from the coach at Guildford I inquired about the same, but could not hear of any vehicle returning; nor was there any public conveyance. If it had not been for my heavy luggage I should have walked the ten miles. I waited nearly two hours, hoping some chance vehicle might turn up. Then I ordered a "fly," as I knew I must reach Farnham that night and it was getting very late. To my surprise, instead of a "fly," a post-chaise and pair came to the door, and before I realised it was meant for me, my luggage was put in. If I had had my wits about me I should have steadily declined the post-chaise and waited till next day; but in the hurry, and not knowing how to act, I yielded and got in. Of course I had to pay highly, eighteen shillings.

Arriving late at night in a coach and pair made the Sankeys think very badly of me, as I found out later. Unfortunately, I was shy and did not explain the circumstances.

My cousin, on first receiving me, was very much afraid lest I should, because of my first cousinship to them both, take liberties. But I am sure I was more deferential to him and his wife than was Hodson, who was (I considered) very free in his language, and acted (I considered) decidedly rudely towards Mrs. Sankey. For instance, on one occasion, he would persist on keeping up a long conversation with her as to the impropriety of first cousins marrying; and on my telling him, on leaving the room, that Mr. and Mrs. Sankey were first cousins, he said he knew it. Having always found it difficult to read with attention in company of others, I spent a great deal of my time in studying in my bedroom, and I find that my cousin, in writing to my father, accused me of going to my room to doze away the time. What I especially disliked there was having to sit for about two hours after a late dinner over wine and dessert, and then another hour in the drawing-room, when I must confess I found it most difficult to keep my eyes open, and sadly deplored the utter waste of time.

Another thing I disliked there was the Sunday. Sankey always gave us two long sermons of fifty minutes or more each, and between services you were expected to be idle, and sit about and talk. He strongly disapproved of a quiet Sunday walk, and so I could not go. What time I could I spent studying theology, but I had no books on the subject there, so I am afraid I often fell asleep.

I was heartily glad when October came so that I could go into residence at Wadham.

I did not go home first, so my mother sent things straight to Oxford for me. Amongst other things was a set of new shirts with frills. These I picked off, as no young fellow then wore them.

Directly I went into residence, of course, the first thing, I reported myself to the Warden of Wadham. He, finding that I knew no one up just then, sent for Joseph Walker, who had just taken his degree, and told him to introduce me to some steady man. So Walker introduced me to H. D. Skrine, who asked me to wine, where I met John Cooper, afterwards sub-warden; and Edward Tufnell, afterwards Bishop. Shortly afterwards Tufnell asked me to wine; and I was delighted with his rooms, which were up Corner Staircase, No. 5, garrets overlooking Trinity Gardens, the bedroom not opening out of the sitting-room, but from a short passage between the oak and the sitting-room door. I determined if ever I got the chance to get possession of these rooms, which I afterwards did.

The first rooms of my own that I had were in the Back Quad, in the garrets up No. 9. My opposite neighbour on this staircase was Henry Mitchell, brother of Dr. Mitchell, afterwards Head of Magdalen Hall.

I soon found that the name of Ellman was in bad repute in Wadham. My half-uncle Henry had been there and had been very wild, and certainly no credit to the college.

During my first two or three terms of residence I frequently spent the whole week without exchanging a word with any of my fellow collegians. But at Easter John Rusbridger came into residence. His father (who was steward to the Duke of Richmond, had long been acquainted with my father) having selected Wadham for his son that we might be companions. When in 1833 Mr. Rusbridger heard that my name was down for Wadham, he invited me to stay at Goodwood that his son and I might become acquainted.

After Rusbridger came up we soon became constant companions. His rooms on the ground floor of No. 4 Staircase were expensively furnished, and he himself was very neat and particular about his dress. He had been well educated under Ayling at the Grammar School, Guildford, and I thought was sure for a second class, as he had very good abilities and was by no means idle. He read with Robert Lowe as his private tutor, and one long vacation went with Lowe to read at Granville; but, somehow or other, I believe his health or eye sight failing, he delayed going into the Schools, and at last only went in for a pass.

Robert Lowe was a celebrated tutor at that time, and with his white hair, ruddy face and pink eyes was quite a character at the University. He was so short sighted that he always held the book six inches off his eyes; and it was said that he employed his long nose to cut open the leaves! No one suspected then that he would ever become a statesman.

Rusbridger and I used to take a constitutional walk together daily over Magdalen Bridge, as far as Sandford Turnpike Gate, which we calculated was exactly four miles from Wadham.

We always started punctually at 2 o'clock and were back by 4.

We used to meet in the Quad, and if the New College clock, by which we always went, had done striking before I appeared in the Quad, I was sure to be reminded of the fact.

On coming out of Hall we adjourned to each other's rooms on alternate days, took two glasses of wine, and when New College chimed half-past six separated to read, coming back at half-past seven, when we found cups of tea poured out. On New College striking eight we separated for the night.

I always attended morning chapel, and, the first Sunday or two, evening chapel; but being dazzled by the blaze of wax lights, I gave up going on Sunday evening.

I was never found fault with for not attending college chapel of a Sunday evening, and did not go, not knowing then that every man was expected to attend twice on a Sunday, and once on other days of the week. But after a term, learning that such was the law of the college, I again attended on Sunday evenings; and about this time a sermon was instituted on Sunday nights.

Once, on the first day of term, I was sent for by the Warden and asked why I was not at chapel that morning. I assured him I was, but he would hardly believe me, as he said that he had never known the Bible clerk to make a mistake.

On my last term before going into the schools, Robert Walker, the mathematical tutor, offered to take me at 7 a.m. if I could come then at that hour at his residence in Beaumont Street; on which occasions, of course, I missed morning chapel. On those days, though I intended to go to evening chapel, when the time came I always forgot it.

OXFORD LIFE

In the course of two or three terms Tufnell moved into larger rooms, and I immediately secured those he vacated. There were no rooms in the college more suited for quiet reading. No one overhead; even my opposite neighbour was shut off by a short passage. My advice is, always avoid, if possible, rooms on the ground floor.

Idle men are much more likely to look in on you and lounge in your rooms than they will be if you are up two or three pairs of stairs.

I tried various experiments as to hours of reading. The whole of one term I did not shut up my books till 1.30 a.m., but I found that that would not do. At last I always commenced reading at 5.l5 a.m., but then I never looked at anything that required very deep study after 2 p.m. For a long time I read fourteen hours daily. Cockey's, the tutor's rooms were just under mine, and being on the same staircase he, of course, knew that I was a quiet, reading man. Shortly before my going into the schools, he expressed a hope to me that I did not overwork myself, when I told him that for some months I had not read any deep subject after 2 p.m. This being so different from the time of most men's reading, he expressed surprise.

He also questioned me as to my knowledge of the Bible, in which so many men fail; that being a sine qua non for Great-go. He asked me a question or two, but I soon floored him, he saying that I was right so far, but would not positively assert that my while answer was right, without himself referring to the Bible.

I am convinced, from my own experience, that one hours' reading in the morning, when the head is clear, is worth two hours' reading at night by artificial light.

Another reason why I preferred morning reading is that my eyes have always been weak, especially since 1831, when I was ill in Guernsey.

During my first term at Oxford, as there were no vacant rooms for me to have, I was put into the rooms of a man who had been rusticated, and used his furniture, spoons, crockery, etc. (I mentioned before that as I went straight from Farnham to Oxford, my mother sent me a box of linen to Oxford. On opening the box, amongst other things I found dinner napkins, which of course were taken back at the end of the term without being used; tea spoons with the crest, which likewise I did not use, not choosing to pay the duty; and shirts with frills, which I ripped off.)

The room I was put in was a large room on No. 4 Staircase; the walls were adorned with sporting pictures and pictures of actresses, which I was ashamed to see around me, but not being my own room I did not like to interfere with them.

In the middle of the term, about 8 o'clock in the evening, whilst I was reading in my shirt-sleeves, a rap came to the door. I answered, "Come in," and to my surprise there was my father, who on his way to Gloucestershire determined to take me by surprise, to see that I was not going on as his half-brother Henry had done. On seeing the indecent pictures on the wall my father was at first taken aback. I made him a cup of coffee, and appointed to go to him at the Star the next morning. But I could not stay long with him, as I had four lectures to attend that morning, and I liked to show him that I would not ask leave to absent myself from them.

I should mention that in pre-railway days Oxford was on the direct coach route to Gloucester, Cheltenham. etc., and that a very large number of coaches changed horses in the city. The principal coaching inns being in the High, on the site of the new schools, and the Star in the Corn Market is now transformed into the Clarendon.

One coach, which left the Bolt-in-Tun, in Fleet Street, at 6 a.m., travelled through to Hereford, reaching there at 10 at night. During my Oxford residence a man made a bet that a certain horse should leave the Bolt-in-Tun after the coach and reach Hereford before the coach. And then he made a second bet on another horse to do the same thing.

I saw the poor horses coming through Oxford, where they had gruel, and rested about two hours. They were led by two men on other horses. But I heard that on one stage, as they neared the end of their journey, as extra horses could not be obtained, they were themselves ridden. Both bets were won, but it proved the death of one horse and the other was not fit for much afterwards.

No more at college than at school did I take other exercise than walking. Three or four times during my college career, when asked, I have joined in a four-oar, but that was all.

In the spring of 1835 I went in for my Little-go, and I think I had a narrow shave, for I had to translate a second piece into Latin. I was in the Slow lectures, Herodotus and Livy, and in Vores'

Sophocles lecture, which, when Vores left, was taken up by Cockey, who then became tutor in his place. I shall never forget the scene at the conclusion of Vores' last lecture, in his farewell address to us. He himself was in tears, and so were several of the men.

Vores afterwards went to Hastings, where he was very much beloved. I saw him but a short time before his death, when we talked over our Oxford days.

I was one of about a dozen men at Wadham, who started a debating society on some subject connected with the schools. We arranged to meet one evening weekly. At our first meeting each term we were each to write down a subject for discussion, and then the members selected one for each weekly meeting, the man whose subject was chosen for the evening, opening the discussion with a written essay. They were such subjects as the comparison of Thucydides and Herodotus as historians, and Aeschylus and Sophocles as tragedians. The last was my subject. Another of my subjects was that mathematics was a better groundwork than classics for education. By this time I had learnt how absolutely necessary mathematics are to navigation, astronomy, and mechanics, etc.

As I had made up my mind to go in for mathematics I had to take up logic for my Great-go.

One long vacation I read with Walker for six weeks at Dover, where his mother resided (1835), and in the next long vacation, for thirteen weeks at Fareham, where his wife's relatives (the Paddons) lived.

I think it was during my first year that Queen Adelaide came to visit the University, and the Duke of Wellington, as Chancellor of the University, came to receive her. I most especially remember the Iron Duke at the theatre; some honorary degrees were conferred, and he had to make a Latin speech, which he could not do with out a great deal of prompting from the Vice-Chancellor!

In my time there was, just over Magdalen Bridge, an auction room for the sale of books, the auctioneer being an old man named Wise. There were very frequent sales, supplied either by men leaving Oxford, and not wishing for the expense of taking their books with them, or by stocks collected by second-hand book sellers. Two or three lads with marked catalogues were generally present. One one occasion when I was there, there were in the catalogue two copies of Parkhurst's Greek Lexicon, the second was Hugh James Rose's edition, the publication of which had rendered the original edition almost worthless. The second lot (Hugh James Rose's edition) was thrown down on the table before the previous lot. I bid for it and got it for a few shillings, and then at once took it up, telling the auctioneer I would not trouble him to send it to my rooms, but would take it myself. The worthless edition was then thrown on the table, for which there was a good competition, and it was knocked down at a good price, the book-seller's boys relying on their marked catalogue as being Rose's edition, they only going by the number of the lot.

Another time, just as I was passing Wise's, there came on a heavy shower, so I stepped in out of the rain, and soon three volumes were thrown on the table. One was a very ancient translation of Xenophon's "Ana basis." I began the preface, "Not to excite you to military cogitations," etc., and then gave a bid, and the lot was knocked down to me. The shower soon being over, I went for my walk, and on returning, two hours later, looked in to see what the other two books were. Not caring for them, I told Wise to re-sell them for me. Two or three weeks later he paid me, after deducting his expenses, sixpence more for selling the two than I had given for the three. So I got the book for sixpence less than nothing!

Talking of book sales reminds me that when I was in Dublin in 1837 I was struck by the large number of well-bound books (several of them being odd volumes) that were for sale on the street bookstalls, and also in the numerous second-hand book shops. I spent an evening at Mr. Marland's, and there learnt from him that these books had been purloined by servants. He told me of a gentleman who, on finding several leaves torn out of a book, accused his maid of doing so. She remarked that she did not see why he should make such a fuss about it, that a few leaves could not make much difference, and that when she wanted some paper to light a fire she was very careful never to go to the same book a second time! On examination of the other books this was found unfortunately to be correct. He told me also that it was very difficult to get any but Roman Catholic servants, and that one must be very careful what you said before them, as in confession they told everything to their priests, and were as spies in the house.

He also told me about the Irish character; that those who go over to England harvesting, do so to obtain money for rent of the few acres they cultivate, as they are too proud to work at home for another man.

OXFORD STILL –
DESIRE TO BECOME A NAVAL CHAPLAIN

I can hardly tell when it was decided that I was to take Holy Orders. Somehow it seemed to be taken as a matter of course, and I never thought of being anything else. But though I wished to be ordained I did not want work on land, but always thought the life of a naval chaplain would be what I should like the best. I loved the sea, and the discipline, order, and systematic regulation of the hours appealed to me. I had a great desire, too, to see the world, and always liked sailors. But I mentioned to no one my desire, which as I grew up became stronger.

I remember one very pleasant Sunday that I spent on board the "Cornwallis," off Spithead, in the summer of 1836. Interested as I always had been in the Navy, I was very glad when my brother Spencer wrote to me at Farnham inviting me to spend a Sunday with him on board. We had only met once during the twelve years he had been in the Navy (on board the "Hyperion" at Newhaven) as he had hardly been at home for more than a day or two at a time, and each time I had been in Guernsey, and I felt it might be long before we met again, so I was very glad to take advantage of being comparatively near him. I arrived on the Saturday and remained till Monday.

My brother gave up his cabin to me, and slung a hammock for himself elsewhere. To make more room in his cabin he had had his berth fitted up across the cabin instead of lengthways, so the bed was only five feet six inches long. How he slept in such a doubled up position I do not know. I could not get much sleep. During his watch we walked the quarter-deck together and I much admired the rapid carrying out of orders and the rigid discipline.

On the Saturday evening, just before sunset, as we walked the deck, his eye detected a loose end of a rope high up, that had not been properly stowed away, and he ordered a man up aloft to see to it. Half-way up as the man was racing to complete the order before sun set, when the gun announcing that the sun had set was fired. He instantly ordered the man down, and gave the order, "See to it first thing in the morning." The man said, "I won't be a moment, sir"; but he was not allowed to do it then, as the orders were that no man was to be sent up aloft between sunset and sunrise except in a case of necessity. Spencer was very strict, but the men always liked him, as he was a good officer and always just.

The next day was Sunday, and I thoroughly enjoyed the heartiness of the morning service on board. The chaplain preached an excellent sermon on the text, "Behold how good and pleasant a thing it is for brethren to dwell together in unity." But what most struck me was the devotional order and behaviour of the men. (I observed this same devout demeanour when I attended some years later on board the "San Josef," at Devonport.) It being Sunday, the captain, Sir Joshua Rowley, was a guest of the ward room mess, as well as myself. At dinner we were waited on by six boys, who were the perfection of neatness in their white trousers and shirts, with turn-down collars and bare feet.

It was my brother's watch from 8 p.m. to midnight, so I went on deck with him, and very soon one of the sailors came up in blue cloth trousers. My brother immediately sent him below to change, as at that time of the year white trousers was the regulation till after sunset.

Another man for some slight neglect was ordered on to the quarter-deck, and there put in charge of the sentry till 10 o'clock. It is this strict attention to details that makes the good sailor.

The next day Spencer came on shore with me and took me over the dockyard, where we went on board various ships of different types, which I knew well by name. But what I was most especially pleased with was the block machinery, of which I had often heard, and which was invented by Sir Isambart Brunnell, and excelled (I believe) any other machinery then invented.

I also visited the ship biscuit manufactory, which was an excellent invention to save labour, the wheat being delivered at the top of the building, and with very little human intervention being converted into biscuits at the bottom. (But this is far surpassed by what I have seen at Huntley and Palmer's biscuit factory at Reading, where the biscuits actually go into the oven and when baked come out again, without anyone going near them.)

After the visit to Spencer on board the "Cornwallis," I more than ever desired to become a naval chaplain. In those days the chaplain was also naval instructor, and I knew that to teach navigation mathematics were essential.

At Portsmouth the party I was with included an assistant medical man who had just returned to England. He said he must go and see his old friends at Haslar, where he had seven years previously been on the medical staff. He invited me to go with him, and as Spencer had to return on board I was only too glad to accompany him, while waiting for the coach. We at once proceeded to the lunatic side of the hospital. His old lunatic patients recognised him at once and were delighted to see him. The doctor gave me the history of several of the men. One man fancied that his mouth was full of worms; another wanted to bring a new invention, of which he had drawn plans, before the Admiralty for a new kind of rigging for a boat which would sail either backwards or forwards, and save all tacking.

On the whole they seemed happy. I only saw one man who was said to be violent. He was in a room by himself with bars in front. He amused himself by making balls.

On passing a Quaker's meeting-house on our return, one of our party related to us an anecdote of two middies passing the Quakers' meeting-house one day when a meeting was going on. One midshipman remarked that he had often looked in and waited to hear someone speak, but that he had never done so, as unfortunately the Spirit would not move them; whereupon his companion made him a bet that he would go into the chapel and before he had been there two minutes the Spirit would move some of them. The bet was accepted, and so they walked in. The second middy pulled a handful of nuts out of his pocket, saying, "Here, my friends, here is a scramble for you." Two or three Quakers immediately jumped up and began to reprove him, whereupon he quietly walked out, saying to his companion, "I have won my bet."

When once I was in a coffee-room at the Royal Hotel, Devonport, a party of midshipmen came in, and one of them suggested they should do as another party of middies had done, who, having just come from foreign parts and heard no news for a long time, called for cigars, a newspaper, and a boy to read aloud, directly they entered the hotel, so that they could all enjoy their smoke while listening.

OXFORD

My father had strongly impressed upon me that I must be as economical as I could and not waste time or money at Oxford, so I was fully resolved to get through and to go in for a Great-go as soon as possible. As I wished to be a naval chaplain I knew that I must qualify myself well in mathematics, or I should not be fit to be a naval instructor.

When I was a boy, arithmetic was a great stumbling-block to me. I could not understand or work upon the rules given. At school my masters certainly were not good at figures. My cousin, Richard Sankey, too, knew nothing of mathematics. But when I came to Oxford, with the assistance of Walker, the mathematical tutor of Wadham, I went ahead. He, having several times been public examiner, well knew the style of questions likely to be given, and indeed, when the time came for my going into the schools, he had supplied me with, and I had gone through, all the mathematical papers that had been set for the last two or three years.

I would never trust to a formula, though it shortens labour, knowing that the smallest error in memory as to A plus or minus would make it more than useless. Walker grounded me well as to how each formula was constructed, and therefore I was always ready to construct a formula for myself if needed. The fifth book of Euclid I never even went through, but having satisfied myself from the first two or three propositions of the method of reasoning I passed on to the sixth book.

I resolved to go in for honours, and by working hard I hoped to get a class. I found that it was possible to go in during my fourteenth instead of waiting till the sixteenth term, and determined to do so.

When I put down my name for the examination, and gave in my list of subjects, I think the examiners were rather astonished with my long list, which I think comprised about a dozen subjects, including mechanics, astronomy, optics, hydrodynamics, hydro-statics, etc.; not that I felt myself perfect in all these various subjects; but my object was to induce the examiners to give questions on each different subject, and then I might take my choice of what I would answer.

When the examination came on I felt so overdone one after-noon, and had such a splitting headache, that I did not attempt anything beyond a full description of the Kaleidoscope and the Gregorian telescope. On meeting Walker the same evening, I told him that I had not felt up to doing anything that afternoon, and that therefore my paper was a failure.

But the next days he told me that Cockey (who was one of the examiners) had told him that my paper was by no means a failure, for I had written very lengthy and most accurate descriptions of the two instruments. Indeed, as I did not wish to try my head with fresh problems, I had employed the three hours in giving full descriptions of these instruments with the angles of incidence, reflexion, refraction, etc., showing that I was fully up in the principles on which they were constructed.

One day of the examination, owing to its being a Saint's Day, the schools did not open till a later hour, so I took the opportunity of going down to Spier's and had my hair cut as short as possible

132

to cool my head.

Cockey was the first to tell me and to congratulate me on my First Class, waylaying me as I came out of chapel.

One stimulant to me had been a bet between Rusbridger and the Senior Procter, the Rev. James Butler, who was something of a sporting man, and having formerly been private tutor to Lord March, was on very intimate terms with John Rusbridger.

It came about thus. They were talking of likely men to take honours, when Rusbridger mentioned my name, saving he thought I should get a First. Rusbridger offering to bet him ten pounds that I got a First Class, he at once said he would accept the bet, as the odds against any man getting a First were so great.

He lost, and paid the bet.

As I only went in for a Pass in Classics, I was rather surprised at getting an Honorary Fourth; for I had always considered myself so dull as Classics. I suppose it was my history that did it, of which I was only obliged to take up one subject, but took up two, corresponding with those portions of Herodotus and Livy, which I took up. Travers Twiss examined me in my Livy History, and as he had spent the last "Long" in Switzerland his memory was fresh on the different passes, which he proceeded to examine me on. I got on all right till one question, and then instead of acknowledging my ignorance I made a shot and was floored, as I found out afterwards when I consulted the maps. I suppose, however, that reflection would tell him that it was beyond what could be expected when examined on Hannibal's passing over the Alps to know all the relative positions, with the ancient and modern names of all the different passes.

Petley was the first to tell me of my Honorary Fourth, having been told by his tutor, though the list did not come out for some weeks afterwards.

On coming out of the Schools I hastened into Hall, rather late for dinner, and was immediately asked whether I had got my testamur. I did not know then, but directly we came out of Hall I went to the Schools, and was just in time to meet Purdue (the schoolman) coming out with the testamurs in his hand.

In those days the same examiners examined for Class and Pass, the men who went in for Class simply taking up more books and having a stiffer examination than those who went in merely for a Pass. If any Pass man had Honours awarded him he would be put in the class list.

As I went in my fourteenth term I had a term to keep, which, being Trinity Term, was only a three weeks' one before I went down.

When my sixteenth term arrived I merely went up to Oxford for a day or two in November, and took my B.A.

I greatly surprised my father by my First Class, for I had never given him the slightest hint that I was in for any examination, much less, that I was going in for Honours. I knew if I failed he would be greatly disappointed, and I dreaded letters that would make me more nervous than I already was, so the only thing was to keep my family in ignorance.

And the evening I knew that I had got the First Class I was so worn out that I did not write. However Rusbridger wrote home and told his father the same day and Mr. Rusbridger went at once and told the Duke of Richmond, with whom my father was staying for a few days.

A very few days after my coming down from Oxford I met the Duke in Lewes, who stopped me and was especially warm in his congratulations.

In the spring of 1838 I went up to Oxford to keep my Bachelor's term, and attended the lectures of the Margaret Professor of Divinity, instead of Hampden's the Regius Professor of Divinity, who, notwithstanding his unsoundness, had been thrust upon the University as Regius Professor of Divinity and afterwards was appointed to a bishopric! the protest of the Episcopal bench having been disregarded by the Crown. Few men have passed through Oxford seeing as little of Oxford life as I did.

VISIT TO SCOTLAND

After obtaining my First Class, my father proposed that I should take a tour in Scotland, joining my brother Harvey, who had gone for three or four months to Mr. Archibald Scott in East Lothian to learn Scottish farming. For this purpose he gave me twenty pounds in cash and a cheque for me to get cashed if required.

By my father's suggestion I went first to Bristol to see his old friend, George Webb Hall; then on to Gloucester to see William Jones who had married my half-aunt. Then to Liverpool, where I became a member of the British Association, paying down £5 as a life subscription. Then, when the British Association week was over, I crossed to Dublin, went from there to Belfast, whence I crossed to Glasgow, where I met my brother. We then went on to Lady Wedderburn's (she was sister of Lady Hampden) and after a pleasant visit to her at her home in Haddingtonshire we set out on our walking tour. I soon found out that Harvey had come with an elaborate outline for a tour, and with no money. Knowing that what money I had left would not last two of us long, I proposed to at once deliver the cheque into a bank, but my brother objected to this as he said it would keep us in Glasgow so long, as it could not be expected that any bank would cash a cheque for a stranger, before they could send it to London and get it acknowledged. (We must recollect that there was no telegraph or even quick post in those days, very few railways in England and none in Scotland, so that several days must elapse before the cheque could possibly be acknowledged.) As I have left on record a separate account of this tour, written the same year, I will not enter therein beyond saying, that when I delivered the cheque at Perth I had to wait a fortnight before I received the money.

The following Christmas I had a very sharp illness. I was at Glynde, and there was deep snow, through which I had waded into Lewes. To avoid as much as possible the deep drifts, I walked back over the Downs, where I met my father, who was shooting rabbits with one or two others. He called to me to hold his gun for a few minutes, and to watch at the corner of the "shaw." * I did so, but he was so long gone, having stopped to talk to someone who was watching at an other corner, that by the time he came back I was thoroughly chilled, and was soon laid up.

* Sussex name for a small wood

135

The weather was excessively cold, and though a fire was kept up in my bedroom all night the water in a cup on the mantelpiece was frozen. For a month or more I was very ill with inflammation of the lungs. My pulse became most irregular, sometimes completely stopping. This irregularity of pulse is hereditary, both my grandfather and father having had it. From that time dates my asthma and my peculiar pulse. Whilst I was in Wartling, 1844-46, Dr. Robert Watts told me that though I might probably live to seventy, the asthma would always hang about me, and he has proved correct. I have been recommended all kinds of special medicines as asthma cures. Some I have tried, but with almost the invariable effect of making me worse. The greatest assistance I had was from the late Dr. Brinton, who said I had doctored myself so well for so many years, that I had better persevere as I have done, and only gave me a pill of storax, and a few general directions.

I have before mentioned that in those days the difficulties of travelling with heavy luggage were very great, tedious, and expensive, and the number of travellers was comparatively few.

In my Oxford days I used to leave Glynde in the old gig about 5 a.m., to catch a coach to Brighton about 7, and reach Oxford about 8 in the evening. This coach, however, only ran in the summer. In the winter I would leave Glynde soon after 8 to catch the coach leaving Lewes at 9, reach London soon after 4, and stop the night in London, and go down to Oxford next day.

I was so travelling in January, 1835, and sleeping at the Golden Cross, Charing Cross. I had booked my place by the "Magnet" coach, leaving at 7 the next morning, and was in bed, sound asleep, when about midnight I heard a heavy rap at the door. I immediately answered, thinking it was time to get up. Then "Fire!" was called out. I opened my eyes, and found a strong glare in the window. Hastily dressing, I went down stairs, almost expecting to find the stairs burnt away, but to my surprise the fire did not seem to grow worse as I neared the ground floor. In the coffee-room were some Italians, in deshabille, bewailing their fate. I rushed out in the street to give what help I could. I found there were two or three manual fire-engines at work (steam fire-engines were not invented then).

136

The burning house was a corner place, used as a hosier's shop, kept by the Italian and his wife, whom I had seen in the coffee-room. The Golden Cross Hotel almost surrounded this shop; the bedroom in which I slept, at the very top of the house, being against the burning wall. Finding that there were plenty of volunteers, and that I could not help pump at the fire-engines, and also that I could do no good to the poor Italian and his wife, who was trying to console him, I walked down as far as Fleet Street. By 4 a.m. the hosier's shop was a heap of ashes, but strange to say, the hotel escaped. I then returned to bed, to get up again at 6, in time for the coach.

At the beginning and end of term especially, it was necessary to book your place on a coach many days in advance.

Once, having omitted to book my place long enough before-hand, I could not get away from London till after 4 p.m., and knocked into college just at midnight.

Indeed this was the only time during my whole college career that I knocked in. So the porter did not get much out of me in fees. On the occasion alluded to, my vis-a-vis on the back seat of the coach was John Henry Newman, who did not open his lips once during the whole journey.

Cards were forbidden by the University Statutes, and I am afraid I refused to play rather ungraciously when staying up for the Easter vacation to read. Of course there were very few men up, and Church (now Dean of St. Paul's)* came and asked me to join in a friendly rubber. I did not like to tell him that I would not willingly transgress the Statutes by playing, and moreover was afraid of being drawn into anything that interfered with my reading, so I said I did not play.

To my amusement once, on the occasion when a party of soldiers on the march were resting at mid-day in Oxford, I over-heard as I passed along the High, one soldier say to another, "I wonder what regiment those chaps belong to?" Whereupon the other (who also had been gazing at the caps and gowns) answered, "Don't you know? They belong to the Black-guards!"

* This was written about 1888

By Coach – Old Coaching Days

My father used to go about England a great deal, and many were the stories that he used to relate on his return home. Amongst others was the following:–

He said he had been travelling since early morning and was very tired, when towards evening two young men got into the coach, who were evidently imbued with Chartist opinions. My father wanted to go to sleep, but their loud language, as they found fault with the Government and the laws, quite prevented this. They would not leave him alone, but tried to get him to agree to their opinions. It was useless for him to say he did not. They tried to argue, and again asked him if he did not agree that they were right in what they wanted. Whereupon, he said, he thought the perfection of Government was that of the Bey of Algiers, an irresponsible one! This had the desired effect, and they made no further appeal to him.

Here is another. At another time my father was one of four inside passengers, of whom one was a lady. One of the other two men lighted a cigar, whereupon my father and the other gentleman at once called his attention to the presence of a lady, and requested him if he wanted to smoke to exchange places with someone out side. The man rudely answered that he had paid for an inside place and should do as he liked. The smoking was continued, whereupon at East Grinstead, which was the next place to change horses, out jumped the gentle-man. He hurried to a chandler's shop, went in and purchased a couple of tallow candles, he returned to the coach carefully carrying one of the two alight. My father was rather astonished at this proceeding but said nothing. After the coach had again started the gentleman gravely lighted the other candle, and as soon as it had well burnt up, blew out the first tallow that he had lighted. As soon as the last spark of the wick had vanished, he lighted it again and blew out the other tallow repeating this operation with the two candles for some minutes, till at last the man who was smoking complained of the horrid smell. The lady was appealed to and (seeing the joke) declared that she had no objection to the gentleman using tallow candles. The man was told if he objected he could go outside. A little more candle smoke had the desired effect; and at the next stopping place the man got outside. I do not fancy the present generation are very familiar with the smell of tallow candles, which were at that period in common use. When blown out the smell was particularly disagreeable if no snuffers were used to stop it, the wick would smoulder on for one or two minutes, emitting a thick smoke.

On another occasion my father was travelling by a coach, which stopped for refreshments at Tunbridge Wells.

The table at the coaching inn was laid out with cold meat, sweets, etc., and a charge of half-a-crown a head was made for anyone entering the coffee-room. (This was a very usual custom in coaching inns at that time.) A certain lady got out of the coach, went into the coffee room and sat down with the rest of the passengers and called for a cup of tea. When the time was up and the coach ready to start the waiter demanded half-a-crown of everyone. The woman protested and said she would not pay. The waiter had to call the land-lord, who pointed out the notice that anyone who went into the coffee room was at liberty to take what they liked, that the charge was stated to be 2s. 6d. a head, whatever was taken. He pointed out that in the rush of business there was no time to see what each person took, so the charge was the same for all. She therefore had to pay the half crown, and was just getting into the coach after the other passengers, when it was discovered that one of the wheels was not safe. This caused considerable delay in getting another wheel to put in its place, whereupon the woman immediately returned to the coffee-room, sat down and ate an amazing quantity of food, from all the best and most expensive dishes on the table, whilst the waiter locked on, but could say nothing, as he had told her she could eat as much as she liked and what she liked! When she returned to the coach she informed the other passengers that she had eaten out of spite!

In my young days the pace of the coaches on the principal lines of road was very great. The coaches were heavy, and the roads not nearly so good as they are now.

Five hours was the usual time of a coach between London and Brighton – fifty-two miles. But the "Quicksilver" was timed to do it in four and a quarter hours. I have frequently timed a coach for three or four miles, and the average was three minutes a mile. Once, on a narrow, twisting road, between Odiham and Reading, we did four miles in twelve minutes, and in the next mile only pulled up once to take up a passenger.

On some of the coaches, on coming to the top of the hill, they would put on the skid and go down the hill full gallop, and with the impetus be carried some way up the next hill. (The roads were not levelled so much as they are at the present period, and frequently went over high ground to avoid marshes and floods in winter.) On one occasion my father was travelling by the Brighton to Bristol coach that went the whole distance in the day. When near Bath he heard the guard say to the coachman that he must be careful, or else the shoe (i.e., the skid) would not hold out, so my father asked him why they did not get a new one before starting. The guard told him they always had a new skid every day.

Twice I have come in for what might have proved very awkward accidents, namely, the breaking of the coach pole.

Once was at Uckfield. We were just starting from the Maidenhead when the pole snapped. The driver at once whipped up the horses and got them into a gallop, which he kept up till he began to ascend the opposite hill.

The other time was at Arundel, when the driver made use of the same tactics, though after crossing the river there is no opposite hill to ascend.

At Perth I was witness to a somewhat similar accident. The coachman had evidently no command of his team, for on crossing the river, instead of turning suddenly to the right, he snapped his pole against a wall.

The difference in travelling between those times and the present is very great, not only in time but in expense. For instance, the Lewes coach, which left Lewes at 9 reached Charing Cross at 4, and the outside fare was twelve shillings. They stopped nearly half an hour at East Grinstead, and about ten minutes at each other place where they changed horses, which was at Maresfield, Godstone, and Croydon.

In those days we frequently got down and walked up the long hills, and I have sometimes walked a mile or more before the heavily laden coach overtook me. Where, however, there were many coaches running, as between Brighton and London, or on the Great Western Road out of London to Bath, etc., there was not so much loitering, and the coaches averaged ten miles an hour, including stoppages.

There was an anecdote that used to be told of a Lewes man (but I forget of whom), who, when the coach stopped at East Grinstead, always said he could not afford to waste his time in stopping, but must walk on as fast as he could. This he did, letting the coach overtake him later.

Many of the drivers were very noted for their anecdotes. George Simcox, the driver of the Lewes coach, was especially so, and the box-seat was always sought after for the sake of his amusing conversation.

The driver on the alternate days was Thomas Brian. Once, when we stopped at East Grinstead on a pouring wet day, I followed him into the kitchen, whither I had noticed he always retired, and I found that he had something hot especially prepared for him. So, instead of taking cold refreshments in the general coffee-room, after I found this out I used to go into the kitchen, order for myself, and thus secured a warm and better meal at a low price.

In 1835, wishing to go to Dover, I left Glynde in the old hooded gig at 4 a.m., and went therein as far as Ninfield, where my brother Frederic met me from Battle with another gig, and drove me to Hastings in time for the 9 o'clock coach, by which I reached Dover between 4 and 5, thus taking upwards of twelve hours for a distance of sixty miles.

CELEBRATED OXFORD MEN AND SOME QUEER ONES

For some time when I first went to Oxford, I regularly attended the Sunday afternoon service, at 4 p.m., at St. Mary's, the University Church. John Henry Newman was the incumbent, and always preached at these services. I was delighted with his sermons. I heard him deliver the one on St. Andrew, which is included in his published addresses.

Then the dinner hour at Wadham on Sundays was altered from 5 to half-past 4, for the express purpose (it was commonly said) of preventing any Wadham man going to hear Newman, who was looked upon with great disfavour by the Wadham dons.

After being prevented attending St. Mary's, I regularly used to attend the afternoon service at St. Peter's in the East, of which our sub-warden, Thomas Griffith, was incumbent. But he soon gave it up, and his successor was Edward Denison, whose preaching I always liked. Immediately on his appointment he nominated Walter Kerr Hamilton as his curate. Hamilton's preaching was for a time most painful, as he had the strongest impediment in his speech that I ever heard in the pulpit. It seemed to be the greatest difficulty for him to get out the words, but in the course of six months he had completely cured himself.

Denison and Hamilton were most constant friends. On Denison being appointed to the See of Salisbury, Hamilton succeeded him as Rector of St. Peter's in the East. But Bishop Denison, feeling that he could not get on without his friend, soon made Hamilton his examining chaplain, and gave him a cathedral appointment, and he was as his *alter ego* till Denison's death, when Hamilton succeeded him as Bishop of Salisbury, a most wise appointment, as it ensured the carrying out of various reforms, which they had been jointly instrumental in starting.

I always of a Sunday morning attended the University sermon, which was frequently far above my understanding. I think I may safely say that a large proportion of the University preachers thought more of seizing the opportunity of preaching a learned sermon than they did of preaching one suitable to a congregation composed principally of undergraduates.

Dr. Pusey's sermons were to me most mystical. I never carried away anything from them but a feeling that I was mystified.

Of the Wilberforces I decidedly preferred the sermons of Robert Isaac Wilberforce to those of the future Bishop (Samuel); and

Edward Denison's sermons to those of his brother George, afterwards Archdeacon.

Some of the select preachers were especial favourites with the undergraduates, and none more so than Walter F. Hook – afterwards our Dean, and James Anderson, of Brighton, whose ministration I had constantly attended whilst at school there, 1832-4.

At Holy Communion at St. George's, Brighton, he always secured the assistance of three other clergymen, and even then from the number of the communicants, the services were very much prolonged.

In many churches at this time when there were many communicants, the words of administration were only once pronounced for the whole railful.

Cardinal Newman, after joining the Church of Rome, did not visit Oxford for very many years. But when at last he did he visited nearly all his old haunts, and amongst them his beloved church at Littlemore. When there he was seen kneeling in the church weeping like a child.

My informant was the sexton, when I visited the church a few months later, in August, 1877.

The visit of Newman to Littlemore must have been a private one, during which he evidently did not wish to be known, but he was recognised by the old sexton.

I spent a few days with my son at Abingdon from August 21st to 25th, in 1877. It was during that time that we went to Littlemore and were told of Newman's visit. It has, however, been publicly stated that Dr. Newman did not revisit Oxford again, after he had joined the Church of Rome till 1878.

There was a very great difference between the two brothers, James and Robert Anderson, both in appearance and in their teaching. James was more of a courtier and was, I should think, Broad Church; he was of a good figure and full-faced. Robert Anderson was slight, thin-faced, and looked like an ascetic. He was decidedly Low Church. I often wondered why he had chosen for a wife one who was so fond of society, and seemed so worldly minded. I suppose that he was attracted by her literary powers. She

143

came of a noble family. Her only daughter was a great favourite of the Duke of Devonshire, who, when at Brighton, repeatedly had her to lunch with him.

During my Oxford days, there were some of the members of Wadham who found the greatest difficulty in getting up in the morning, and various were their devices to rouse themselves. One of these men had a large heavy clock weight, which was released by the going off of the alarum. The cord attached to the weight went over a pulley, the other end thereof being attached to his bed-clothes, which were consequently all pulled off on the alarum running down.

The Fellows were all elected from amongst the Scholars, the election being made immediately after morning chapel. The senior scholar, Hyman, never could get up in time for chapel, but in the morning, when he knew it was his turn to be elected Fellow, to the surprise of everyone he appeared in chapel. After the election the Warden said to him, "Mr. Hyman, I see that on such an occasion as this you can get to chapel." His answer was, "Indeed, sir, I cannot," and added that, not wishing to miss chapel, he had sat up all night.

One anecdote of Porson (which I think has never appeared in print) is, that one night when sitting up with one or more companions over a bowl of punch, just as he turned up the bowl to try and replenish his glass once more the candle went out.

Amongst those famous for mixing a bowl of punch I may mention William Davies and F. P. Walesby. The former – a son of the former Vicar of Glynde, and therefore brother-in-law to my grandfather – always had a bright face. Nothing seemed to disturb his temper. He could sing a good song, his favourite being, "A Friar of Orders Grey."

Walesby was a Scholar of Wadham and Fellow of Lincoln, and afterwards held a good position as barrister, and became, I think, Recorder of Westminster. When he was trying for a scholarship at Wadham there was in the examination-room on a side table refreshment for the examiners. In the midst of the examination, to the surprise of all who beheld him, he deliberately left his seat and helped himself to some wine. He was a college friend of my half-uncle, Henry Ellman, and this led to his marrying my half-aunt, Catharine. Whenever he came to Glynde he wanted to make a bowl of punch, which my father frequently successfully prevented his making, by declaring that they had no lemons in the house, etc. Once at a dinner party, on my father making the usual excuse, he directed one of the servants in waiting to feel in his great-coat pocket in the hall, and to bring in the lemons, as he had purchased a dozen on passing the shop in the Cliffe (Lewes).

In writing about Oxford men I might mention the driver of a coach between London and Oxford whom I recollect. He was a dark-faced man whose unshaven face towards the end of the week displayed a crop of coarse grey bristles. My Uncle Barrow told me that in his Oxford days, more than twenty years before, he was commonly known as "Black Will," but that now his coarse hair having changed colour from the lapse of time, a more appropriate name for him would be "Oxford Mixture." It was well known that he had two wives and two families, one in London and the other in Oxford. He did not deny the fact, but said he could not see why he should not have a comfortable home to go to at each end of his journey, as he spent three nights at one place, and four at the other, each week.

Among the Heads, old Dr. Routh was singular. During my Oxford days I rarely saw him, but when I did he always wore a wig. He persevered in wearing this full-bottomed wig till his death in 1855. Maltby (if I recollect right) was the first Bishop who discarded the wig.

ORDINATION

In February, 1837, my father wrote telling me that Mr. Hutchinson, an old friend, Vicar of Firle, and Bishop's Chaplain, had persuaded him to purchase the advowson of Berwick with the view of my eventually settling there.

I was at Oxford at the time, and if I had had the slightest idea of his intention I should certainly have done all in my power to prevent his doing so. All my life I have had the strongest objection – I may say abhorrence – to the sale of advowsons and next presentations.

When his letter came I was very sorry. Strange to relate, up to that time I had not only never seen Berwick, but had hardly realised the fact that there was such a village near.

It had always been my desire and intention to be a Naval Chaplain and Instructor (the two always went together in those days), and this desire had encouraged me in the study of mathematics, and, in any leisure time, of navigation.

I stayed up the Easter vacation to read, so that I did not return to Glynde till after I had gained my First Class. Directly afterwards I was offered work as a mathematical coach, and a Fellowship if I would stay on at Wadham. But I steadily refused, as I did not think myself I should like the work as much as work in the Navy. However, I took care not to mention the offer at home, as I felt my father would urge me to accept.

Soon after I returned to Glynde, I took "Old Hoper" and rode over to Berwick. It was a most beautiful day in summer, and the quiet peacefulness of the village, so retired amongst the trees, pleased me much. I tied up "Old Hoper" outside the rectory gate, got the church key, and looked over the church. It was in a very tumble-down state. One aisle had been pulled down years before, the roof almost touched the ground, and the high pews had been added to and heightened till few people could see over the tops.

Some months passed, and I had not given over the wish to be a Naval Chaplain – at all events for some years – when, in the spring of 1838, the Rev. Harry West, the non-resident Rector of Berwick, who was then living in our old house, Southover Manor, wrote and asked me to call upon him. On my doing so he offered me the Curacy of Berwick, saying that he had had much trouble with his curates, and that hearing I was to succeed him, felt it would be a great relief to his mind if I would accept the curacy. He then offered it me on the same terms he was giving the then Curate-in-charge. The terms were £40 a year, and to live in the furnished Rectory, free of all rates and taxes. I would not consent at once, but took time to consider the matter.

In the end I consented. Mr. West himself had only lived in Berwick for a very few months, and never went near the place. Time passed on, and Mr. West was anxious that I should become his Curate as soon as possible, and wished me to be ordained in the September ordination, which would take place a few days after I was twenty-three. But there was no September ordination in the Chichester diocese or in any of the adjoining dioceses. Mr. West wrote to the Bishop, saying how anxious he was for me to be ordained as soon as possible. So the Bishop sent for me on the 18th of June, and offered to give me "Letters Dismissory" for the September ordination.

On Sunday, September 23rd, I was ordained Deacon at the parish church of Buckden.

On the Monday I left, reaching Glynde on the Tuesday, thankful for a few days' quiet before entering upon my sacred charge.

CURATE OF BERWICK

On Sunday, September 30th, I rode over to Berwick and took the prayers, and the former Curate preached his farewell sermon. In the afternoon I took the whole of the service.

The following Tuesday, October 2nd, I came into residence, and having heard from Mr. Brereton, the former Curate, that he proposed to start at 9, I arrived there before that hour and saw them start, but would not enter the Rectory till they had departed, I thinking it best immediately to take possession of the Rectory without any interregnum.

A wagon laden with my books and goods, and also a Mrs. Seale, a Glynde widow, whom I had engaged as my general servant, had started from Glynde at 6 o'clock and had arrived before me.

It is not good for a young man to have to begin as I did, Curate in sole charge. From the first Sunday I had two sermons to prepare and preach each week. It was not easy to me to compose, and I did not get the help that can be got now from Commentaries. Books were expensive, and I could not afford them, as from the time I was ordained I had to live on £40 a year. Mr. West took no interest in the parish, he never drove over the eight miles from Lewes even once during the six and a half years I remained there as Curate, though he sent his carriage over with his man once or twice to fetch things he wanted.

So I had no training in pastoral work. Mr. uncle, Rev. James Boys, had written entreating my father not to let me settle down at three and twenty in a small village, as he said it would make me lazy. But I do not think it did that. The parish being small, I could give individual attention, and I visited the people constantly. I have always believed that a house-going parson makes a church-going people, and so I tried to influence my parishioners by showing interest in them and their families; to lead them by love.

In those days there was great poverty. The men had very low wages and large families – several had fifteen children, others twelve or thirteen – and morality was at a very low ebb.

I had two services every Sunday, and I believe in 1838 no other church for miles around – even in a town – had two services. At Alciston * there was only service only a fortnight, and should it be wet even that was given up. So it was not unusual in winter that there should be only one service in six weeks, Mr. Moore, Curate of Alciston, living at Willingdon, and walking over from there the eight miles. At Lullington, in 1838, there was only one monthly service, but the year after altered to one fortnightly.

Amongst the people I found at Berwick was my churchwarden, William Stace, and his wife. She was the eldest daughter of Mr. Gell, solicitor, of Lewes, who during the greater part of his life was a Unitarian, and his daughter, Mrs. Stace, had embraced the same views. But she regularly attended church. We had been acquaintances from childhood, but even then she was most peculiar. When we were tiny children, instead of joining in a game of play she would retire to a summer house in her father's garden, and sit there engrossed in some deep book.

* This was written about 1888

She informed me, when I met her again at Berwick. that she had married William Stace "because he had such a capacious mind, and she desired to fill it."

I always considered that she helped to hasten his ruin, for she encouraged him in his wild schemes, some of which, indeed, showed cleverness and ingenuity, but led him into great expense and to neglect what was more profitable. He invented a windmill for ploughing, the machine having four arms, to each of which a sail was attached, and by the revolution of the sails a rope was wound up, to which a plough was attached. After ploughing a few furrows the machine had to be moved, which took a considerable time, besides the employment of two or three men. And then, moreover, it could not be used on a calm day. The way the sails acted, as the arms revolved in an horizontal direction, showed ingenuity. He sent it to the Royal Agricultural meeting at Shrewsbury in charge of two men, and as the rail at that time did not extend beyond Crewe or Stafford, it had to be carried a long distance by road. At the exhibition, on the day of the trial, unfortunately, the wind did not blow.

Mrs. Stace at one time wanted to take charge of several young children, so she procured beds, bedding, etc., for twelve or sixteen boys. When she had furnished the rooms she failed to get pupils.

Once, when I took my sister, Mrs. Scutt, to tea at Church Farm, I found the drawing-room table set out with seven or eight books arranged round the table. I took up one after the other, and found amongst them books in French and Italian, books of Philosophy, and on abstruse subjects, and that the simplest book of all was one on Perspective. Mrs. Stace was very fond of showing off her learning by the way she pronounced certain words different from anyone else.

Another evening, when I went to tea there, Mrs. Stace said that if she ever came to poverty she would go to America and earn her living there by teaching languages to the natives. Her sister-in-law, Mrs. George Stace, who was present, said she would like to go, too, and she would teach the poor natives how to make artificial flowers!

149

She took a Berwick girl, Susan Evenden, into her service, and proposed that Susan should be apprenticed to herself for seven years as servant, and in return she would teach her to play the piano.

On my return to Berwick from Wartling, I found that her religious belief had grown very unsettled, and that she was in correspondence with a Roman Catholic priest, and ultimately she was received into that Church. She told me that, having been brought up in Unitarian doctrines, she had in course of time found how she had been led astray by following her own judgment; that her Roman adviser told her that she was not to think for herself, but to follow implicitly what his Church taught, and that she would be sure of salvation, whereas I would not insure her this certainty of salvation without any care of her own, that by joining the Romanists she would throw all her sins upon the priest, and therefore it was the most comfortable religion.

The Staces left Berwick about two years after my return from Wartling, and shortly after emigrated to America, where she died. I never heard whether she tried to carry out her plan of teaching the Indians.

Another of my parishioners was an old man named William Diplock, who died at Berwick in 1847. He said that if he were a gentleman he would like to travel over England on top of about half a load of hay, drawn by a pair of steady, old oxen. *

SOME MORE BERWICK PEOPLE

When I first came to Berwick certainly more than half the population were Staces, and now for some years not a Stace has been left in the parish. The large families of Staces have all totally disappeared from Berwick. In the forties and fifties many of the families emigrated, some to America, some to Australia, some to New Zealand, and at least three townships to my knowledge on the

* What would Diplock think of motor cars, when even horses were too fast for him?

other side of the globe have been named Berwick by different Staces in remembrance of their far distant native place.

Amongst my other parishioners when I first came here in 1838, were an old couple of the name of Jenner, Mr. Jenner having in the earlier part of this century been tenant of Berwick Court Farm. In his old age, when turned of eighty (before I came to Berwick) he slipped down and broke his arm, which never afterwards properly united. In 1838, when I went to live in Berwick, the Jenners had given up the farm and were lodging at the cottage just opposite the Threshing Machine. He was a large heavily made man, and even before the accident never attempted to move without crutches. After the accident, at every step he took, though his hand had hold of the crutch, the upper part of the arm swung to and fro. He could, however, no longer manage to get up and down stairs, so wooden rails were fixed on each side of the staircase, and a seat made to slide on the same, a pulley being fixed to the wall at the top, which enabled him to be let down or drawn up. These rails are still *in situ*, and subsequent tenants have no doubt wondered what they were for.

Mrs. Jenner came from Isfield. Once, when I called upon her, I found her singing, which led to our conversation turning on church singing. She remarked that she liked the old-fashioned way, with all the different parts taken up. I said I did not know the difference between the various parts, especially mentioning tenor and counter-tenor. So she said she would show me. She selected some well-known old psalm tune – if my memory is correct, I think it was the Old Hundredth – and sung a verse, first in the treble, then took the tenor, the third time sang the counter-tenor and fourth the bass. Her voice, which must in her youth have been a very good one, was still correct, though thin and weak. When she had finished, she turned to me and said, "Do you know how old I am? It is my birthday to-day. Don't you think I am a wonderful old woman, for I am ninety to day?"

I liked the old couple very much, and always was on cordial terms with them, but they could not get on with Mr. West.

It is recorded of old Mr. Jenner, that when in consequence of something he said, Mr. West exclaimed, "Do you know that you are speaking to a gentleman?" his answer was, "I have my doubts about that, sir!"

Another parishioner of that time was John Hilton, of Lower Berwick, who, when he was passed forty, married a woman of less than half his age, who did not prove much of a helpmeet. They had a large family, and the wife was always running into debt and was very shiftless. On one occasion she was much taken with some print in a shop at Alfriston (the next village) which she thought she would like for a gown, but as she could not afford to buy the whole gown then she had three yards cut off, saying she would buy some more another time. Her husband was had up for some debt she had contracted at one of the Alfriston shops, and as he had not the wherewithal to pay he was sent to prison for six weeks. On coming out he said he liked prison, for there he had nothing to do, and meat twice a week. Poor fellow, he evidently would have liked to have been recommitted, for he felt himself much better off there than at home.

Then there was old Mrs. William Hider, also of Lower Berwick. In 1803 an advertisement appeared in the Times for the heirs of a person of the name of Coates, who had died at Hull, having come from Sussex many years previously, and had amassed a large fortune in a Hull manufactory. Mrs. William Hider, by birth Elizabeth Coates, was his nearest relative. But though at the time her attention was drawn to the advertisement, and she knew that old Coates had no nearer relative than herself, yet she would not apply then, but waited fully six years before writing. In 1809 she first wrote to make her claim. In answer to her letter she was informed that Coates' estate was then wound up, and learnt that the money left amounted to £80,000. Now that it was too late she was very anxious to take steps to get the money. Various petty lawyers and others told her that those who had received the money were bound to refund it, and persuaded her to employ them to conduct the matter. But nothing ever came of it, though she expended much money thereon. She had two sisters, co-heiresses with herself, but instead of joining with her in asserting their rights, some members of their families made separate claims, each one trying to secure the entire fortune for him or herself to the exclusion of the others. Mrs. Hider let her claim drop again for some years, but after I came to Berwick in 1838 she renewed her claim, and promised certainly more than one lawyer half her fortune if she would get her the other half. She spent many pounds, but never secured anything. However, she believed that a family descended from a younger sister had been paid something to quiet them.

My old servant, Richard Bean, is apparently concerned in a somewhat similar case of lost property. His great-grandfather was a soldier in the American War of last century. At the end of the war he did not return to England, but stayed for some years in America and then disappeared. He was stated to be the heir to considerable property in Bishopstone and other places, which was afterwards sold to the Earl of Chichester; but what became of the money no one knows. It is supposed some younger members of the family and some lawyers must have got hold of it. In his case, too, the younger branches of the family worked against his claim. Church registers were in the early part of the century got hold of, and when the registers came to be searched, all the important certificates had been cut out.

Mrs. Seale, the widow whom I had engaged as my servant, was not above practical jokes. I had engaged a boy, Thomas Evenden, aged twelve, to clean knives and boots, and to help in the garden, as I was anxious to raise vegetables for the Lewes market and so add to my income.

Mrs. Seale informed this boy that if he could get her a husband she would give him a shilling. The boy set to work, and recommended a little man named William White, and though she afterwards tried to stop him, contrived to bring them together. This resulted in their being married. On their way back from church the boy waylaid them and demanded the shilling that he had earned, and got it. One of her daughters by her former marriage, was married to a painter in London, and during the time of the 1851 Exhibition, Mrs. William White and her little husband took advantage of a week's cheap excursion ticket to visit her daughter.

There was an old gentleman lodging at the daughter's house, who took great interest in the elderly couple, and he gave his landlady five shillings to take them to see the Exhibition. The son-in-law took half a day's holiday to go with them. On arriving at the Exhibition buildings they first walked all round the outside, and then came away without even entering the building, saying they had seen as much as they could carry away with them.

GLYNDE AND THE ROSES

In Glynde Church in 1823 I heard Mr. Tuttee preach who was then ninety-three. I can therefore say that I remember hearing a sermon preached by a man born in 1730, in George II.'s reign, more than 170 years ago. Old Mr. Tuttee was then living at Glynde Bourne. (Written in 1905). His daughters, the Misses Tuttee, once made a complaint to my grandfather of boys bathing within sight of their house, in a pond, and that it was a most indecent sight for any lady to see. The boys, on being spoken to on the subject, said they were so far off that they were sure the ladies could not have seen anything indecent, unless they stared at them through a glass.

In the following year, on the death of Mr. Oliver, who had succeeded Mr. Davies as Vicar of Glynde, Mr. Rose became the new Vicar.

Mrs. Rose was a most superior, clever woman. She had been a governess at a ladies' school in Lewes, whilst Mr. Rose had been a master in Mr. Raymond's school on School Hill, which stood with its large play grounds behind, where Albion Street now is. I recollect Albion Street being built about 1824.

Mr. Rose, after leaving Mr. Raymond's school, became Curate of Little Horsted, and there their eldest son, Hugh James Rose, was born. Mr. Rose there began to take private pupils, of whom the first was my father, and from that time the friendship which had always existed between my grandfather and Mr. Rose was strengthened. My father did not long remain the sole pupil, for he was soon joined by several others of good families, until Mr. Rose had as

154

many as he could take into his house. Amongst the boys were at least two who have succeeded to the peerage, Lord Gage and Lord Abergavenny.

Gage first appeared at Mr. Rose's school in a bright green suit. He was immediately nick-named "greengage," and the nickname stuck to him all the time he remained there. Another thing that made the name appropriate was that some of the first greengages brought to England were cultivated at Firle Place, which was his home.

Lady Gage, his mother, put him under the care of my father, who was a little older, and particularly requested him to look after him.

On his first day at school there was beef pudding for dinner, and when Gage had finished his helping, Mr. Rose asked him whether he would have any more pudding or wait for the goose. The small boy therefore declined the pudding, but when no goose appeared, he asked my father where the goose was, and was told that he was the goose.

In after life Lord Gage became celebrated in cooking. He wrote and published four works, viz.: one on the "Carpenter's Rule," with its various markings, which to an ordinary person are quite unintelligible; one on "How to Cook Fish"; another on "The Rubrics"; and the fourth was a new Catechism, which he wished to be used instead of the Church Catechism.

When abroad, on tasting any particular dish which he especially fancied, he would order another like it, and go into the inn kitchen to see it made, and weigh the ingredients with his private scales, which he always carried with him. But to return to the Roses, I will leave Viscount Gage for the present.

My grandfather saved my father's schoolboy letters, written in the eighteenth century, both from Little Horsted and Winchester, and they are interesting as showing what a schoolboy's life, both at a private and a public school, was more than one hundred years ago.

The Roses had only two children, both exceptionally clever, Hugh James and Henry John.

Hugh James, the Roses' eldest son, would no doubt have been made a Bishop if he had been spared. I agree with Dean Burgon, that the Church is indebted first to him for its revival.

I occasionally heard him at Glynde. His sermons were so simple, exactly suited to the country congregation, mainly composed of labourers and their families. It is seldom that we meet with a University preacher who can preach so simply.

It is a curious fact that both he and his brother Henry John were both Hulsean Lecturers. The two brothers were, however, very different. Hugh was more sedate, weighed down probably by his health and failing strength. Before his seventeenth birthday he was six feet four inches in height.

Henry, after Archdeacon, was always full of fun. He was very forgetful and absent-minded. When dining out he would frequently stuff the dinner napkin into his pocket. I recollect once when dining with him at Glynde Place his mother playfully suggesting to Lady Hampden (the hostess) to search his pockets before allowing him to leave the house!

I consider that neither of the two brothers would have attained to the excellence they did, had it not been for their mother, who was, indeed, a very superior woman. It never struck me that there was anything particularly remarkable in the father. In after years I have several times heard people confusing the two brothers: in fact, thinking there was only one H. J. Rose, Hugh's and Henry's initials being similar. There was to me something most attractive, most lovable, in Hugh James Rose, and I deeply regretted his early death.

Richard Elphick, Mr. Rose's servant at Glynde, was quite a character. I first remember him when he used to drive his mistress at a sauntering pace, sitting mounted upon his little "dicky," often half asleep, and only kept awake by frequent pokes from his mistress's parasol, when his head nodded more than usual.

Richard was fifty years old before he thought of matrimony. He was a very quiet, sober, respectable, peaceable fellow, and he selected a regular termagant as his future wife. After the banns were put up, and they had been asked once, some of the neighbours

156

informed him of the character of his bride to be. One told him that she was called "Thunder and Lightning," and another that her nickname was "Earthquake," and he found on inquiry that her violent temper was well known. Frightened at what he was told, the poor peaceable man asked what he could do to get off marrying her. His informants united in informing him that he must marry her if the banns were not forbidden. So the following Sunday he went to Beddingham Church and forbade his own banns. What the woman said I do not know.

Soon afterwards he married someone else, with whom he could live in peace.

After the death of Mr. and Mrs. Rose he entered my father's service, and stayed with him till his death. He was a most faithful servant and highly esteemed by all the family. "Old Richard" (as he was always called, even before he was really old) was coach-man and head gardener combined. He prided himself upon having everything in apple-pie order, and took great delight in conducting visitors over the stables, the conservatory, the pits, and the grape-houses, his honest face beaming when praise was expressed.

One day my father suddenly sent out word to the stables that he wished to be driven at once to Lewes. On receiving the message, and knowing that his master did not want a moment to be lost, old Richard sent the servant back to ask whether he was to put on his breeches, meaning, of course, was he to go hastily home and change his stable clothes (in which he was working in the garden) for his livery, or was he, to save time, merely to slip on his livery over his stable clothes. My father, always full of fun, sent word back, "No, he was to go without them!"

A donkey-cart was kept at Landport (my father's house after he left Glynde), for fetching the mid-day letters, or for parcels. On one occasion, when the boy who usually went with the cart was out of the way, and something was wanted in Lewes, old Richard was told to take the donkey-cart and fetch it from the town, at which he was highly indignant. He went to his master and asked if he was to be donkey-boy. My father answered, "Yes, and donkey, too!" Poor Richard! but he knew and loved his master.

Richard always drove his master and mistress to church, going in good time, so that he could put up his horse and be in church himself before the services began. And regular as clockwork would the carriage come round, on Bench days, with Richard on the box, to drive his master to the Court. In my father's last illness Richard often sat up with his old master. He was with him the last night, but though in the room he had dozed off to sleep. I, who was the only one present with him, would not rouse the old man.

A few years afterwards, in May, 1874, his death was sudden. He was found dead on the Downs near the Brighton racecourse, having evidently fallen down dead on his way from Brighton to Ovingdean, where he was then staying with his daughter.

LOCAL PEOPLE

I mentioned before, Lord Gage, of Firle Place, who, as a small boy, was at school at Mr. Rose's, at Little Horsted. As a young man, when travelling in Italy, he was present at a ball in Naples, at which Lord Nelson attended, a very short time before Trafalgar.

During the riots of 1830, when there was so much stack burning, he would himself go about at night to see whether the farmers were on the watch, and on one occasion at least he ran a great risk of being shot. For he went to a stack with a dark lantern, and when close to the stack he suddenly exposed the light. The farmer, who was watching near, raised the gun he carried to fire at the supposed rick burner, when a man who was with him stopped him just in time as he recognised the Viscount.

On one occasion Lord Gage, with two or three of his friends, went for two days' shooting to Hellingly. They drove in the morning to the King's Arms, Horsebridge, secured beds and ordered dinner. On the landlady inquiring what they would have, Lord Gage said they could have nothing better than a beef pudding, and that they did not want anything else. The landlady, however, did not think it right or correct to give them only one dish, and thought she must provide a little more. So to the amusement of the party when they sat down, there was the beef pudding at one end of the table, a chick pudding at the other, and a Sussex hard pudding as a side dish, and an apple pudding to follow.

Lord Gage was very careless about his dress, and had a very shabby old smock frock, and a hat equally ancient that he was very constantly to be seen in, and that for years seemed to remain in the same condition. On one occasion at Glynde he came over one morning early, hoping to catch my father before he went out. When he rang the servant did not recognise him, and in answer to his question, "Is Mr. Ellman in?" said, "Yes, and you had no business to come to the front door. Go round to the back and wait for him." My father being told a man wanted to speak to him at the back door, went round and found Lord Gage, who was very much amused at the mistake.

I only recollect Lord Hampden as an old man, leaning on his stick or on Lady Hampden's arm. Lady Hampden was much taller than he was, especially when he became bowed down by old age. She always took great notice of us, and in the estimation of everyone was a delightful person. And so was her sister, Lady Wedderburn. When in Scotland, in 1837, with my brother Harvey, we went to see her. That was the last time I saw her.

One delightful resident at Glynde Place of whom as children we were very fond, was Dame Cornwall, the superannuated housekeeper. She survived till 1830, dying at the age of ninety-five. I recollect her taking us on one occasion into the inner court of the house, which was then planted with evergreens, to show us the large number of birds' nests which were there.

At that time Glynde must have been a very healthy place from the number living to the age of ninety or more. One old woman at Glyndebourne lived to one hundred and two.

My father's old nurse, Dame Beach, lived to the age of ninety-eight at Glynde. My father's mother, after his birth, never really recovered, she had always been delicate, and died when he was three years old, so my father was brought up from the time he was one month old entirely by Dame Beach, until his father married again.

From the time my father took up his residence at Glynde in 1829, he always gave his nurse a hot dinner on Sundays, and afterwards sent it to her daily, promising it to her as long as she lived. Once on his going to see her, she told him that she considered it "a regular dead take in," for she was sure he would never have made such a promise if he had thought she would have lived so long.

On the birth of my eldest sister's eldest child in 1837, she expressed a great desire to see it. And on the nurse's taking it to her, she said that she had now seen five generations of the family. "And who knows but I may live to see a sixth!"

Talking of old age, at Glynde there was one old man, Tom Eager, who always said that he was going to live to be as old as Methuselah; for he had found out that Methuselah had lived on bread and cheese. So nothing would persuade the old man during the last twenty years of his life to touch any other food. I cannot say what his age was at death, but I fancy it was not quite ninety.

When we were little children our grandfather always saluted us with, "How beest thou, my dear?" The old-fashioned affectionate address I always liked. I fancy someone in his childhood used the words to him, for he evidently liked them and used them only for us children.

At the end of the last century Coomber, of Lewes was the best known clocksmith * in this part of Sussex. He went out of his mind, and it was decided to take him to St. Luke's Hospital. The paper for his reception was properly made out and entrusted to the person who was to take him up to London. He was very quiet and well behaved on the journey and when they reached London he was taken to an inn very near the Hospital, to await the proper hour of admission. Whilst waiting in the coffee-room the keeper left him for a few minutes; and on returning, to his consternation, missed his charge. But the lunatic soon came back again, and he remained very quiet until the hour for admission to St. Luke's arrived. He made no scene but quietly accompanied the keeper.

When Coomber was brought before the Board, he bowed and said, "Gentlemen, you understand this case." Whereupon the house-surgeon whispered some thing to the others, the keeper

* Watchmaker

handed in the paper, and it was announced to be correct. The attendants came forward and secured the keeper, and Coomber was suffered to depart quietly, which he did, whilst the person who had brought him to London, notwithstanding his vehement protestation and endeavours to seize Coomber, was detained.

It appeared afterwards that directly Coomber had been left alone in the coffee-room, he hastened to the mad house, and requested to see the house-surgeon at once, saying he would not detain him. He then told the doctor that he had brought up a patient, but that to induce him to come quietly, he had entrusted the lunatic with the certificate, allowing him to suppose that he had to bring him to the hospital, that he, Coomber, was in fact that man who had been sent in charge of a lunatic.

It was some little time before the ruse was discovered. Coomber's quietness, and the violence of the other man in his anger at being detained, while his charge was allowed to depart, completely deceiving the medical board and attendants.

Ultimately, however, Coomber was sent to St. Luke's and was very quiet so long as an old clock was found for him to clean.

Another Lewes lunatic was Verrall, whom I myself remember. He was a tallow chandler. On one occasion at a meeting at the Bear Inn, he sat down on the fire, and ignited his clothes, and then rushed out and jumped into the river. He got out a little lower down, behind some buildings, then went home and changed his clothes. He then returned to the Bear, and found several men dragging the river for his body, being told in answer to his inquiries "That that madman Verrall, had purposely set himself alight, and then drowned himself."

Amongst my father's most intimate friends from boyhood were the two Hopers, George and John, James Ingram and Harry Hurley.

CHURCH LIFE IN SUSSEX
EARLY IN THE NINETEENTH CENTURY

In 1819, when the new turnpike road was opened between Lewes and Eastbourne, the only resident Incumbent was Mr. Capper, of

Wilmington. Almost every Incumbent had two parishes, in neither of which was he probably ever seen except on Sunday. No parish even in Lewes had more than one service on a Sunday, and the time of these services was frequently changed without notice, the ringing of the church bell summoning the people when a clergyman came in sight. Even in the latter half of the century in some churches – for instance, Alciston – the old clerk never would begin ringing till the Vicar, who lived in the next parish, arrived. Over and over again he was urged, the Vicar saying, "You know I shall not fail." But the old man would not be moved out of his custom. "How can I tell that you are not ill or dropped down dead as you were coming," he retorted. Churches were regularly whitewashed, old stone, old marble, all covered up with white or sometimes yellow wash.

It was a time of dreadful deadness amongst the clergy, but here and there earnest laymen sought and reverently used every means of grace that they could. Sermons were long, services dull, but those who wanted to go went.

In churches built in the commencement of this century (written 1888) the usual place for the pulpit was in the middle of the nave, immediately in front of the Communion table, with reading-desk and clerk's desk attached. Sometimes the reading-desk was on one side of the pulpit and the clerk's desk on the other. And I have seen the Communion table placed in front, the Communion rails extending in a semi-circle. In such churches there was no chancel. As examples, I may mention St. Michael's and All Saints' Churches in Lewes, in both cases the chancels being modern additions. In Lewes formerly there were fourteen parishes, but their number was reduced to seven.

At St. James's, Guernsey, the pulpit was actually attached to the east wall of the church, a door through the same admitting the preacher.

Such churches generally had galleries on three sides, and the pulpit was of an enormous height to suit the gallery audience.

In building a church in those times the principal thing that seemed to be considered was to make as large an auditorium as possible, and all the arrangements were made as if preaching were almost the sole object of having a church.

Of all the curiously shaped churches that I ever was in, I think that All Saints', Newcastle, must take the lead. It is oval, and filled with mahogany pews. When I attended service there in 1838 I was struck by the preacher preaching in his surplice, an unusual thing, I thought, in a town church at that time. On inquiry, I was told that in that diocese, as also in the diocese of Exeter, the black gown had never been introduced.

In country parishes, I believe, in all parts of England, it was not unusual to see the surplice in the pulpit. When there was so much controversy about the black gown in 1843, the Rev. G. M. Cooper, Rector of West Dean, introduced it, to the astonishment of the people, who said they had never seen such a thing before.

On the other hand, when I was in Guernsey, 1829-1832, I never saw a surplice, the whole of the service of the church being conducted by a black-gowned clergyman.

Sermons in those days were very long, especially in towns, generally from twenty-five to forty-five minutes.

One evening, when I was present at Farnham Church, Gerald Noel's sermon lasted two and a quarter hours. This was in 1834. Even since I have been in Orders, at a visitation in Archdeacon Hare's time, I have been detained in church four hours, of which the Archdeacon's charge occupied two hours and the sermon about an hour. The preachers selected for the occasion on three different years embraced the opportunity of condemning the High Church party and what was called Tractarianism. This naturally was productive of much ill-feeling, and instead of (as usual) at the subsequent luncheon being thanked for the sermon, hearing strong disapprobation expressed thereon. It was therefore thought wiser to discontinue the sermon.

The Bishop, or the Archdeacon, whichever held the visitation, selected the preacher from those incumbents in the diocese who had not preached before at a visitation, and apparently without any regard for their fitness to preach on such an occasion. Extemporary sermons were rare, and generally contained much repetition.

The altar was usually a very common, small deal table, covered with a moth-eaten cloth, and a huge cushion for the clergyman to rest his arms upon.

We must remember that the beautiful old altars had in most instances been broken up by Cromwell's men.

In Berwick Church, at the time I restored it, I found the broken remains of the old stone altar. It was of Sussex marble – now worked out – and had the remains of five small crosses cut on it. I thought the best thing to do with the pieces was to make altar steps out of them, and the biggest piece I put at the bottom of the Easter sepulchre.

When any part of a church was in danger of falling, instead of restoration, a wall would be pulled down and the size of the church reduced.

Thus in Berwick Church, when the spire was struck by lightning and burnt, in the eighteenth century, and the tower much injured, a buttress was built against the tower to hold it up and nothing rebuilt. The north aisle was in an unsafe state, so it was pulled down, the arches separating the nave from the aisle filled up to make an outside wall. In Beddingham Church an aisle was like-wise pulled down and not rebuilt.

The clerk was an important person. He could read, and he made the responses and gave out the Psalms to be sung.

I remember hearing at the time of a Tunbridge Wells clerk, who on the occasion of a Bishop being present, composed a psalm for the occasion, which he gave out two lines at a time (this being frequently done then). Of the production I only remember the refrain: –

"The hills . . .
Ye mountains why ye hop?
It is because ye come to see
My good Lord Bishop."

As a rule the singing was left to the choir, who generally sat in a place of honour in the gallery.

Clerks were often partly paid by having certain rights over

certain land given by people long ago.

During the summer of 1839, at the request of Mr. Cobb, the then Incumbent of Lullington, he also being Curate of Alfriston, I took the services at Lullington Church for that summer. Mr. Cobb was a poor man, and had left the neighbourhood, but did not want to resign the living till Michaelmas, as every penny was of importance to him. The income of the living was then about £20 a year, with no house. There was a service once a fortnight in the afternoon, and as I had that summer evening service at Berwick, I could attend to Lullington. The internal measurement of the church is only sixteen feet square. Originally it was much larger, the present church being only the chancel of the old one. The foundation of the nave can be seen here and there in the church-yard.

On one occasion I counted forty heads inside the church and thirty more crowding around the outside of the open door. The church was crammed and there was hardly standing room. The Rev. T. Scutt, who was present, sat within the Communion rails. Three boys I had with me in the pulpit, which also served as a reading desk. If anyone had told me that such a number were present at the service, I should have thought it impossible, if I had not counted heads myself.

As the population of Lullington was then very small, there only being one farmhouse and two cottages left in the parish, the congregation must have come from the neighbouring parishes. In proof of this I may mention that Mr. Walter Woodhams, the farmer at Lullington Court, once told me that as he was the only man in the parish to do anything, of course he was a churchwarden, over-seer, etc. Once when he went into Lewes for the annual meeting of overseers, when the magistrates' clerk had passed the accounts, he inquired why Mr. Woodhams had not charged his expenses to the parish, and insisted upon his doing so, though Mr. Woodhams pointed out that as the only ratepayer in the parish, he would have to pay himself. The Woodhams family held that farm for three hundred years.

CLERICAL NEIGHBOURS

At Christmas, 1838, I tried to get a clergyman to come and give my people a Celebration, but I could not get anyone, and we had to go without. At Easter I did succeed in getting a Celebration for my people on Low Sunday, but not for myself. Every clergyman had two or more churches to serve, and Holy Communion had to be administered in each. The only way I could get a clergyman at Easter was by persuading a neighbour to change duties with me on Low Sunday; I could not afford to pay for help.

I was hoping to be Priested in the autumn, but there was no Chichester Ordination, and I could not afford to travel elsewhere. So it was fifteen months before I entered upon the Priesthood. For some reason, best known to himself, the Bishop put off the Christmas Ordination from the Sunday after Christmas to the first Sunday in January.

I would not let my people go without a service, so I paid a clergyman to come and take the services that Sunday.

I had learnt to be very economical. I kept pigs and worked hard in my garden in my leisure hours, sending what I grew to the market at Lewes. I had started a Dame's school in a cottage, and Clothing and Coal Clubs, and all required money, which I had to supply myself. It was seldom that I had any butcher's meat, and my suit of clerical clothes lasted me four years before I could buy more. To make them last me as long as possible, I wore the clothes I had had as layman when working in the garden. Newspapers and books were luxuries I could not afford.

I was very thankful to be in Priest's orders and to be able to celebrate the Holy Communion.

My clerical neighbours did not at all like it because I would not give up one of my two Sunday services, but would only give them one at some other hour if they could not take their own duty. Over and over again I have been told that it was not worthwhile for a parish to have two services. But I was often in request and took three services, and as I was resident in Berwick and most of my clerical neighbours were non-resident, they often asked me to take

166

funerals or weddings to save them.

When I settled at Berwick in 1838, the first to call upon me was Mr. Robinson, Rector of Litlington and Curate of Jevington, where he resided. He was very urgent in pressing me to visit him often. He told me that there would always be a knife and fork laid for me at his table, and that if he were not at home, his daughters would be delighted to welcome me.

He afterwards went to reside at Eastbourne. I was once told that he complained that he did not know how it was, but try as he would he could not get any of his daughters off his hands. He supposed it was that at Jevington he was so shut in by the sea on one side and the Downs on the other, that young men would not come forward.

Some years after I was present at luncheon at Alfriston Vicarage, and heard an amusing dialogue between Bishop Gilbert and Mr. Robinson. The Bishop began by asking after his sons. In reply Mr. Robinson stated that he was thankful to say they were no longer any expense to him, but were off his hands. The Bishop said, "I wish I could say the same of my sons." Mr. Robinson immediately said, "I have eight daughters and only one of them is off my hands." The Bishop remarked, "I also have eight daughters, and not one of them is off my hands."

In the parish of Litlington is Clapham House, that used to belong to my sister's father-in-law, the Rev. T. Scutt. When he left Clapham House to reside in Brighton, my sister went there to live. The first Sunday, on my Sister going to church, she found that the service was advanced as far as nearly the end of the Psalms. After service, Mr. Robinson came up to her, before he had left the church, and apologised for beginning the service, saying that if he had known any of the family were at home he would not have thought of beginning the service twenty minutes earlier than usual, but he thought only the poor people would attend that day.

One warm day, seeing my sister untying the strings of her bonnet in the middle of the sermon, he stopped and called out to the clerk, "Open that window, don't you see that Mrs. Scutt is fainting?"

Another time while preaching, he saw that it was beginning to rain, so he called out to a man to go outside and cover up his carriage.

His churchmanship can be judged from the fact that his numerous children were baptised in batches, two or three at a time, as the Litlington registers testify.

One Sunday he brought his wife with him to Clapham House and told my sister that as she had said she would be pleased to see Mrs. Robinson, he would leave her there, whilst he went to Brighton. He left her there for a week. The only luggage she brought with her was a small handbox containing her cap. Mrs. Robinson had very good means, having been a Miss Wigney; the Wigneys being the bankers and brewers of Brighton.

Another of my queer neighbours was the Rev. Charles Bohun Smyth, Vicar of Alfriston. Alfriston had then no Vicarage, so the Smyths lived in Litlington Rectory. Mr. Smyth was very eccentric. He was at Wadham with my uncle, James Boys, who told me that even at college he was very peculiar. He was one of my earliest callers. On my going to Litlington Rectory to return the call, he pointed to his wife, who was in the room, and said, "Look at Harriet (meaning his wife); isn't she pretty?" I was very shy, and really did not know what to say, especially as I was not struck with the lady's beauty. After a pause, finding me silent, he said, "I married my first wife for money – my second for beauty." Another time he said, "I married my first wife for money – my second for love."

Sometime in the thirties, he and his wife being childless, they thought they would adopt a boy. Accordingly, they looked about, and finally fixed upon a very pretty boy of about six, belonging to some poor parishioners. The child was given up to them, and told that he was to have nothing more to do with his own family. He was handsomely dressed, and taken out driving in their close carriage. For a few days all went well. Then Mrs. Smyth took him for a walk and passed his home. The child caught sight of his dirty little brothers and sisters playing in the gutter, he rushed from Mrs. Smyth's side, and in his blue velvet dress embraced one of his common little brothers. The Smyths were horrified at his ingratitude to them and at his low tastes, and he was sent back to his parents in disgrace. They never adopted another child.

Mr. Smyth was a clever man, fond of taking up various studies and pursuits. I once heard him say that he devoted seven years to each pursuit and then gave it up. One seven years was devoted to the study of Anglo-Saxon, another to music, etc. One of his pursuits was painting, and on leaving Litlington he presented each cottager with one of his pictures.

One evening that he spent with us he brought his guitar with him, and wished to give my nieces lessons on it.

One Sunday evening I had walked over to Alfriston Church after my own services, and during the sermon I heard him say, "I daresay you have all noticed a grating over a grave just outside that window," and then proceeded to say that an opening was left for the escape of the spirit. Another time I heard him say that he always liked to select some principal event from the daily papers for the subject of his sermon on the following Sunday. A short time afterwards, while waiting at Berwick Station, I overheard the remark, "What a horrid thing that prize-fight was the other day." Whereupon a farmer living in Alfriston parish remarked, "The best account I have heard yet was from our pulpit on Sunday evening."

On another occasion, meeting my wife in the street of Alfriston, after speaking of some wrongdoing, he exclaimed, "Madam, the devil is in this place."

Yet one more anecdote of Mr. Smyth, who was really a very pleasant man, but queer. He and his wife strongly disapproved of Confirmation, and he always got out of a Confirmation if he could. The Bishop evidently thought it strange that in a large village there should be no candidates. So he decided to have a Confirmation in Alfriston Church, and stated the fact by letter to Mr. Smyth. Other clergymen were told to take their candidates to Alfriston.

It was a very hot summer day (August, I think). The Bishop arrived and the neighbouring clergy, but Alfriston Vicarage was shut up and its Vicar away. The clerk was told to conduct Bishop Gilbert to the vestry, where he could find luncheon before the service. He followed the clerk into the vestry; a bottle of port wine, a glass, and a plate of sandwiches were on the table, and a roaring fire was in the grate. The Bishop retreated to the churchyard! One more anecdote of Mr. Smyth's sermons. In the middle of one, he said, "It is sad to think that out of the whole congregation here present only six will be saved" – he paused and then added, "and I could name them, too."

VICAR OF WARTLING

My life at Berwick has been a very quiet one. In all the six and a half years that I remained Curate of Berwick I was only absent once – two nights – and that was when I was Priested.

Mr. West was very quarrelsome, but by being firm and refusing to take offence, he could not pick a quarrel with me. He made several attempts to lower the £40 a year I received, several times trying to get me to pay rates; but this I steadily refused as he had offered me the Rectory furnished and free from rates and taxes.

In the autumn of 1843 I received a letter from him saying that he had just found out that it was not usual to supply clocks in furnished houses, and that on turning to his accounts he found that the one in the Rectory (which was indeed only a timepiece, as it did not strike) had cost five guineas; that if I liked to pay the same as he had given for it, I might have it at that price, if not he would take it away. I, of course, declined. I had no clock of my own of any description, but I could not afford to pay for it.

In the course of a day or two he sent over his carriage with one of the Lewes watchmakers after the timepiece, who was directed to obtain a customer for it. But the man could not, though he offered it in his shop for two guineas. When I left the Curacy the next year it was sent back to the Rectory, and after Mr. West's death was sold at his sale for twenty-five shillings. I have wondered whether the watchmaker was again paid, as well as the turnpikes, which were very heavy then, for taking the clock back.

My successor at the Curacy was a Mr. Pruen. When he came over to see the house he complained of the scanty furniture. I explained that some of it was my own, and that the stove in the hall belonged to me, and that I should take it with me. I said, with my asthma, I found it a great comfort, as the passages in the old house were so cold and draughty. Mr. Pruen went to Mr. West and said he could not take the Curacy unless he too had a stove and more furniture. So Mr. West tried to get me to leave the stove: "Surely I could not think of taking it away." Then he tried to persuade me to part with it very cheaply. I wrote back in answer that I intended to take the stove with me to Wartling Vicarage, but, on turning to my old accounts, I found that the stove with its pipes, fixing up, etc., had cost me so many pounds, shillings, and pence, that if he liked to pay the same for it he might have it: if not I must take it away. It was reported to me afterwards that he had said he was sure he could not put in a stove cheaper than Mr. Ellman had done. So he agreed to take it.

I had no thoughts of giving up the Curacy till the beginning of 1844, when I received a letter asking me if I would accept the living of Wartling. The late Vicar, Mr. Pratt, had been accidentally shot the previous September, and the living was in the gift of his father, the Rev. John Pratt, who was undecided what to do, whether to sell the advowson or not. Would I accept the living and vacate it on the death of Mr. West (who was then over eighty), as he understood that I was very likely to succeed him? I replied, thanking him, and adding that I could accept no living under such a condition, and declined it. Notwithstanding my refusal, in the course of a few days I received the presentation with Mr. Pratt's signature.

I felt that Wartling was a place that sadly needed someone who would work it, and that I was a young man, and that experience would be good for me, and accepted.

In the summer of 1845 Mr. Pratt sold the adowson of Wartling. Since then both advowson and the living have repeatedly changed hands.

Wartling was then a large and scattered parish. One house was seven miles from the church, several five miles. Since my time two districts have been carved out of the parish – Bodle Street Green and Gardiner Street – so that there is now no house more than three miles at most from the church. It had been utterly neglected. Many of the parishioners had never seen the outside of the church, but only vaguely knew in what direction it was. I was asked what I wanted when I began a house-to-house visitation, and the door was often held that I should not enter, or shut in my face. But I gradually won my way. I made a census of the population, and before entering a house refreshed my memory as to names, ages, etc., of the children.

There was a parish doctor who very much neglected the people. One poor woman said she would say this of the doctor, "He did not torment poor people, but left them to die." My knowledge of drugs came in usefully, and I won my way in many cottages by doctoring and giving medicine. Soon after I went to Wartling there was a very bad epidemic of measles; the average number of cases I visited in the day was over eighty for two or three weeks, adults as well as children. In one lonely cottage I found a father and four grown-up sons all ill with measles. The old man had lost his wife many years before and no woman ever entered the house.

One of the first things I did was to establish six Dame schools in various parts of the parish. These I visited twice a week to give the religious instruction.

I found that beginning at 9 a.m. and visiting till 6 p.m., when I returned home to dinner I could only visit each cottage in the parish once in six weeks, except in the cases of illness, when I went oftener. The cottages were, many of them, scattered across fields. I tried at first having "Old Hoper," my father's pony, but I found I must do the visiting on foot, for often after visiting a sick case I would hear of another and go on across fields, when I would have to return a mile or more to where I had tied the pony up on going to the first cottage.

The Church, as I have said, was in a very bad state, and the roof of the Vicarage was off; it was being repaired when the former Vicar died, and as his father had presented me to the living, of course, I could not ask for dilapidations. As I had no money I therefore did the best I could, got what repairs I could done to the Church, and the Vicarage roofed in, and paid as soon as I got my tithes.

I found that many of my parishioners would be willing to stay for the afternoon service, if only they had somewhere to rest in between services; so I gave up the drawing-room and gave dinner to various people; and others brought food with them and ate it in the vestry. From amongst these I obtained my Sunday school teachers. I was careful not to eat my dinner with any of my Sunday guests, as I thought that, being a bachelor, it might make talk, as several were maiden ladies; besides, I was glad of the quiet and to rest my voice, so I had my dinner sent to me in the study.

I found that the work was really more than I could properly manage by myself, so as soon as I thought I could manage it I thought I would get a Curate to help me. I was in correspondence with a young man, when Mr. West rather suddenly died, and I had a letter from my father offering me Berwick. I felt very much over-worked and knew that I could not stand the strain much longer, so I gladly accepted Berwick. But I determined not to leave Wartling till my successor was appointed, as it was most important that the parish should not be neglected. So I stayed on at Wartling Vicarage, and rode over to Berwick twice a week to look after the parish and take Confirmation classes, leaving the church wardens to provide for the Sunday services.

As soon as an appointment was made I was instituted to Berwick, but I did not go into residence. The old Rectory had been in such a tumble-down state that it was necessary to rebuild it entirely. Mr. West would never pay for necessary repairs, and his Curate could not.

When the sale of Mr. West's things took place at the Rectory, to increase the number of lots, the bells, bell wires, and grates were pulled out and sold, which still further knocked the walls about.

RECTOR OF BERWICK

I had no money of my own, but the dilapidations were adjudged at £900, and as I was my own architect, this was almost enough to build the new Rectory. The remainder I paid by degrees out of my tithes. Many people asked me why I built such a good house; as a bachelor I could not need so large a one. But I considered that a man must not only consider his own requirements, it might happen that a future Rector had a large family. So I built the style of rectory I considered suitable for the living. While it was building, I stayed at my father's at Glynde, riding over to Berwick daily.

As soon as the house was finished I moved in with my two servants, Elphick and his wife, and in a week or two my sister and her children came to live with me.

As soon as I had paid off the bill for the rectory I began saving to build a school and restore the Church.

I have now been Rector over fifty years, * and it is a long period to look back upon. Little did I think when I was first ordained that I should live to be eighty.

The subject of my first theme at school was "In medio tutissimus ibis." I was told the various parts into which I ought to divide the theme, simile, example, etc., and I was so impressed with this, my first attempt at composition, that (I think I may say) "Medio tutissimus ibis" has been my guide through life, as I have ever been careful against being led into extremes, and striven to keep a middle course. I never liked excitement.

Whenever I have heard anyone spoken against, my desire has always been to make some excuse for him. When anyone has been angry with me, there has generally arisen in my heart a feeling of pity that he should have given way to anger.

I have shown a desire to shrink from any attention being shown me, and when attention has been shown I fear I have answered ungraciously. I have ever been desirous to make everybody happy. I do not think I have ever shown favouritism. I have always had a strong sense of duty. Being ever ready to make allowance for a fault, I have been too gentle in the management of children and others, fearing to act unjustly. This has made it difficult for me to govern and keep order, and I have often thought that had I been an army man I should have made a much better private soldier than an officer. Even at school competition did not succeed with me; I

* He was rector sixty years when he died

174

would help others to maintain their position above me in class. I was never ready of speech, and consequently boys who had obtained their knowledge from my going over the lesson with them beforehand, got the credit of the knowledge which I had imparted to them, whilst I remained at the bottom of the class. I have ever been too mild in dealing with offenders, having in my school days been continually punished for supposed idleness or imaginary faults, has made me too ready to find excuses for others, for fear of being harsh or mistaken in my judgment.

I have tried to lead my people, not to drive them.

It is of the greatest importance to get hold of the children. What a child learns in his earliest years makes a lasting impression upon him. A young child's mind is like a blank page; you can write upon it what you will, for good or ill. Therefore I consider it most important that in every parish there should be a Church school, and that the clergyman should attend to the religious instruction himself. I have never once had a child withdrawn by his parents from religious instruction. Church people and Dissenters alike, every child has been taught the Church Catechism, and taken to church with the school for the Lent services.

I consider that every soul in the parish is given into an Incumbent's charge, whether they are Church or Chapel. To show harshness or neglect is not the way to win Dissenters.

My uncle, the Rev. James Boys, entreated my father not to allow me to accept a Curacy in a small parish like Berwick, saying that it would get me into idle ways, etc.! and that I should end by neglecting the parish. But the fault has rather been with me in the opposite extreme, that by devoting myself to the school and parochial visiting as I did, now that I can no longer keep it up, the people have grown careless. As a youth I never cared much for society. I have ever striven to carry out my duty, and as a boy joined very little in boyish games. (Written in 1892).

One day, after having been a short time at Berwick, on meeting my father's schoolfellow, Mr. George Hoper, he asked me how I got on at Berwick as Curate in sole charge. On my replying that I found no one to help me, he said, "Be thankful, young man, that you have no one to hinder you."

I have often thought of his words since, but I think it far better for a young man to learn work under a good man, than to be put, as I was, in the month I was twenty three, in sole charge of a parish. However much I had neglected the parish my Rector would neither have known or cared. I never could get him to take any interest in the parish, and latterly I very seldom went near him.

When I was a boy there was great laxity amongst the clergy, and the services of the Church were very slovenly taken. Anything in the shape or form of ceremony was avoided as much as possible, and regarded as "Popish." The services were long, the sermons very "dry," and as a rule above the understanding of the rural working classes, but there was here and there certainly deeper and more childlike faith than is common at the present time.

When I started chanting the Canticles and having flowers, it was considered a startling innovation. The high chancel screen, with its doorway that could be locked if needful, that I had made from good parts of the old church oak, when the church was restored was in the eyes of many "Popish." But I carefully felt my way, and introduced nothing that could not be a help to my people, and that the parishioners did not appreciate. By degrees I got more frequent Celebrations. It is a great mistake to force any change upon a parish.

When I was first ordained I preached, as everyone else almost did in the thirties, in a black gown, but as soon as I could, gave it up; but as it was a non-essential I did not hurry

In my boyhood I never saw a cassock, and I do not think they were ever worn in country parishes before quite the middle of the century. The black gown was worn about the early middle of the century, after all the disturbance in 1844, when there was so much stir about black gown versus surplice in the pulpit. It was the unaccustomed sight of Dr. Raynes in a black gown, with, I fancy, puffed out "pudding bag sleeves," that excited my attention at three years old, in Firle Church, in 1819. There were several letters in the papers on the subject, but *Punch* did more good than all by publishing some rhymes, in which a man was represented saying that his wife preached to him in a black gown by day and a white one by night. Hat pegs on church walls were not an unusual sight. I cannot recollect hearing, in my early days, of any church in which the Holy Communion was administered above once a quarter. Afterwards in town churches (about 1828) it began to be administered monthly, and so it continued to quite recent times.

Even in our Cathedral there was only a monthly Celebration till the Rev. C. Marriott, when he came as First Principal of the Theological College, induced the Dean to establish a weekly Celebration.

BISHOPS OF CHICHESTER

Of our Bishops I do not recollect anything of Bucknell, the old Bishop (as he was usually called). He was of great age when he died in 1824. His successor was Carr, who had for many years been Vicar of Brighton and was a boon companion of George IV., when Prince Regent. He was raised to the Bishopric by him when he came to the throne, to enable Carr to pay his debts. He confirmed me in 1829.

He certainly did not make a good Bishop. When he was translated to the See of Worcester, Maltby was made our Diocesan; his only qualification (as far as I could understand) being that he had edited a Greek lexicon. I was astonished at a sermon of his at Brighton in 1833, wherein he asserted that the Baptist when cast into prison despaired of Jesus being the Christ. In 1836 he was translated to Durham. Of his successor, Otter, who had been head of King's College, London, I have already written, as establishing various works for the good of the Diocese. He was a most lovable man, but I doubt whether, if he had been spared long, he could have effectually and well carried out the various schemes he had originated.

Then came Bishop Shuttleworth for two cures, who was succeeded by Bishop Gilbert, whom I always found most friendly, and by no means the stiff don he had always appeared to be at

177

Oxford when he was head of Brasenose.

During his administration of the Diocese energy in the different parishes greatly revived, and as various old Incumbents died, there was a gradual improvement. He was in truth a Father in God – and his advice was always fatherly.

Dr. Gilbert was succeeded by Bishop Durnford, who had been for thirty-five years Rector of Middleton, in Lancashire. When he first came his ideas evidently were for carrying on the administration of his office, as he would have done in a thickly populated district like that from which he had come. But he quickly learnt to accommodate himself to circumstances, and has proved an excellent Diocesan. (Written 1890) He has continued – notwithstanding his great age – most indefatigable in work, ever ready to preach at the re-opening of a church after restoration, himself to induct a new Incumbent. He has greatly increased his number of Confirmations and in the various towns has held Confirmations annually. He has instituted annual Diocesan Conferences, and never (unless absolutely obliged) absents himself from any Diocesan meeting, and thus gets through an amount of work which few men, ten or fifteen years his junior, are physically able to perform.

By bringing Bishop Tufnell into the Diocese and using him as a coadjutor, he has by no means spared himself, but done it so that the amount of work done is increased.

I never met with anyone better acquainted with parochial business, and I have heard that when he was in the large parish of Middleton he made a first-rate chairman. He is also a good botanist and archaeologist. Once, when I was with him at Alfriston, he had no hesitation in pronouncing the Star Inn to be of the period of Richard II., and gave his reasons for so doing.

The first time I met him was a few months after his Consecration, at a Confirmation at Firle in 1871. The then vicar, Mr. Smith, was too ill to venture out, so I acted as cicerone to the Bishop. On going into Firle Church his quick eye immediately caught sight of a mural tablet of very recent date. He asked by whose authority it was put up, and said that he wished it to be generally known that nothing of the kind was to be erected or done without applying to him for a faculty, and then added, "And if they do apply I shall not grant it."

A very short time after this the Vicar of Firle died, and the Bishop was anxious to divide the two incumbencies of Firle and Beddingham, which for many years had been held together. He thought he would find out for himself the state of the parishes, and also inspect a house that had been suggested as a future vicarage. So he paid a surprise visit by himself to Beddingham. He found the proposed vicarage inhabited *pro tem*, by a party of harvesters, the children running about in a state of Nature in the house. And these people gave him such a wretched account of the ague there that he gave up the idea.

Bishop Gilbert thought it was very undesirable that anyone should be Incumbent where he had been known in his youth. After the Confirmation at Alfriston this year (written 1898), an anecdote I had just related was repeated to the Bishop (Wilberforce), and he immediately came up to me and strongly urged me to send him an account of my early remembrances of Church matters in this Diocese, saying it would be helpful to him in preparing his Visitation Charge. Of course, I have done so, and have just sent off three foolscap sheets with accounts of the state of the Church in the Archdeaconry of Lewes in the first half of the century.

ARCHDEACONS AND DEANS

Of our successive Archdeacons of Lewes I cannot say much for Raynes. Two anecdotes of him that I have written show that his Churchmanship was at a very low ebb.

His successor, Dean Birch, was a shade better, but still not much of a Churchman.

Then came Hare. He was very vigorous against some things, such as pews, which he compared to cattle pens, and black stove pipes being visible in the church. He was the means of the Rubric being better observed throughout the Archdeaconry as to Baptism after the second lesson. His charges were immoderately long. One was more than two hours in delivery. He was more suited to be a Cambridge don than a parish priest.

His church at Herstmonceux was two miles from his Rectory, and quite away from the population of that extensive parish. He restored the church at an expense of upwards of £950, and he told me that he regretted that instead of doing so he had not removed the church to Gardiner Street. However, he secured good men as Curates, of whom I knew two, J. N. Simkinson (who wrote the life of his brother-in-law, George Wagner), a most excellent, energetic and successful priest, both as Vicar of Dallington, and afterwards of St. Stephen's, Brighton.

Simkinson was succeeded in the Curacy of Herstmonceux by Edmund Venables, who established a mission service at Cowbeach. He wrote an account of Herstmonceux in the Sussex Archaeological Collection, and afterwards published various works. He is now Precentor of Lincoln Cathedral. During Archdeacon Hare's time the walls of Herstmonceux Rectory, passages as well as the rooms, were lined with his library, which he afterwards left in his will to his college at Cambridge. When I was at Wartling, the next parish, our two large parishes had a mutual boundary of some miles.

I had several discussions with him, even as to points in his Charges, and he would take down his old folios to show me his authorities. I frequently took funerals for him, and learnt that he was very unpunctual, often keeping a funeral waiting an hour or more.

He was succeeded in the Archdeaconry by Otter, an amiable man like his father the Bishop, but he did not appear to me to be much of an administrator. He astonished me once at a Chapter meeting at Ripe, by asserting that we might take the word "Communicant" to mean one who was entitled to communicate, though he did not do so.

After his death, Hannah, Vicar of Brighton, was appointed Archdeacon. Bishop Durnford, being so vigorous an administrator

180

himself, did not leave much for his Archdeacons to do, and consequently Hannah shone more in Convocation, and as Vicar of Brighton, where he was instrumental in breaking up the parish into independent vicarages, and doing away with pew rents in a large number of the Brighton churches.

On Dr. Hannah's death, Robert Sutton, of Pevensey, was appointed Archdeacon of Lewes, whose administration of his office has commenced most energetically. (Written 1888). Of the Archdeacons of Chichester, Manning was a good writer – evidenced in the part he took of the early proceedings of the Diocesan Association – a good and effective speaker, and an elegant and taking preacher. I looked upon it as a sad blow to the Church when he and Archdeacon R. T. Wilberforce joined the Church of Rome.

Garbett I did not think much of. I never could understand why he was made Professor of Poetry at Oxford. He was clearly brought forward merely to oppose Isaac Williams, who was a noted member of the High Church party, which at that time was so much dreaded by many, who imagined it tended to Rome. He was no doubt a clever man.

His successor, Walker, was an energetic mall, and Bishop Durnford, whose Curate he had been in Middleton, knew his working powers, and made good use of him. His death was a sad blow to our old Bishop, but he immediately did what he could to replace the loss by appointing his kinsman, Francis Mount, in his place. Mount was at Firle and Beddingham for seven years and then became Incumbent of Cuckfield. He is an excellent man, but I do not think comes up to his co-Archdeacon (Robert Sutton), in administrative power.

Of our Deans Chandler decidedly made a good one. He contributed largely himself to the restoration work of the Cathedral, and insisted on the Canons Residentiary doing the same. It was in his time that the roof of the south transept of the Cathedral was again raised to its original height.

He was succeeded by Hook. His energy, his work and his writings are too well-known for me to comment thereon. I but add my testimony to his work.

In his time the Cathedral spire collapsed and was rebuilt. At the re-opening of the Cathedral after the rebuilding of the spire, I was present when Hook communicated to a whole railful of Bishops. I doubt whether at any other time a whole railful of prelates had ever been communicated by one not in Episcopal Orders.

When Chichester Cathedral tower was rebuilt, about four feet extra walling was built under the windows to raise them clear of the roof. Otherwise the new tower and spire are exactly like the old. He might have been a Bishop, for he more than once refused a bishopric when offered to him.

Once when he was preaching at Seaford, his daughter, who was in church, fainted. She was, of course, attended to at once; but it was most trying to the preacher, who, immediately his sermon was concluded, descended from the pulpit and sat down beside her. Burgon, as a Dean, I did not think much of. He was a clever, studious man, and did good work by his writings. Even at meetings he did not shine, except it was by his eccentricity. At one of the Diocesan Conferences at Chichester, one of the subjects was the burial of Dissenters. Burgon said he had no objection to bury Dissenters He should, in fact, like to bury them all!

Burgon's being appointed Dean did not increase his usefulness, beyond giving him an income, which enabled him to devote more time to literary pursuits.

It is too early days yet to say much of Pigou's administration of the Deanery. (Written about end of 1889). I think he promises well. He has taken advantage of his position to preach special sermons in various churches of the Diocese.

NEIGHBOURING CLERGY

When, by the death of Mr. Lewis, in 1844, Bishopstone became vacant, Carnegie, who was Vicar of Seaford, was appointed, he thinking that, with the assistance of a Curate, who might live at Seaford, he might work the two parishes, and thus ensure better parochial visiting for the large Seaford population.

Carnegie was a good Churchman, and thought it right to act as strictly as possible up to the Rubrics and Canons.

He consequently, amongst other alterations, in conducting the services of the church, revived the order for always using the prayer for the Church Militant. This gave great offence to the people, whereupon Carnegie referred the matter to the Bishop. Bishop Gilbert's answer was to the effect that Carnegie should consider what a length of time these orders had been neglected. That he was ready to uphold him if he thought he ought strictly to adhere thereto, but he must recollect that if by anything he might do he lost the confidence of his people he destroyed his usefulness in the parish.

Carnegie soon resigned Bishopstone, and John Harison was appointed Vicar. John Harison lived at Sutton, two miles from his church. One Sunday morning, on reaching Bishopstone Church, he found a strange clergyman in the reading-desk, already commencing the service. He quietly went into a pew and let the stranger go on. At the conclusion of the service he spoke to the strange clergyman, and then found out that the cleric, who was staying at Seaford, had undertaken to take the service at Blatchington, and had mistaken the church.

Meanwhile a congregation had been waiting in Blatchington Church, and did not know what to think. After a long waiting, Mr. Catt, the churchwarden, stood up in his seat and read the prayers. The matter was referred to the Bishop; but as Mr. Catt evidently meant well, he merely received a kind letter from the Bishop, pointing out to him that he did wrong and must not do the like again.

Writing about Bishop Gilbert makes me think of a discussion I had with him about forcing dogs to draw hand-carts on the high road. He thought the law for bidding it pressed very hard upon the hawkers of fish. I maintained my point, that dog's feet were not suited to the work and that it was cruelty to make them draw a cart on a hard and stony road. I said I had frequently seen a lazy fellow sitting on his cart and urging his dog forward at a rapid pace.

I don't think I have before mentioned Bishop Gilbert's twinkling eye when telling a good story. This I especially remember on his telling one against Mrs. Gilbert, one day when they were both at this Rectory. It appeared that on one occasion, shortly before Mrs. Gilbert went to the Royal Academy, just before the opening day, being desirous to obtain a private view, she thought she could get in, but was refused admittance by a policeman who was guarding the entrance; so she said to him that she was the Bishop of Chichester's lady. "Even if you had been the Bishop's wife you could not go in," was the answer.

When I was engaged to be married from no one did I have more cordial, hearty congratulations than I had from Bishop and Mrs. Gilbert. I did not know that anyone knew of it, when at a meeting at Brighton of the C.D.A., Mrs. Gilbert pressed her way through the crowd to congratulate me, and a few minutes later Bishop Gilbert came to me and declared how pleased he was at the news, that he would be delighted to welcome one whom he knew would make such an excellent clergyman's wife, into his Diocese.

One of the first fruits of the institution of the Rural Decanal Chapters in 1840, was the building of the Dicker Church and the formation of its ecclesiastical district. The largest subscriber thereto was Mrs. Capper, the widow of the Vicar of Wilmington, and as an acknowledgment her grandson, Owen Vidal, was selected as the first Incumbent.

He and his twin brother, James Henry, had never been separated, either at school or at college, and they were so much alike that they were often mistaken the one for the other.

I recollect on one occasion at a Chapter meeting at Firle, Mrs. Hutchinson saying laughingly to Owen Vidal, "Is it you or your brother?" Whereupon he playfully answered, "It is my brother, ma'am." His disposition was most amiable.

He was afterwards chosen as the first Bishop of Sierra Leone, owing to his great facility (it was said) in acquiring languages. His brother was appointed to Chiddingly, so that even in parochial work they were hardly separated. James was by nature of a much less peaceful spirit than Owen, and was much more ready for contention. On the death of Owen Vidal, in writing to James Vidal a letter of condolence, I especially spoke of his brother's mild and peaceable spirit, and the good effect it had on the Chapter, his very presence restraining other members, who disagreed with him and held opposite opinions, from speaking harshly.

James Vidal immediately wrote and thanked me for what I said; and from that time forward he was much quieter in the Chapter, and evidently strove to act (and with success) as his brother had done. The Bishop died at his post in Africa; James died outside the gates of Jerusalem. He was travelling in the Holy Land when smitten down with fever. Months before, at a missionary meeting, he had spoken of the happiness of dying at Jerusalem. On the day of his death he was borne as rapidly as possible to the Holy City, but when he arrived in the evening the gates had just been shut, and no one is allowed to enter at night. His tent was set up just outside the gates, and there he passed away. His young daughter, his only living child, was with him. The English Consul and his wife took care of her till there was an opportunity of her returning to England.

The majority of the members of our Rural Decanal Chapter did not belong to what is called the Evangelical school, the only three exceptions being the two Vidals and Mr. Bedford, of Denton.

The Vicar of Seaford, Carnegie, who retained his buoyancy of spirits to the end, on one occasion, in order to arouse Mr. Bedford, expressed himself in a higher church tone than he probably otherwise would have done. Whereupon Mr. Bedford exclaimed, "Really, Mr. Carnegie, one would think that you were a Catholic priest!" "I trust I am," Mr. Carnegie simply replied.

Mr. Bedford on one occasion, at a Chapter meeting, informed us that when he had given what he considered a particularly good sermon in the morning he repeated it in the afternoon.

Mr. Pitman's (Vicar of Eastbourne for sixty years) predecessor as Incumbent of Eastbourne was Dr. Alexander Brodie, a brother of Sir Benjamin, who died in 1828 from injuries he received from being thrown out of a gig on the Downs.

Once, on a Saturday evening, a person called upon him and

offered to preach for him the next day. His visitor was a perfect stranger. He hardly liked positively to refuse the assistance, and yet was not inclined to accept it. Dr. Brodie therefore said that he was not accustomed to allow strangers to occupy his pulpit, that no doubt the stranger was an excellent preacher, but that if he allowed him to preach it would afterwards make his hearers disappointed with himself; whereupon the visitor disclaimed being an excellent preacher, and declared that he was not nearly so good as Dr. Brodie himself. The doctor hastily closed the interview by saying that he was a poor enough stick himself, so he certainly could not let his pulpit be occupied by one worse than he was.

This remark reminds me that on one occasion, after service at Glynde, when Henry John Rose had preached, his mother remarked that she had seen one stick in the pulpit, but never recollected having seen three there before. The heavy sounding-board, which was getting rather loose, had been propped up by two pieces of wood! Henry John Rose had something of a drawl, and his voice was rather harsh and not nearly so pleasant as his brother Hugh's.

Trinity Church, Eastbourne, was the first addition to the parish churches of Eastbourne. It is seldom that an Incumbent is spared to see such a vast increase of church accommodation as Mr. Pitman saw during his long incumbency of upwards of sixty years, but then the population of Eastbourne increased about tenfold during the same period.

When Trinity Church was consecrated in December, 1838, Mr. Gilbert gave a luncheon to the clergy, and I was there. I was one in the procession of clergy at the consecration in 1838, and this year (written 1888) again took part in its jubilee. Looking back on those fifty years, I thank God for the wonderful increase of Church privileges given during that period.

VARIOUS CLERGY

When my father was appointed churchwarden at Firle (about 1810) he found that it was the custom to distribute the alms collected at the Holy Communion, immediately after the service, to the poor who had stopped to the Celebration, but on his protest this was stopped.

When he was churchwarden of Beddingham, in 1814, the south aisle was, by order of the Rural Dean, Mr. Baker, Vicar of Stanmer, pulled down. It was in a very dilapidated state, but would not have been pulled down if the order had not been given. It was rebuilt in 1858, during the incumbency of the Rev. C. E. Hutchinson, who, for his first wife, married Mr. Baker's daughter, so he may have considered himself almost bound to repair the damage done by his father-in-law's orders. He succeeded Mr. Baker as Rural Dean, holding that office till he resigned it in 1860. Mr. Hutchinson was one of a large family; his father was Incumbent of Beeding, or one of the other small parishes in the valley of the Adur. He was at the Grammar School, Lewes, when the then Earl of Chichester applied to the headmaster, Dr. Merriman, to recommend him a boy to come and stay at Stanmer as companion to his son (then about seven years old) and to start him in the elements of the Latin Grammar. The choice fell on Hutchinson, which ultimately led to his being appointed Vicar of Seaford, and then, after a very brief incumbency, to Firle.

It is a curious fact that three boys who were together in the same class at the Grammar School, Lewes, each became Vicar of Seaford; Clark, 1816; Hutchinson, 1817; Carnegie, 1824.

The population of Brighton has vastly increased within my memory (my first visit to Brighton was in 1822). Mr. Wagner, who was Vicar of Brighton from 1824 to 1870, was instrumental in building many churches there. Indeed, as soon as ever one church was opened he started another.

On one occasion, in 1833, I was present at St. James' when Simeon preached, but he mumbled so (being very old) and as I was in a gallery behind the pulpit, I could hear but little of his sermon.

When she was at Brighton Queen Adelaide used to attend constantly at the afternoon service at St. George's. She was always accompanied by a lady-in waiting, and, occasionally, by some member of the Royal Family.

Nowadays many clergymen wear hair on their faces – I, myself, in my old age, have given up shaving – and few people would know the commotion a beard on a clergyman's face made a few years ago. The Rev. C. Bradford, once Vicar of Arlington, on returning to England after several years' absence, requested permission of Bishop Gilbert to officiate occasionally in the Diocese, at the same time he mentioned that by the advice of a Servian doctor he had given up shaving. At that time it was most peculiar for an officiating clergy man not to be clean-shaven. Shortly afterwards, Mr. Bradford appeared in the reading-desk at St. Mary's Brighton, to take the prayers, whereupon as soon as the service began, one of the congregation immediately left the church (or chapel as it was then called), went home, and wrote a letter to the Bishop. His letter said that he was sure his lordship would not approve of anyone with an unshaven face officiating in the Diocese. It was a fact to which he himself had been witness in St. Mary's. He added that he could not stop to the service, as he felt it his duty to show his disapprobation, and at once to inform his lordship. My informant was the Rev. Henry Browne, the Bishop's Chaplain. He said it was amusing to see the Bishop's eyes twinkling as he told him of the letter he had received, mentioning that he himself had given permission to Mr. Bradford to officiate in the Diocese, "with an unshaven face," and adding, "What could I say, when I look at the portraits of these, my predecessors," pointing as he spoke to the unshaven faces of the Bishops whose portraits adorn the walls of the dining-room at the palace.

When my brother-in-law, Rev. W. E. Light, became Rector of St. James', Dover, he selected as his Curate the Rev. Henry White, who was afterwards for so many years Chaplain of the Savoy. I first met him at my mother-in-law's, Fort Lodge, Margate, when he came down to see Mr. Light previous to his engagement as Curate. On that occasion he managed somehow to upset the lamp on the table, but fortunately without any very serious mischief being done. He was a general favourite, but often got into scrapes through carelessness; losing his purse when away from home or some other *contretemps*, but he did not suffer anything to trouble him. From what I saw of him I never expected that he would become a favourite of Royalty as he did in after years. Shortly after officiating at the almost secret marriage of Lady Burdett-Coutts, he was summoned down to Windsor. The Queen cross-questioned him about the marriage, and he narrated how he acted on the occasion, whereupon the Queen said, "Mr. White, you are a brick!"

When I first came to Berwick there was a branch at Alfriston of the London Society for Promoting Christianity amongst the Jews, of which the Rev. D. W. Cobb was secretary. On his leaving I took his office for the next few years, till I left for Wartling, and on one occasion we had as our deputation Dr. Alexander; the first Bishop of Jerusalem, himself a converted Jew.

I have always found it most interesting to meet a Jewish clergyman. The effort he must have made to embrace Christianity shows an earnestness which is reflected in his after work.

The Rev. Joseph Kahn, Vicar of Bishopstone (in later years) was also a converted Jew. The history of his conversion was as follows:– To escape the conscription he was fleeing his country, and was waiting at a seaport in Holland when he was spoken to by a stranger, who recognised him as a Jew and spoke to him of Christ. The stranger stated that he himself was a Jew by birth, but a convert to Christianity, and urged Kahn to become one too. They embarked together in a small sailing vessel, hoping to reach England in safety. During the passage they were nearly lost in a storm. While in the midst of the storm his fellow Jew increased his urgency, and exacted from Kahn a promise that if they escaped safe to land he would read the New Testament, and study the subject. After a fearful passage the vessel arrived at an English port. Mr. Kahn was thus led to study Christianity, and ultimately to take Orders in our Church.

In a list of questions for Archdeacon Hare's visitation returns one was, "Is there a decent pulpit cushion?" My answer was "No; and I should like to know the authority for the same." The question has never been repeated in subsequent lists.

Archdeacon Hare tried to revive the Rubric for Catechising before the congregation. The only instance of it having been done within my memory was in Southover Church, by Rev. J. Scobell, but I did not think it very edifying. I, however, tried to act at the Archdeacon's call, but grievously failed. The children were nervous, and seemed as if they could not answer before the congregation; and when, on one occasion, I got an answer from one of my boys, "I renounce the pomps and vanities of the Christian Faith!" I gave it up.

At the time the Rubrics were drawn up there were no Sunday schools, or any provision for teaching the Catechism, beyond the injunction to godparents in the Baptismal Service. But as I always taught it in the Day school, and also in the Sunday school (which was at that time held in church), and constantly preached on the different parts of the Catechism, I felt that I was carrying out the spirit of the Rubric much better than by obeying it literally. I evidently had not the gift of doing it properly.

I have since heard it done, and done well at St. Bartholomew's, Dover, by Churton, now Bishop of Nassau.

The Berwick children became nervous, and though they could answer well in school utterly lost their heads before the congregation.

A few years later, an old cousin of my wife's – James Hammond – was catechising in church. He inquired, "Who is your ghostly enemy?" A boy called out, "Granum, sir." "Your grandmother? nonsense, now –" " But she is, sir, because she larrups (whips) me so."

Another time I heard a girl who was highly nervous, in answer to "In whom do you believe?" "I believe in the Virgin Mary!"

Once in the Day school an examiner asked a girl, "How many Commandments are there?" "Eleven." "What do you mean?" "There were ten, but our Lord said, 'A new Commandment give I unto you.' "

CHURCH DECORATIONS

Whilst I was at Wartling an elderly parishioner told me that he had once lived at Alciston, and on one Sunday a strange clergyman took the service there at 2 o'clock. He hurried from thence to take service at Berwick (one mile across the fields) at 3, and then hastened across the fields to Alfriston, another mile, and took service there at 4. The man said he had followed the clergyman to each church and so heard the same sermon three times in one afternoon. It must have been a very short one, rather different from the usual long ones.

Writing this reminds me that some years ago it w as the custom in His Majesty's Navy, for those ships which did not carry a Chaplain, to pay a clergyman a guinea for a Sunday service, when they could get one. At Jamaica, when a fleet has happened to put in, one clergyman has been known to take as many as six services, hurrying from one ship to another.

From boyhood I could not keep up my attention for a long period, and sermons in those days were not as a rule interesting, and seldom under half an hour in length.

In my younger days I never heard of there being service on Ascension Day in any church in this neighbourhood, in town or country, before I myself started an Ascension Day Service in l 841. On Ascension Day, 1843, the Vicar of Seaford, Mr. Carnegie, being ill I took a service there in the evening, using the same sermon which I had preached here at Berwick in the morning. In those days sermon writing was very difficult for me. From my very first Sunday I had two sermons weekly to prepare, and not many Commentaries to help me.

When I was first ordained anything like church decoration was dreaded; the cross or even the candle sticks on the altar was looked upon as Popish. Flowers were considered the same. The only decoration ever indulged in was at Christmas. These decorations consisted of pieces of holly or other evergreens stuck on the tops of high pews, holes being bored in them to hold the branches.

I first introduced Easter decorations into Berwick Church after the restoration (Easter, 1857), persuading Mr. Shoosmith, church-warden, from whom I feared opposition, to give me flowers for the altar for the occasion.

After this I soon introduced flowers at Ascension and

Whitsuntide, and then very soon altar vases with flowers on every Sunday.

I would add that Christmas was the only season before that I ever knew of any church being decorated Gradually the other churches around were decorated also. *

About 1870, when church decorations were more thought of, the then Curate of Wilmington, the Rev. Samuel Ward, took great interest in the subject, and visited every church in the neighbourhood that he could, to see the Christmas decorations. He was told that the Arlington decorations were out of the common, so through rather deep snow he went to see them. He found great red flowerpots in each window, with a branch of evergreen stuck in each; nothing else. But he said the church walls were green with damp moss, and plants which had vegetated of their own accord were in the damp window-ledges. In the west window tall nettles were growing.

It was even a few years later that the Rector of West Dean (who then lived at Seaford), going over on a Christmas Day, found what the clerk styled "Taxts" up. The "Taxts" were three in number; what one was I forget. One was "A Merry Christmas," over the altar, and the third consisted of three letters, "M.B.P."

The Rector puzzled over in his mind during service as to what "M.B.P." could mean, and thought it must be something about the Virgin Mary. But the clerk explained that it was the initial letters of "Mr. Bannister's Pew," and had been put up over that seat.

The rest of the decorations consisted of bent willow boughs across the aisle, from which dangled some oranges, which were afterwards to be given to children. The clerk was very proud of his decorations.

It was customary to whitewash the church walls. Arlington was regularly shut up for whitewashing every year. On one occasion is

* In the early sixties, amongst my earliest memories, are church decorations, seeing my father mark out texts and devices on white calico, which my mother, the village schoolmistress and my nurse worked over with leaves and flowers, under h i s personal supervision. In Holy Week the school children were always, instead of lessons, on Wednesday and Maundy Thursday afternoons, taken into the fields to

192

was kept shut six weeks.

The Deanery of Malling, in the County of Sussex, consisted of "Peculiars," i.e., parishes exempted from the visitation of the Bishop of Chichester. In these parishes the Archbishop, by a Commissary, held a special visitation. It was said that the Archbishop could, from the diocese of Canterbury, visit all the Peculiars without going through any parish under the jurisdiction of the Bishop of Chichester; but this was not quite correct, for there was a break between the Cliffe parish and Stanmer. In 1834 I attended this Visitation by special invitation, and afterwards joined the clergy at dinner. There was but a small party of fourteen or fifteen, and on obtaining permission to give a toast, I proposed "The Universities," coupling therewith the name of Dr. Wordsworth, the head of Trinity, Cambridge, who was present as Rector of Buxted with Uckfield annexed. Dr. Wordsworth, in returning thanks, embraced the opportunity to explain the circumstances under which he had admitted to Trinity College, Cambridge, the two sons of the Duke of Wellington, who had been expelled from Oxford, for which he stated he had been found fault with.

It appeared that at Christ Church all the Canon's doors were found one morning to have been painted during the night a brilliant red. It was traced to the Duke's sons, whereupon they were expelled. But Dr. Wordsworth said he had received a special letter from the Dean of Christ Church, saying that though he felt compelled to make no difference between the Duke's sons and others, yet he hoped that Dr. Wordsworth would not refuse to receive them at Cambridge.

It is a curious fact that, at three separate Visitations for Peculiars at Lewes, almost (if not quite) the last three special preachers were Goodday, Goodchild and Goodenough.

CHURCH MUSIC

In the first forty years of the century the Psalm-singing was generally accompanied by one or more musical instruments, and

St. Anne's Church, Southover.

the hymns most frequently used were either the "Old" or "New Version of the Psalms of David," which we so commonly see bound up with the Prayer Book, in the same way that "Hymns Ancient and Modern" are now. One version was by Tate and Brady and the other by Sternhold and Hopkins.

It is from the old version that we get the beautiful rendering of the hundredth Psalm: "All people that on earth do dwell," besides other less well-known but beautiful hymns. Of course some – nay many – to the modern taste are quaint and crude and unfitted for the purpose for which they were written. Still, many linger in my memory with pleasant associations, and their quaint phraseology appealed to and comforted many old fashioned, God-fearing people. The tunes to which they were sung were often quaint also. Some have fitly gone into oblivion, but others have found a place amongst our modern tunes, and still more might, I think, be revived. There was more real music in many of these forgotten tunes than in half the modern ones.

In most churches the Psalms (metrical version) were sung in parts, and in many cases the third or last line was repeated three or four times, or sometimes one word only was repeated.

A story was told me by my mother-in-law that on one occasion she was asked to visit a Penitentiary, and the girls were told to sing. One line to be sung was "Poor polluted creatures." It was rendered thus:– "Poor, poll-poll-poll-poll-poll-poll-luted creatures." She said it sounded ridiculous.

In many places choral singers composed various Psalm tunes. At the end of last century there was a carpenter living at Winton Street who composed several tunes; one called "Berwick," another "Seaford," and a third "Winton Street." These were all sung at Berwick when I came here in 1838.

At Glynde my grandfather practised over the Psalms in the house with the choir for the Sunday service, leading the men with a flute. In my father's time a violoncello was first added for the bass, and gradually other instruments.

When I first came to Berwick, Mr. John King, farmer, of Berwick Court, led the choir with a flute, and when he left Mr.

195

William Jenner succeeded to the post, and, after a time, when Mr. Vallence came as partner to Mr. Stace at Church Farm, he assisted with a violin. For a short time we lost both our musicians, and the choir had to rely on a pitch pipe.

In 1862 I purchased a harmonium, which was used in church till we had an organ in 1880. When we first had a harmonium John Shoosmith, junior, accompanied with a cornopean, and very well it sounded.

I was secretary to our Rural Decanal Chapter, and in 1853 I proposed to our Rural Dean that we should ask for a return from each of the seventeen parishes of the R.D., as to the musical part of the various services. I made a copy of the return. Briefly, it is as follows:–

Ten out of the seventeen parishes stated they had no instrumental music whatever. Seaford had an organ, two churches had "finger organs" – (it was necessary to state that they were not barrel organs) – two had each a flute, one a pitch pipe.

Eight years later, in November, 1861, I asked for another return, this time as to what churches had chanting, what hymn book was used, etc.

Arlington and Blatchington returned that they had "no singing of either Psalms or Canticles"; nine churches had chanting; nine churches still used the Tate and Brady Psalms and hymns, five "Hymns Ancient and Modern"; and one a local hymn book.

The return for Bishopstone was that they had barrel organ tunes. In the previous return they had had no instrumental music. Jevington was not in our Rural Deanery, being the other side of the Cuckmere Valley. As a village, it always prided itself upon being very musical. For about a hundred years it had the reputation of being the most musical village in the neighbourhood. Some time about the thirties, before railroad days, the good people of Jevington decided to have an organ, of the kind that could be played by simply winding up a handle. A farmer's wife – as a wagon had to go to London to fetch the organ – decided to take advantage of the wagon and have a washing machine down from London at the same time.

Saturday night came, and with it the wagon. It was late, and by some mistake the box washing machine was put in church, and the organ left at the farm. However, early next morning the mistake was discovered, and an exchange made in good time for service. The man who was to manage the organ studied it, and was certain that he knew how to manage it. A large congregation assembled. When the Psalm was given out, the organ was wound up, and went beautifully and the singing was most hearty. At the end of the Psalm, about four or six verses, the congregation left off singing, but the organ went on. It was necessary to stop it. In his flurry the poor man forgot exactly what he had to turn or push in; he however did something, and the Psalm tune changed into "Drops of Brandy." He made fresh attempts, and the tune changed into "Go to the devil and shake yourself." Playing this air, the organ was carried out of church and put down in the churchyard, where it by degrees played itself out. Of the truth of this story I cannot vouch, but it was told me as a fact when I first came to Berwick. These grinding organs usually had three Psalm tunes (one long, one common and one short metre), and the remainder of the tunes were secular.

I started chanting the Canticles in Berwick when the church was restored in 1857. Old Mr. Hider was very much impressed, and said, "It was heavenly." I believe I was the first for miles round to have chanting.

James Susans, of Alfriston, was for many years a prominent member of the Berwick choir. He was also local correspondent to the "Sussex Express," and on one occasion, after describing a choir supper, which I had given at the Rectory, he wrote to the paper, "that the ladies were drunk!" meaning, of course, that their health was drunk.

He was very fond of long words, of which his pronunciation was amusing and peculiar.

During a choir practice one night I overheard him tell the other members of the choir that a certain tune, "Aurelia," had so pleased the Rev. S. J. Stone, that he wrote "The Church's one Foundation" to go with it, and registered it on the spot in Stationers' Hall.

He latterly lived by himself, and was found dead from bleeding of the nose, to which he was subject.

In the early part of the century church singers were vastly proud of themselves. Sometimes the two last lines of the last verse were repeated six times over.

Edward Bodle, who lived at Winton Street, was a carpenter, and his name is cut high up on the north pier of the tower arch, as repairer of the church. He was a carpenter by trade, who lived in the eighteenth century, and, I believe, a member of Berwick choir.

The hymnal used in Berwick in 1838 was one printed specially for Jevington and the other churches in the neighbourhood. I was soon asked to supply more copies of this hymnal, and was very glad to find that it was out of print. I therefore introduced a selection from the old and new versions of the Psalms, printed by the S.P.C.K. About 1870 I introduced "Hymns Ancient and Modern," which was not in existence in the thirties.

Mr. Scobell, of Southover, about 1825, introduced a selection of hymns of his own. Altering some of the verses, such as in Ken's beautiful morning hymn, he put, "my public thoughts and private ways," and spoilt other hymns in like manner."

CHAPTER MEETINGS AND EDUCATION

In our Rural Decanal Chapter meetings, about 1842, we agreed, after other business of the Chapter was finished, to consider the Church Rubrics; but we soon found that we had so little time left after the Chapter business, that we agreed to hold special meetings to discuss the Rubrics, etc. These meetings we agreed to hold monthly at one another's houses, by invitation. This also enabled us to inspect the different churches in the Rural Deanery, as well as to enter more fully into the subject under discussion than we could do at the fag end of a quarterly Chapter meeting.

We soon found that there was a great want of uniformity in the different parishes. This, we felt, was bad for our people and therefore we strongly desired to correct it if possible. We therefore agreed that when our opinion on any Rubric was unanimous we would all observe it, but if the opinion was not unanimous the point should be referred to the Bishop.

The reserved points were, after all, never submitted to him, but the mere discussion led to much more uniformity than there had previously been.

One of the greatest benefits of meeting together in Chapter I always considered was to draw us closer to one another by learning that there was not that difference which extreme men fancied there must be on almost every point between them and those of the opposite extreme. Thus the rubbing off the sharp angles led us to greater unity.

It was in 1840 that Bishop Otter had revived the Rural Decanal Chapters. When our Chapter was revived, the Rev. C. E. Hutchinson, Vicar of Firle, became our first Rural Dean, and the Rev. Henry Latham, Vicar of Selmeston, acted as secretary till 1847, when Rev. James Carnegie succeeded him, and on Mr. Carnegie's resignation in 1851 I was appointed secretary; and as such, when Mr. Hutchinson resigned, by the Bishop's direction, summoned the Chapter as usual, and at his request continued secretary when Rev. R. S. Sutton was appointed Rural Dean. I received a like request from Bishop Durnford when he became our Diocesan.

The Diocesan Association was established by Bishop Otter in 1838. I believe I was the first to suggest that there should be a training institution for women as school teachers in this Diocese.

In the summer of 1839, when a training school for masters either had been proposed or was just started, I received a notice asking about certain school returns. I appended to my answer a letter, giving my opinion and reasons for so doing, that in our country districts there was but very little demand for school masters, that for teaching the girls needlework school mistresses were necessary. That, considering the early age the boys were taken away from school for farm work (about seven years old then) I thought that women were much more successful in teaching the very young boys as well as girls.

I know that Bishop Otter considered over my letter, and he

communicated with me about it. It was very shortly after this that the Brighton Training College was started. In a few years the Chichester Training College for Masters broke down, and the buildings were then converted into a Training College for Mistresses.

In these days of School Boards and compulsory attendance, it seems to me that there is not the regularity and punctuality in attendance that there used to be.

The most effectual punishment for a child (or rather the child's mother, for in her does the fault chiefly lie) for irregular attendance, or any serious fault, was to strike the name off the books, and thus I have kept a child away from school for three months, with good effect, not only to the child, but also in the example to the others. But such a punishment would not now be allowed. Not only in the lower grade schools, but all schools, punctuality was much more enforced. At the Grammar School, Lewes, there was a fine of a halfpenny if a boy was not in school by the fixed time. During my six and a half years I never once incurred a fine.

Later at Kemp Town, Brighton, a titled lady who had been staying at Brighton for some weeks, came to Dr. Proctor, and, as she was returning home the day before the school broke up, requested that her boy might return with her.

Dr. Proctor told her it was against his rules to allow it, but that she could take the boy away if she liked, though if she did he should not allow the boy to return after the holidays. Lady pointed out the inconvenience it would cause her if she had to leave someone behind to travel with her son, the – as she thought – useless expense, that she could not delay her own return, having been hastily summoned home; but the Doctor would not relent. The mother took the boy with her in her travelling coach, and he was not allowed to return.

The Chichester Theological College, as well as the Training College, was started by Bishop Otter. To him we are thus indebted for the vast improvements in the work of the Diocese since the days of my youth.

Bishop Shuttleworth's episcopacy was too brief to have much effect, but under Bishop Gilbert and Bishop Durnford diocesan work has gradually increased and improved.

I have always held that it is most essential to have sound Church teachers for our children, and that the children should be in day as well as Sunday school taught the truth of our most Holy Faith. The Church Catechism is the very best ground-work for teaching, and should be taught on week-days as well as on Sundays. You cannot begin too early to teach it to a child. The Bible and Prayer Book I have always looked upon – as Article VI. declares – as containing all things necessary to salvation, and therefore I have never assented to some things taught by the Fathers or in subsequent ages. Though I highly value the Fathers as interpreters, yet I never could receive their teaching unless supported by Holy Scripture.

Many of my brother clergy are not careful enough as to those they engage when they want clerical help. In two instances in this Rural Deanery men who were not in Orders have officiated. In one case, many years since, the truth was not found out for weeks; but now, fortunately, such things are not possible.

Rectors of Berwick have had long records. This is now the twentieth century. (Written about 1905). I have been Rector nearly sixty years. My predecessor, Rev. Harry West, was Rector forty-nine years, being instituted in 1797, so that I was the only man instituted to Berwick in the nineteenth century, and between us we have been Rectors 108 years. Two other Rectors of Berwick were here a long time – Rev. John Jeffres from 1566 to 1617 (fifty-one years), Rev. John Hawes, senior from 1694 to 1743 (forty-nine years).

A strange fact is that the last three Rectors of Berwick have all been Vicars of Wartling, the Rev. Harry West, Vicar of Wartling, having exchanged livings with Rev. Jeremiah Smith, Rector of Berwick in 1797.

POOR LAW

The law of settlement till the last few years acted most unjustly. A ratal of £10 a year, or an apprenticeship, gave a settlement.

Since I have been on the Board of Guardians at Firle we have had several hard cases brought forward.

The first remedy was that a pauper was not to be removable from a parish where he had lived for three years with parish relief. John Russell left Berwick as a lad, married and lived in Alfriston many years. He lost his work, and, being a native of Berwick, applied to the Firle Union for relief. Our answer was that he was irremovable from Alfriston, and must apply there. A fortnight after he applied again and said that he had given up his house in Alfriston the day before and had the previous night slept in Berwick parish, in the Berwick end of Comp Barn, the other end of the barn being in Alfriston. The irremovability being thus broken we were obliged to admit him, his wife and eight children into the union house as a Berwick pauper, instead of being chargeable to Alfriston.

William Russell had been a shepherd at Rottingdean for forty-two years. Being past work he gave up his house and went to stay with a married daughter at Preston for a few weeks, to break his irremovability from Rottingdean. He applied for relief and we had to admit him into the union house.

A servant girl, aged twenty-seven, was admitted to the Brighton union with an illegitimate child. The Brighton Guardians made inquiries and could not find that she had ever made a settlement, so they inquired into her father's settlement, which appeared to be Ripe, which parish he actually left twenty years before his daughter's birth. Yet we were compelled to admit her and her child.

Another man had not slept a night in Berwick for seventy-two years, and yet we had to admit him as a Berwick man.

But enough of these examples, though I could give many more. It was not only a hardship to the poor to remove them from their lifelong friends to a strange union, but it was a great hardship to rate-payers to have to provide for paupers whose working years have been spent in other parts.

The law now is that a three years' residence gives a settlement, and one year's residence within a union an irremovability, which law appears to be working well.

When the South Coast Railway from Lewes to Hastings was proposed, many considered it a wild scheme, as one coach and a small omnibus on alternate days was quite sufficient for the traffic.

I don't suppose the railroad line would have been sanctioned by Parliament, had it not been for the Duke of Wellington, who urged the importance of coast defence for Dover being connected by a coast line with Portsmouth.

At first it was only a single line, but in two or three months the traffic was found to be at least four times as great as was expected when the Bill was before Parliament (which estimate was then considered extravagant). And accordingly it was with as little delay as possible converted into a double line, and as soon as ever the loop line from Lewes to Keymer Junction was made, it competed favourably for the London and Hastings traffic.

At first the South Eastern Company seemed to despise the South Coast Company, but the Brighton Company put on trains to carry passengers within two hours for five shillings from St. Leonards to London Bridge, which led the South Eastern Company to give way and to agree to share with them the traffic, instead of competing one against the other.

At that time the line to Sevenoaks was not made. The South Eastern's original line was to turn off from the Brighton line at Godstone Road; but to save making another long tunnel, they got permission to make use of the Merstham tunnel, and the use of the Brighton line as far as Redhill.

In the Bill for the South Coast line, as it appeared before the House of Commons, there was a clause that there was to be no station on Berwick Common without the consent of four-fifths of the proprietors. I had suggested that a station on the Common would throw a great expense on the parish of Berwick for maintaining the road, which had hitherto been scarcely ever used, towards which the railroad would contribute so little, inasmuch as their extent of mileage within the bounds of the parish would be very small.

The clause was, however, struck out in the House of Lords, because it was represented that Berwick was the most convenient spot for the traffic from Hailsham on the one side and from Seaford and Newhaven on the other, it being little imagined then that these places would ever be reached by branch lines, and have stations of their own. My ground of objection has been proved to be correct, for the Berwick highway rate has year after year been half a crown in the pound, whilst the highway rate of adjoining villages have been only four pence or sixpence at most. (This was written about 1888, before the County Council took over certain high roads.)

Before the railway was made there was a considerable traffic of lime from Alciston Pit flint from the Downs and beach from Long Bridge, which were all carried over the Selmeston roads. But since the road across Berwick Common has been improved for access to Berwick Station, this traffic has been diverted to the Berwick road, and yet Selmeston receives a much larger share of assistance from the railway company than Berwick, Selmeston having about two miles of railroad within the parish, while Berwick has less than half a mile. When Chilver Bridge was rebuilt the expense fell on the Hundred of Long Bridge, which comprises the parishes of Litlington, Wilmington, Folkington and Berwick.

I think it is important that the rates should be kept down as much as possible. I have always considered it very hard that if a poor man, by dint of carefulness and rigid self-denial, has saved money enough to buy a small cottage or bit of land to retire upon in his old age, he should be forced to pay and help to keep those who by drink, carelessness or waste are thrown upon the rates. By hard work the one has laid by just enough for his old age, whereas if he had been lazy or given way to drink, he could not possibly have put by for his declining years.

I have always noticed that it is not the men who earn most who save and have the most comfortable cottages.

If possible, when paupers come on the rates, a difference should be made between those who, through no fault of their own, are in distress, and those who have brought it upon themselves.

ANECDOTES OF MARRIAGES

Once whilst performing a marriage at Wartling, the bride fainted, and I had to wait some time before she was sufficiently recovered for the service to be continued.

On another occasion I had a bride who positively refused to sign the marriage registers. I had to tell her that I could not allow her to leave the vestry until she had done so. After waiting some time vainly for his wife to be sensible, as last the bridegroom said that that he should go away without her. And he and the rest of the wedding party left the church, leaving me alone with the bride. Immediately they had gone the bride seized the pen and wrote her name in the register, and then hastened after her husband, whom she found awaiting her at the church door.

Another time at Berwick, the bridegroom had been put out by finding out that the bride intended making a will leaving the £50 that her old mistress had left her, to her own family. Directly he had signed his name he hurried out of church, leaving his bride and the witnesses to sign and follow as quickly as they could. I believe, however, he did not go beyond the churchyard.

The following was told me by the Rev. Richard King-Sampson, who was Curate of Hooe. It took place, as far as I remember, in the 'thirties. Two sisters were to be married; the old Vicar knew them, but did not know the bridegrooms. When the service began the bridal pairs were wrongly sorted. The men and women standing in two pairs, the old Vicar proceeded to marry them. Each couple repeated after the Vicar in turn the vows, but the men changed names. After the service in the vestry the mistake was found out, one man saying, "Please, sir, you have married us to the wrong girls."

He did not know what to do, the marriage was completed, all except signing the registers. The bridal party requested to be left alone a little time to talk the matter over. The Vicar agreed, and shut them in the vestry and himself paced up and down the aisle considering how he could act. He had quickly come to the conclusion that the marriages could not be dissolved, and that an appeal to the Archbishop of Canterbury could not help matters, when soon the vestry door opened. He was called back to the vestry and found everyone cheerful. He was informed that they had talked the matter over, that the marriages did very well, it was all right as it was, for they had all known one another so long that it could not matter and they were quite satisfied. So the two brides left the church perfectly content though they were wives of men whom when they entered the church they had no thought of marrying. Richard King-Sampson was Curate of Hooe at the time. The Vicar was usually non-resident and did not know much about his people.

On one occasion King-Sampson told me that his old Vicar preached the same sermon that he had preached the previous Sunday. After the service he suggested to the Vicar that next time he came to preach it would be as well to compare notes, so as not to repeat the sermon preached the previous week. This reminds me of an anecdote related to me by Rev. George Miles Cooper, of Wilmington, of himself in his courting days.

He was engaged to Miss Catharine Smith, daughter of the Vicar of Newhaven (the same Miss Smith, whom as a child I had refused to kiss at Mrs. Newton's Christmas party). Mr. Cooper arrived at Newhaven one Saturday evening intending to preach there the next morning. On arriving at his destination he took his sermon out of his pocket and pushed it on the top of some books on a bookcase. The following morning before service he went to the same book-case and took what he thought was his sermon, which he put into his pocket, and did not discover that it was not his own until he got into the pulpit to preach. It was someone else's sermon. However, he felt he must make the best of it. So he gave out the text, when he at once became conscious that his intended father-in-law, who was sitting under him in the three-decker, was gazing at him in surprise, which grew more marked as he proceeded. It was the sermon Mr. Smith had preached the previous Sunday and had thrust away on the bookcase as done with.

Few people I have met are so ready with anecdotes as the Rev. W. D. Parish, my neighbour at Selmeston. His Dictionary of the Sussex Dialect * surely contains much that must have been invented to illustrate the meaning of the words. But many of his illustrations are from life. One of the most genial of men, with a

* Reprinted by Country Books

keen sense of the ridiculous, he loves to relate a good story.

I remember two that he told me at different periods – both took place at Selmeston. The first one, the bride was from his parish, a Selmeston girl. The bride groom was a jockey from Alfriston, from which parish his best man also came. The service began and all went well till the ring was placed on the bride's finger. Then, while still on his knees, the bridegroom solemnly saluted his bride. (It is an old Sussex custom, but fallen into disuse). The best man, who with the bridesmaid was kneeling just behind, with the best intentions in the world, evidently thought it part of his duties to do the same by the bridesmaid and kissed her. He was instantly felled to the ground by a stinging box on the ear. Mr. Parish had to make peace before he could proceed with the service – the poor man vehemently protesting that he only did it because he thought he had to.

On another occasion the bridegroom was a native of Selmeston, the bride was not. It was Mr. Parish's custom if he found that any-one wishing to be married had not studied the service, to have them up to the Vicarage, go over the service with them, and explain it. On this occasion the man was in a good position and had received a good plain education. They read the service through until they came to the words, "With my body I thee worship." The man started to his feet. "Worship, worship! I don't worship Fanny. I won't worship her!" He evidently thought that he was asked to break the Second Commandment.

One more marriage anecdote – a Litlington one this time. The maid of Miss Scutt, my sister's sister-in-law, was to be married, and her young mistress attended the wedding. The bridegroom, on seeing the young lady, hung back, whereupon the bride dragged him up the church and, stopping before her young mistress, said as she bobbed a curtsey, "Please, miss, he be so shy." Before the time of railroads especially, the men in our country villages were much more shy than the women.

My wife before she married used to do a great deal of Church work at Margate. Among other things she had a district. On one occasion a woman in her district informed her that an old woman, a butcher's widow, had suddenly married her butcher boy. Not believing it my wife soon after went to visit her. The door was opened by the woman in deep black and her widow's cap. "I am so glad to see you, for I had heard such a silly story about you that you had been so foolish as to marry a boy." The woman looked very confused, and bobbing said it was true. She thought Bob could help her in the business, and he had said as she had such handsome mourning she might just as well wear it out.

Another woman in her district told her she always thought "Marriage such a solitary thing."

I was asked to take a wedding at Alfriston at 8 o'clock in the morning. The man was a butcher, and as I walked through Alfriston on my way to the church I saw him busy in his shop. The party were punctual, and when the wedding was over I lingered a few minutes in the vestry putting by the registers, and then started to walk homewards. I met the bridegroom already in his shirt sleeves carrying his basket of meat to his customers.

At a Chapter Meeting one of my brethren said that shortly before saying "Name this child" at a baptism, the godmother had produced a long string of names beginning with Arabella and going through the alphabet – each name being the longest she could pick out. After the service he asked what she had given such a lot of names for. She replied it was to spite the parents, as she did not wish to stand.

I remember at one Chapter Meeting the Rev. George de St. Croix, Vicar of Glynde, spoke strongly as to the right of god-parents to choose the name, and said that in his own case he left it to them. He had several children. One man present, I think it was Parish, then said he had stood godfather to one of de St. Croix's boys. When de St. Croix said, "Name this child," the godmother looked at the godfathers, and they looked at her; all had forgotten to inquire what name the parents wished. They asked Mr. de St. Croix. "It is your business to choose the name," he rejoined. The god mother suggested "William" (I think). "It is already the name of one of my children." A second name was suggested with the same answer. At the third name the father baptised the child.

CRICKET

I was never anything of a cricketer myself though both my father and my grandfather were keen cricketers.

In an MS. book of memoranda, written by an old man named William Wisdom, who was born at Glynde in 1756, is the following description. The John Ellman alluded to is my grandfather. He writes:–

"When the present Mr. John Ellman and his brother Richard came with their father from Hartfield, in 1761, to the Great Farm at Glynde, Mr. R. Ellman was much the best hand at Cricket; but Mr. J. Ellman began to use the Game. He learned to play it scientifically, that is, to guard the Wicket by holding the Bat upright, and bowling what is called a length Ball. Being a powerful young man he also bowled so hard that it required some skill to keep the ball off the wicket. He soon got to be much superior to his brother, and played very successfully for many years. He played at cricket. He danced. He sang – was excellent company – always Liberal, 'Merry and Wise,' and knew when was the proper time of Life to drop such kind of amusements."

At Winchester my father was the best bowler of his time. The best batsman of the time being Woods, afterwards Member for Gloucester, who I have heard spoken of as a gourmand and a miser. One school anecdote I have been told of him was that on one occasion he left a woodcock roasting before a fire, giving strict charge to the boy who fagged for him to watch it. He was looking forward eagerly to the enjoyment of eating it. As an accompaniment, he had provided himself with a bottle of old port, which, to prevent anyone touching, he had labelled "Poison." On coming in to enjoy his repast, he found only the bones of the wood cock, the boy drunk, and an empty bottle. The boy, on recovering his senses, confessed that whilst watching the roasting he smelt the delicious odour, and could not resist picking off little bits of the bird to taste. He took a little more, and a little more, until he had finished the bird. He was then so frightened, fearing Woods' anger, that seeing the bottle of poison he determined to poison himself, and so drank the entire bottleful.

I liked to see my father play cricket. The way he handled the bat or ball showed that he knew what he was about. Of course, the only bowling he had ever practised was underhand bowling. Round-handed bowling (if I recollect aright) was first brought in by Lillywhite.

I recollect one one occasion, at Glynde, my cousin, Frank Barrow (afterwards Recorder of Rochester), a favourite nephew, who was staying with us, wanted to get up some cricket and failed, so my father offered to give him a few balls, at which he was very pleased. Frank proceeded to put on his cricketing shoes, leg pads, etc. At last he was ready, and standing at the wicket. My father asked if he was ready, he replied that he was. Swiftly came the first ball, which took the middle stump. Frank said he was taken by surprise. So he tried again. My father again asked him if he was ready, and he again said "Yes," whereupon my father delivered the ball which again removed the middle stump. At that Frank Barrow said he did not understand such bowling, and would not be induced to try a third ball.

I remember one occasion when my father, hearing that there was to be a match at Seaford between Public and Private School men, drove over to witness it.

On appearing on the ground he was at once seized upon by the Public School team and entreated to play, as one of their number had at the last moment suddenly failed them. He pleaded that he had given over playing for many years. Then he pointed out a piece of water, which he said did not allow of a large enough field. Both sides laughed at the idea of the possibility of sending a ball as far as the water. In the end my father was persuaded to play. When batting, on the first opportunity he had, he sent his ball into the middle of the sheet of water, where it could be seen floating about, and so could not be called a lost ball. On that ball my father obtained twenty-four runs before anybody waded into the water after it.

But this is by no means the largest number of runs I have known made from one ball.

On one occasion, my father's old school friend, Henry Hurley – one of the partners in the Lewes Old Bank – was playing on the summit of Cliffe Hill, when he sent the ball so far that it rolled down the hill. One of the field went down after it, and another stood on the side to catch it. Not having a firm footing, he failed to do so, and the ball again went to the bottom. It was again thrown up and again missed. At last the fielder climbed up the hill with the ball in his pocket. By the time he at last reached the top Hurley had secured upwards of seventy runs. The laws of cricket are so altered that such a thing could not occur now.

I never played well enough myself to be chosen in any eleven. My usual post when present was to score.

There was a man, whose name I now forget, but whom my father several times mentioned, who offered to meet and to beat any four players belonging to the same family. His family team consisted of himself, his wife, his boy, and his dog. His dog was a splendid fielder and quite entered into the game.

In the early part of the nineteenth century there was no special dress for cricket. Men simply stripped to their shirts when playing. When leg pads, etc. first came in, old cricketers looked upon them with disdain.

ANECDOTES OF ANIMALS

I have always liked animals, and so naturally I have taken a deep interest in the intelligence shown by them at different times.

As I write many amusing and, in some cases, remarkable incidents occur to my mind, and I feel inclined to record some of them. Of course, I have heard many animal tales but these natural history facts have either been seen by myself or I know them to be true.

People talk of "a cat and dog life" when two people quarrel. I consider it the fault of the owners in training dogs and cats when young if either are quarrelsome in later years.

I was always fond of watching animals, birds, and insects, and

Anne of Cleve's House, Southover.

observing their characters and habits. At Southover we boys kept
rabbits. In one hutch on three separate occasions we discovered a
full-sized dead rat, which must have been killed by the doe. On
each of these three occasions she had a nest of young.

The largest rat I ever saw or heard of was caught on the Rectory
premises. It was the size of a full grown rabbit. At that time I kept
fowls, and was continually losing chickens. One night as many as
thirteen disappeared, so I sent for the rat-catcher. For a long time

he could not find a rat, though he found the young chickens laid up in the space between the ceiling of the harness-room and the floor above. At last the old rat sprang from the eaves of the stable-roof into the yard, where he soon fell a prey to the rat-catcher's dogs.

I never entered into field sports, either hunting or shooting. In my younger days it was only flint and steel. I recollect when percussion caps were invented. However, I was always ready to watch ferreting for the destruction of rats.

Once, at Southover, I watched for some time a rat, with a very white belly, sitting on its hind legs, and after licking its forepaws washing its face with its paws. A few days afterwards the rat-catcher came and caught more than a dozen, all white bellied. Rats are very clean animals, and they avoid anything that dirties their fur.

My uncles, at Betshanger, in order to get rid of the rats, once propped up a heavy door with a stick to which a string was attached, and for three or four days running placed under the door some oatmeal. Then when the rats had fed for some nights with impunity, they, very late one night, suddenly pulled the door down on the vermin, and then immediately ran and jumped on the door, which quite rolled under them. When all was quiet they lifted the door and found they had destroyed about thirty full-grown rats.

I once caught alive three mice in one trap; the three must have entered together. In the same trap I once caught a rat that had squeezed itself all in with the exception of its tail.

At one time, when I had the glebe in hand, I built an oat stack in the stable yard. It was much infested with mice, but many of them fell a prey to the hens, who used to watch round the stack, and directly a mouse appeared seize it with their bills. I myself saw several mice caught by the hens in this way, killed, picked to pieces and eaten.

This reminds me that when I returned from Wartling to Berwick, the fowls which I had brought from Berwick more than two years previously were, on their return to their old quarters, perfectly at home. The first night they, of their own accord, went to roost in the hen house, through the hole cut at the bottom of the door, as if they had never been absent a single night.

My cows also I had taken to Wartling. I sent them back to Berwick Rectory in charge of a lad who had never been far in this direction before. On his return to Wartling I asked him if he had had any difficulty in finding the way (more than nine miles across country. He said he had not had the slightest trouble — all he had to do was to follow the cows. Directly they were let out of their field at Wartling and headed away from the Vicarage, they started off walking, kept well ahead of him all the way, and then waited at the gate of the field they had left two years earlier for him to open it.

Animals have wonderful memories of any road they have ever traversed, or people whom they have known.

Still more wonderful is the instinct which enables them to find their way home when shut up in box, or bag, and conveyed to a distance.

I have heard of a fox being sent from this neighbourhood in a bag into Cumberland, and finding its way back to its old quarters in a very short time.

Two or three times foxes have taken refuge in the Rectory garden. On one occasion a fox, which was being hunted, put up its feet and looked in the dining room window. Seeing us m the room it rushed away and took refuge in the coach-house, the door of which stood open. The children's nurse, who was looking out of the nursery window, saw it run into the coach-house she rushed downstairs and locked it in. It was a young one, and when it was caught was afterwards for many months chained up to a dog kennel at Church Farm. Close by was another kennel to which a dog was chained. The animals soon became great friends and used to play together. I don't know what eventually became of it.

When we lived at Southover we had two dogs, "Daphne," a Sussex spaniel, and "Tiny," a terrier. When either dog had puppies, whenever the mother left them the other dog would take her place, lie down and take care of them till the mother's return. "Tiny," we suddenly lost in 1824, and four years afterwards we learnt her fate. Some boys crawled into a narrow passage called "The Dark Lantern," in the Priory ruins, and there discovered her bones with the collar she used to wear. "Daphne's" death I was especially grieved at. Before she died her hindquarters were paralysed.

My grandfather had two favourite spaniels, "Daphne" and "Flora." Our "Daphne" was named after the Glynde "Daphne."

I remember once as a boy entering my grand father's dining-room and finding that "Flora's" puppies had somehow got hold of some poor kittens; one they had killed and the other they were in the act of pulling asunder.

Another dog that I remember in my boyhood was a young sporting dog that my father sent to my Uncle Henry, at Milmains. It was conveyed there in a covered cart with some sheep. (My father used to send animals: rams, and sheep, very long distances in a cart; as far as Gloucestershire and Wiltshire). The dog, on first being tried with a gun, behaved very badly, for which it was scolded, and ran off. My uncle wrote to say that the dog had run away. But the dog appeared at Glynde as soon as the letter!

The most wonderful dog story that I know to be true is the following:

My uncle, Rev. Richard Boys, was one day crossing a street in the East End of London when he was suddenly fawned upon by a dog. This dog he had given away and left in St. Helena some months before, when he gave up his Chaplaincy there. The dog was very faithful and devoted to him. He tried but never could trace how it got to England. He always imagined that the faithful animal, finding he had gone away by ship, voluntarily went on board an East Indian ship calling at the island, in search of his master. Once landed in London it had evidently been searching the streets for some time, until it luckily came across its owner.

In those days, between 1815 and 1822, almost every ship coming home from India called at St. Helena, but not the outgoing vessels, the course of the wind there being almost always from the south-east, consequently ships from England had to hug the American coast to a latitude considerably south of St. Helena, in order to obtain a wind to reach the island.

About the same time, whilst my uncle, the Rev. James Boys, was in India, one night while sleeping in a tent with his little dog

215

asleep on the pillow on which his own head rested, he was suddenly awakened, and beheld a tiger going out of the tent carrying off the little dog.

I have known many instances of animals adopting the young of another species and bringing them up as their own; dogs stealing and bringing up kittens; and cats bringing up rabbits.

NATURAL HISTORY

I have made a list of eighty-four Berwick birds that I have myself seen, amongst which was a hoopoe, which for several minutes sat on the front gate. On three different occasions in different years have hoopoes rested in the garden. Apparently not the same hoopoe, as the first one arrived over fifty years ago, the second thirty years later, and the last only a year or two ago. Of course, hoopoes may have paid many other visits when I did not happen to see them.

I have never seen a quail in the parish. About 1840 a quail's nest was found in the White Links, but I did not hear of anybody seeing the old birds.

Twice I have seen woodcock: the first time in the meadow in front of the Rectory, the other time one was picked up exhausted in the churchyard, and brought into the Rectory to see if it could be revived.

Of our summer and winter visitors I have noticed that the same birds return year after year; the old birds to the same tree or place is possible.

We have had several piebald birds; one rook had nearly a whole white wing; another two long white feathers. One year a hen black-bird was so light that she looked almost white.

Before the church was restored we had a colony of owls in the belfry, who frequently were heard during the service. It is recorded that on one occasion before my time, a preacher (Rev. H. Knox, who had come over to take service) was much disturbed by their snores. He paused, then called out "Mr. Churchwarden, I must request you to wake that person asleep in the gallery." "It is only the owls, sir," was the reply.

216

Since the restoration we have only had owls in the old elms in the Rectory garden, and though year after year they evidently have young ones, these seem to disappear and I have never seen more than four at a time.

Of late years our most common butterfly seems to be the "Red Admiral."

I had often heard of insects crossing the British Channel, and naturally supposed that they would cross the Straits of Dover, but on one occasion, as I was crossing between Newhaven and Dieppe, when out of sight of land, in mid-channel, we met a large flight of white butterflies, several of whom settled on the vessel.

The longest English snake I ever saw was one killed by our groom at Southover, about 1823. He hung it up against a wall and I calculated that it must be very nearly, if not quite, five feet long.

I have been reminded of a fishing incident by reading Frank Buckland's "Anecdotes of Fishing," which I found very interesting.

Once, about 1828, we boys went to Southease to see the old river (a part of the Ouse) dragged. One drag was especially successful, as when the net was emptied there was about a bushel of small fish, principally roach, and under these a pike of twenty-eight pounds; two other large pike, the smaller weighing over eleven pounds, being taken in the course of the day. There were two other boys with us, Henry Gage (father of the present Viscount), and Henry Brand, now Lord Hampden. I should like to ask the latter whether he remembers that day. * Henry Gage was so excited that he jumped in and swam behind the net to help in the work.

To show the power of sound in certain states of the atmosphere, I may mention that on one occasion, whilst fishing in the same old part of the river, we distinctly heard the ringing of the hand-bell at Southover Manor, four miles off.

In the Cuckmere river I have many a time seen salmon trout. When the river was low they were very fond of playing in the deep holes near Sherman's Bridge, but of late years they are not so plentiful, from all accounts.

* This was written some years ago

Frank Buckland's account of the celebrated White Horse in Berkshire leads me to leave on record that the White Horse on the side of the hill below Alfriston, opposite Litlington, was cut out about 1840, by James Pagden, of Alfriston, and one of his brothers.

There has been much controversy as to the age and the origin of the Wilmington Giant, which is cut into the turf on the side of the Downs above Wilmington. The theories about it are many; I have even heard people declare it to be a huge sun-dial, cut by the monks belonging to Wilmington Priory. A sun-dial on the north side of the Downs does not seem to strike these people as an absurdity.

The theory I myself formed is that it was one of the giant figures of a kind of basket-work or wattles, mentioned by Julius Caesar, as the places where the Druids sacrificed the victims taken in war. We know that at that period, and for some centuries after, Sussex was very marshy and thickly wooded. The inhabitants lived almost entirely upon the higher ground, going down to the forests to hunt.

If the basket-work figures filled with victims stood upright, the bottom part would burn first and the victims escape. If the victims were enclosed in a fence, shaping out a figure, the warriors could stand around and prevent the victims escaping.

No doubt the monks from time to time cleaned out the figure. When I was a young man the huge figure was growing very indistinct, the turf only in certain lights showing the outlines of the Giant. About thirty years ago a fund was raised and the figure was carefully outlined in white bricks.

Of rare British animals I had always looked upon badgers as long extinct in this neighbourhood, but a few years ago one was seen and unfortunately killed in a coppice at the neck of the Common just in Berwick parish; and in 1891 one was found and taken from its burrow on the hill above Alciston. It was kept for several months at Berwick Station.

Otters are now very rare, if not extinct, at the present time in the parish. However, I believe there are otters in the river higher up. The last otter that I have heard of being actually seen was in the moat at Mitchelham, now some years since.

Only in 1891 I saw the remains of three or four pound fish (evidently the fragments of an otter's feast) close to Sherman's Bridge, on the Berwick side of the Cuckmere. Their principal home is, I believe, a little above Mitchelham, where the banks of the Cuckmere river are well wooded.

Once I saw three trout caught in the river not far below Sherman's Bridge. Close to the bridge is a very deep hole, in which it was said salmon (but I believe it was rather salmon trout), up to six or seven pounds weight, have frequently been caught. Within a mile of the bridge, on the upper side (still in the parish) I have known of a jack of over twenty pounds being caught.

I once saw a famous haul of grey mullet taken from the Cuckmere at Exceat.

We do not often have squirrels in the Rectory garden. One hung about the churchyard and garden for some weeks in 1892, and the last that was seen only remained a few days, about five years later. I have often seen them in the Vicarage grounds at Wilmington, and most likely our visitors came from there.

In mentioning the wild animals found in Berwick, I must not forget to write that I have also seen stoats. One winter, some years ago, one was hanging about the Rectory for some days. It had a pure white coat – a regular ermine.

Polecats, I believe, are now extinct in the neighbourhood, it must be sixty years since I even heard of one being seen in the parish.

About 1840 I saw some little red harvest mice (first described by Gilbert White) in the field at the back of the church.

TRAVELLING

The speed of travelling by railroad was not anticipated when the railroad between Liverpool and Manchester was opened in 1831, that railroad being principally made for the carriage of cotton and other imports to the large manufacturing town of Manchester. And when on the day of opening the unfortunate accident happened to Mr. Huskinson and the engine, "The Rocket," returned to Liverpool for medical assistance at the rate of thirty miles an hour, it was thought almost incredible.

The fastest run I recollect recording was in 1850, on the G.W.R., having run from the fifty-first mile post to the first post, the fifty miles in forty-six minutes.

In making the new turnpike road from Lewes to Eastbourne in 1819, the only actual new portions of the road were from Ranscombe to Beddingham, from the crossways at Beddingham to the top of the hill where stood the turnpike house, and from Alciston to Polegate. As much as possible of the old road or path was widened and improved for the new turnpike. On the Lewes side of Ranscombe, however, the road was altered, being made lower down the bank to ease the hill, and where it joined the old road at the corner the bank was pared down. This exposed the sites of two pits cut out in the chalk, and filled up with earth. I used to fancy that these were graves, and have wondered whether they could have anything to do with murders committed there. Immediately opposite there is a lane leading down to the marsh, which used to bear a very bad reputation. Many were afraid to pass the spot at night. The lane was said to be haunted, a ghost in the shape of a woman without a head would (it was said, often appear at the top of the lane.

About forty years since – (written 1888) – a short distance on the Ranscombe side of the corner, early one morning, after a heavy thunderstorm, a cart was found upset, with three people dead who had all been struck by lightning.

Very soon after I became Rector of Berwick, I was appointed a Commissioner of Laughton Levels, but I never acted or attended any of the meetings. On these commissions were almost invariably country clergy, the number of country residents duly qualified being very few.

I was appointed Commissioner of the Lewes and Eastbourne turnpike road, and shortly before the final expiration of the trust I was left the sole Commissioner. Before the road was made in 1819, there was an old turnpike road which went by Ranscombe, round by Glynde, with a turnpike gate where Glynde Station now is, then up to Firle, and at the back of Firle Park (that portion of the old road being shut up when the new road was made), then on to Tilton Barn and Bo-peep, where was another turnpike gate, than under the Downs as far as Winton Street, then down Winton Street over Longbridge and then up the Downs by Windo'er and through Jevington.

I once read that about 1770 it was proposed to tunnel the hill between Jevington and Eastbourne, but that idea was given up when the new road was made. In 1819 turnpikes were put up at Southeram; also between Glynde and Firle, and where the road turns off to Ripe, against the ground where the union house now stands. Another at the top of the hill near Milton, and at Polegate, at each of which, except the first two, which cleared each other, the toll was threepence a horse and threepence a wheel.

Consequently whenever Mr. Thomas, of Ratton, took his family to a ball at Lewes, returning as he did after midnight, he had to pay sixteen shillings for turnpike gates. On going to a ball he always drove four horses. After upwards of seventy years the tolls were lowered, but still remained high. We were, however, sorry when the trust came to an end and the gates were done away with, as it threw the expenses of the roads on the parishes, instead of their being kept up at the expense of those who made use of them.

When I first knew Lewes the whole of the streets were paved with boulders. I think it was about 1823 that the boulders were taken up and the roads macadamized. The boulders, however, remained in some of the side streets for many years, and I am not sure whether some of the steep lanes leading from High Street on the south are not still so paved.

The Cliffe was very narrow, barely room for two vehicles to pass each other, but in 1831 the street was widened, the fronts of most of the houses on the south side being thrown back some feet. About the same time the bridge over the Ouse was also widened.

There was then only one footpath, and that was separated from the road by a wall. This wall was removed, and on the south side a second footway was made supported on brackets. These were great improvements, as there was a great deal of traffic into Lewes through the Cliffe.

It was proposed to throw a second bridge over the River Ouse at the bottom of North Street. This would have made a much better and shorter entrance to the county town from Uckfield or Ringmer. I believe the principal hindrance to the scheme being carried out was the opposition it received from the Cliffe, the trades people feeling that the would lose much of their custom if so large a portion of the traffic were diverted from passing their shops. This, indeed, afterwards in a large measure occurred when the railroad was opened.

In like manner did the Lewes tradespeople for years refuse to allow the cattle market to be held anywhere but in the High Street, for fear they should lose their trade.

Before there was a railroad there were in Lewes two large wholesale grocers' firms, which supplied the various country shops for many miles around. When the railroads were opened the country shops obtained their stores much more largely from London. The gentry also, and especially the ladies, instead of making their purchases at Lewes, went by train to Brighton, which was vastly increasing in site and importance. The consequence was that the trade of Lewes went down, and the shops gave up keeping goods for which there was no demand.

Brighton has increased enormously since I first knew it. The first time I went there was in 1822, when my eldest brother Spencer was at school at Ayres', in St. James' Street.

In the beginning of the century long distances used to be undertaken on horseback. In fact, I have heard from my father of long journeys over England, and even into Scotland, that he went on horseback. When he was a lad my father went to Betshanger, in Kent, to learn a different system of farming, and my uncle, Henry Boys, at the same time came to Glynde. This led to his knowing my mother, and as they were engaged for over six years he must have gone to Betshanger in 1803 or 1804.

The distance between Glynde and Betshanger is upwards of

seventy miles, and was always done on horseback, the traveller generally sleeping one night on the way.

Notwithstanding his large family (thirteen children), my Grandfather Boys took agricultural pupils into his house. My father told me he had two or three fellow pupils. One, Bob Wright, as he was commonly called, was made the butt of his companions. One evening he went to bed very early, as he was to be one of a shooting party who had agreed to start very early the next morning on their expedition, as they had several miles to go. About 10 o'clock, when his companions were going to bed, they put on their shooting jackets, sporting boots, shot belts, and with guns in their hands, went into his room and aroused him, telling him to make haste. Wright accordingly sprang up, hastily dressed himself in his sporting attire, and then, not finding anybody about, and lights out downstairs, thought that the others must have started without him, but at last found out it was only 11 p.m. instead of 5 a.m.

My father was as fond of a practical joke as anyone, and joined in many a one played on Bob Wright, afterwards writing various rhymes describing these exploits.

In my young days the breed of horses was much stronger and more capable of endurance than horses are now. Even the race-horses were stronger. For instance, the King's Plate at the Lewes races was always run in four-mile heats, and if the same horse did not win the first and second heats, there were at least three more four-mile gallops for them; and the weights carried were much greater than what is now usual.

I recollect in my childhood, my father and mother, with my sister Emily, then probably about three years old, arriving at Southover in the old chaise, having left Wingham (Kent) the same morning, a distance of seventy two miles, one horse having done the work.

When my mother visited her old home she was always driven by my father, and they stayed one night on the way to rest the horse. The party would consist of my father, mother, the baby with nurse, and, of course, necessary luggage.

Anecdotes of Storms, Etc

On October 29th, 1836, there was a heavy fall of snow, three or four inches deep.

That day month, November 29th, 1836, there was the most destructive hurricane that I ever heard of in Sussex.

In the gale a vast number of trees were destroyed, and forty barns within ten miles of Lewes were blown down, including two at Berwick. The gale was most violent in the south-east corner of England, but raged over the greater part of the country. I was in Oxford at the time, and even there it was very violent, tiles and trees being blown down. When I went back to Glynde for Christmas I counted sixty-three large elms prostrate in Glynde alone.

That Christmas, 1836, was the one and only time that we all were together.

My eldest brother was at sea when my youngest brother was born, and was very little at home after that his home-comings being few and far between; for it so happened that he had only two or three days' interval (not time to come home) before being gazetted to another ship.

On the evening of Christmas Day there commenced a very heavy fall of snow, which stopped all traffic in this part of England.

The snow covered everything, and pathways in the roads had to be dug out. In one place, where a narrow passage through had been dug, the snow was considerably above my head on either side. Someone at Glynde Place – I forget who it was now, a visitor staying with the Hampdens – had an invitation to the Pavilion at Brighton, and offered a man ten shillings (more than a week's wages at that time) to take a letter to his Majesty. By avoiding the roads and keeping at a distance from the hedges, the man managed to wade through. He brought back word that no one else had reached Brighton from Lewes. The snow was not all melted for three months.

The following winter there was another snowstorm, but though not generally so deep as that of 1836, it overhung Cliffe Hill

(Lewes) in wreaths, and falling down in an avalanche it crushed eight houses, burying sixteen people, of whom eight were dead when they were dug out. On the spot now stands the Snowdrop Inn, so named because the snow there dropped.

In the winter of 1846-47 there was another heavy fall. I was staying at Clapham with my sister at the time, and walked through the snow to Berwick, intending there to take the train to Lewes, where I had a meeting. On arriving at Berwick Station, finding that the railroad was blocked, I waded through the snow to Lewes, and then on to Landport. There was no mark in the snow of anyone or any vehicle having preceded me till I reached Lewes.

In 1881 the railroad was again blocked. A train was snowed up near Polegate, and a lady passed the night in a signal-box, as she could not even get to the station.

About 1827 I recollect snow in July, which remained under the shelter of some trees two or three days before it melted.

Talking of railways, I may mention that in their early days there used to be a seat on the top of the "railway coaches," as they were then called, at either end, meant, I believe, for the guard. In 1838 I travelled from Newcastle to Carlisle, occupying one of these seats, and thus had a magnificent view of the Tyne Valley. I had to look out for the bridges under which we passed, and duck down, otherwise I should have lost my head.

Passengers would not now be allowed to travel on the top of the railway coaches, but no objection was raised to our doing so. At that time many of the coaches were open, and some third class carriages had not even seats.

Writing of railways reminds me of an incident that took place some years later. When the Chichester and Midhurst railroad was being constructed, one of the navvies meeting Miss Hutchinson, daughter of the Rev. C. H. Hutchinson, Vicar of West Dean (son of my old friend, the Vicar of Firle), began making rude remarks and tried to prevent her passing. Her father, who either overheard him or was summoned, came up, and gave the man a sound thrashing. The navvy was so twitted about the same by his mates that he left the neighbourhood and joined a gang higher up the line. The report followed him, and in the end he was quite driven away from the works by the laughter of the others.

The muscular Vicar gained by his conduct such favour from the navvies that his congregations were swelled by them as long as they were anywhere in the neighbourhood.

In the early part of this century a great deal of smuggling was carried on all round the coast, but accounts of smuggling have been written, and I think I have little fresh to record. The only thing I can think of at this moment is that a Firle man, who lost his arm in a contest with the coastguards, procured a brass or iron fist, which he fastened on to his arm in place of the lost hand, in order that he might give a hard blow in case of another affray.

On one Sunday, when Mr. West came over from Lewes to take service at Berwick, he found no one in the church but the clerk, who informed him that all the people had gone to a wreck in Seaford Bay. This must have been between 1820 and 1830.

Numerous were the hiding-places for the smuggled goods. Large monuments erected in churchyards were sometimes used, and it was no unusual thing for farmers to find a keg of spirits lying outside their doors, in payment for the hire of the farm horses, taken at night-time without their master's knowledge.

During storms off the coast the roar of the waves on the beach can be at times heard in the Rectory garden.

The shingle all along this corner of the coast seems to be always travelling eastward, and in stormy weather much shingle is washed out of Seaford Bay.

In front of the Tide Mill at Bishopstone several groins were erected to arrest the beach, and if a sufficient number of groins were erected all along the bay it would, no doubt, be very beneficial.

About 1850 it was decided to form an enormous groin by blowing down a portion of the cliff to the eastward. Chambers to hold gunpowder were made in the cliff, and the powder, amounting to some tons, was fired by electricity. I witnessed the operation. A mound about sixty feet high, and running a long distance into the sea, was at once formed, but, as no steps were taken to retain it, it was all washed away in the course of a few months. *

About 1860 the sea again broke through the shingle into
Seaford, as it had done twenty-five years before. Shortly before it
broke in it had been arranged to build terraces and good houses on
the shingle-covered land near the sea, it being thought that the
high, thick shingle bank would keep out all further inroads.

To prevent another irruption, I understand that a trench has been
dug along the highest part of the beach and filled up with concrete,
which prevents the salt water soaking through, and has since
resisted the storms.

THE BRITISH ASSOCIATION

I was always fond of mechanical pursuits and liked to know how
things were made. In my Lewes school days, if I got the chance, I
would linger for two or three minutes on my way to or from school
to watch the work going on in a carpenter's shop or the forge as I
passed. I especially liked to see the blacksmith get a light by
hammering a piece of iron. It was not till 1831 that lucifer
matches were invented. At first they were very expensive, half-a-
crown a small box, but they soon got down to a shilling. I found
them most convenient when at school at Brighton to get a light for
my early morning reading, and did not scruple to give a shilling for
a box of matches. I kept them in the drawer of my washstand, but
box after box was taken away, and I dared not complain, knowing
that they were supposed to be so dangerous. At first, instead of
being struck on the box, a folded piece of sandpaper was supplied
with each box.

When I became a member of the British Association, at the
meetings most of my time was spent in "G," the mechanical
section, as the papers describing new inventions (many of them
illustrated by plans or even experiments) had a great charm for me,

* Note – a few months before my father's death he was much interested in reading
in the newspaper that a charge of gunpowder had been found in the cliffs; evidently one chamber had not exploded, and the fact was not discovered for fifty-

as also had any factories which were open to the members, and of which I visited as many as possible.

In the first years of my membership it was seldom I could afford to go, but whenever I could I was intensely interested. Once I happened to go to a Birmingham factory where they manufactured metal teapots, at the same hour as Farraday. The managers, finding who their visitor was, ordered various processes of the works to be carried on, and hence I came in for much that was not usually known.

The impressing a pattern on metal plates by passing them through rollers, and then taking the metal plate and turning it into the shape of a teapot without destroying the pattern, astonished me. Another process shown was the manufacture of brass-tapering bedposts with twisted flutes.

The machinery departments of the Exhibitions of 1851 and 1852 also greatly interested me, knowing that these various wonderful machines could never have been devised without a knowledge of mathematics. I always had a greater love for the latter than the for the dead languages, the study of which, in my youthful days, I could not see the benefit of.

When the British Association met one year at Southampton, one evening Buckland, who was to give us an address, had been spending the day in the Isle of Wight, and when the time came, stood up and produced his red pocket-handkerchief full of seaside curiosities, upon which he gave us a very interesting address. On that occasion Prince Albert was in the chair.

That same year I first heard of the existence of the planet Neptune. It was some weeks before its discovery, and calculations were being made as to when it could be seen, and the following 1st of January was fixed upon for its appearance.

But Adams and Verrier managed to anticipate the day, the former being the first to record the requisite observations, but the latter, by working his observations out, was the first to announce the discovery.

In 1837, at Liverpool, I heard Dr. Lardner declare it to be impossible for vessels to cross the Atlantic under steam. The next year, 1838, the Association met at Newcastle, after the passage by steam had become an accomplished fact. He was called upon for an explanation of his previous year's statement. I heard his attempted defence of his previous assertion, which amounted to the fact that he had only meant that it would never pay.

I had certainly understood him to declare that no vessel could carry coals enough for so long a voyage. Dr. Lardner was a very short, thick-set man. I have seen him sitting on a table swinging his legs, and his appearance was certainly very much against him. His wife deserted him, evidently preferring Captain Heaviside, who was quite a contrast, being six feet seven inches in height, slight and bony.

One great interest I had from attending meetings of the British Association was the number of clever, noted men that I met. Amongst them I may mention the Arctic travellers, Captain James Ross, Captain Back, and Sir John Richardson, with whom I visited Knowsley, sitting next him at the lunch that Lord Derby had provided for us.

Then I may mention Sir David Brewster, to whom on one occasion, when he came into the room late, I had the honour of explaining what had been said in the paper that had just been read – an optical subject; whereupon, as soon as the speaker ceased, Sir David got up and spoke, optics being his special forte.

Then I would add the names of Whewell; the two Brunells – father and son; Sir John Herschel, who always struck me as a universal genius in all branches of science; Peacock; Adam Sedgwick; Murchison; Owen; Airey; Faraday; Lyell, and Robert Stevenson. Many others I saw and heard, but with those mentioned, I had more or less intercourse.

THE CORN LAW, ETC

About 1813 or 1814, there was a Board of Agriculture, of which George Webb Hall was chairman, and my father vice-chairman. This led to my father being very frequently in town, sometimes for weeks together.

He was a great writer on matters connected with agriculture. Most of his letters were published in the *Farmer's Journal*, and he had printed various pamphlets and letters, addressed to various Members of Parliament, of which copies were sent to a large number.

He was over and over again urgently pressed to allow himself to be elected member for the county, the promise being made that the election should not cost him a shilling. But my mother's earnest appeal to him not to consent, reminding him of the late hours, the worry and tear of a Parliamentary life, and the being obliged to be away even more in London than he already was, supported his resolution to resist, and each time he steadily refused to be elected.

However, he was always keenly interested, as was my grandfather, upon any matter that had to do with the food supply of the country. I am certain if it had not been for my mother's great dislike to a public life my father would undoubtedly have yielded.

On the occasion of a county meeting being called on the question of the Corn Laws, my father was chosen as president and chairman, and his speech filled the whole of one side of a newspaper, and excited at the time great attention. He was summoned to London, and largely consulted by members of both Houses on agricultural matters. It was my father who suggested the sliding scale duty on corn, and the Bill was drafted; but when the scheme came before the House, instead of being such a scale as had been proposed, it was altered in the higher part into a jumping, instead of sliding scale. He at once wrote to the Duke of Wellington, then Prime Minister, and pointed out the evil of the alteration. I am in possession of the Duke's answer, expressing his regret at the alteration, but saying that the matter had proceeded too far to alter it. It turned out as he predicted. My father's object was to keep wheat at as steady a price as possible, to encourage the importation, when, by the rise of prices, it was shown that wheat was wanted; or rather to let it out of bond, having been imported at a time when the low prices showed that it was not wanted.

At that time the burdens on land were very great, and my father calculated that sixty shillings a quarter was a fair price for wheat. By the scheme brought into Parliament, and which afterwards became law, as soon as ever the price rose to sixty-seven or sixty-eight shillings, the duty was lowered about four shillings for each shilling rise. The consequence was, that as it approached that price, the importers and merchants by fraudulent sales or otherwise, forced the price of corn up above seventy shillings to the detriment of the general consumer, without benefit to the English farmer.

We must recollect that at that time the population of England was not half what it is now, that the principal industry was agriculture; that almost all the corn imported came from Russia or Germany, and that the only mercantile ships were sailing vessels.

The sliding scale was a protection for all classes, and during its continuance the average price of corn was never so high as it had been before or has been since.

In 1842, the evil of the jumping part of the scale was remedied, and the new law was working very well, when Sir Robert Peel repealed the Corn Laws altogether in 1846.

The Whigs proposed a ten shillings duty, but this my father highly disapproved, and said he would sooner see corn perfectly free. He fully agreed with a saying of Mr. Hutchinson, "Let the corn be the product of our own labour, and the cheaper the better." Circumstances have changed, but seventy years ago it was most important that we should not be dependent upon foreign countries for a large proportion of our food.

Now that we can import from our own Colonies such large stores of grain, and we have ocean steamers and railroads to reach these corn-growing countries, there is no fear that we may not be supplied, at a moderate cost, with as much corn as we can possibly want.

When the Free Trade Corn question was at its height, urgent appeals were again made to my father to allow himself to be sent into the House. As it was, he was almost constantly up in London on various Committees, or being examined before the Board of Agriculture.

Of course, at the time, it was fully understood that if England

231

led the way with Free Trade the other countries were going to follow. It is needless to say that their promises have been broken.

When the Militia Training was revived, my father and Sir Henry Shiffner, as Deputy-Lieutenants, were selected by the Duke of Richmond, the Lord-Lieutenant, to act with him in arranging about the depots, etc., and this led to three or four visits of a day or two at a time to Goodwood, and to the cordial feelings that ever after the Duke of Richmond seemed to feel for my father, to whom, as the years went on, he showed marked friendship.

SOME MORE ANECDOTES

A neighbour of mine for many years has been the Rev. W. D. Parish, Vicar of Selmeston and Alciston – one of the most genial of men – who possessed an ever-ready fund of humour. For some years now he has been an invalid and as I cannot drive so far we shall never meet again.

I knew him first when he was ordained to the Curacy of Firle and Beddingham, in Hutchinson's time – now many years ago. When Foster left Selmeston he was appointed in his place. He has always been a favourite with all classes, an amusing conversationalist, as all his friends know well. While Curate of Firle he acted for a time as a School Inspector. One day he had to examine the West Firle Union children in divinity. He was endeavouring to get an answer to his query, "What is a miracle?" No child seemed able to give a proper answer. So Parish said, "Suppose you were to wake up and saw the sun shining in the middle of the night what would you say it was?" "Full moon." "But supposing someone told you it was the sun and not the full moon. What would you say then?" "It's a lie." "I don't tell lies, if I told you–" "Ye be drunk." I have of late years seen in print this anecdote, but without mention of the name of the questioner or the place. My informant was my father, immediately after it happened – I rather think the same day – on his return from the Union.

On another occasion while inspecting a school, suddenly a

232

Rev. W. D. Parish, Vicar of Selmeston and Alciston.
"One of the most genial of men – who possessed an ever-ready fund of humour."

small girl burst out crying. The mistress hastened to find out the cause, and then Parish heard her scolding the child. He inquired what was the matter, and the mistress had to inform him that the child said she cried because she wanted the inspector to kiss her! He immediately gave the little one a kiss and the tears vanished. Parish had plenty of money, so when be took a holiday he could afford to go where he liked. In the early 'sixties, during the American war, he had a fancy to go to America and see what was going on. He took up his quarters at a farmer's, but he said he soon found out that the farmer's only farm implements were a revolver and a bowie-knife, so he hastily left. During the siege of Paris he had a great desire to try and get into that city to see what was going on, but he yielded to the wishes of his father and did not make the attempt. He is a confirmed bachelor, but somehow strangers often think he is a married man. I remember at a Chichester Diocesan Conference held at Eastbourne some years ago, Parish, speaking of the tithe on hop gardens, said it was only an extra ordinary tithe. Not one of the reporters present noticed the witticism. His speech was altogether an amusing one. The next speaker, who did not know him well, never imagined he was a bachelor, and said, "It was all very well for Mr. Parish to speak as he had done, surrounded in his pleasant Vicarage by his wife and children." Up jumped Parish, "My lord! My lord!" cried he to the Bishop who was the chairman. "I beg to contradict the speaker. I beg to state that I have no children! I am not married!" in the most droll manner, much to the amusement of the Bishop and the meeting generally.

Once I tried hard to persuade Parish to subscribe to the "Clergy Widows' Fund" for the Lewes Archdeaconry, of which I have so long been secretary. He refused on the ground that he was helping the society already by not marrying.

On one occasion, to his delight, a bill was sent in to him in all good faith by a London firm, for a large amount for doing up Mrs. Parish's sealskin jacket. Instead of writing back and saying there was no Mrs. Parish, he wrote to the firm to say it was a mistake, as Mrs. Parish did not possess a sealskin jacket.

I remember one Chapter meeting when he left early to go to St. Leonards to meet, at his father's house, two brothers, one whom he had never seen, and the other whom he had not seen for twenty years.

There is a Dissenting chapel at Alciston at which a Dissenting minister preached every Sunday. This preacher came from (I think) Tunbridge Wells, he was unmarried, and certain of his followers thought it would be well if he were a married man. Great satisfaction was given when the man one Sunday brought a wife with him. Not long afterwards he turned up on a Sunday with another woman, whom he also declared was his wife. This his followers did not approve of, but the man declared that what was sin for them was not wrong for him. Some of the Dissenters went to consult Parish on the subject and wanted him to condemn the man. This he would not do, but instead told them that he considered they had only themselves to thank; "you wished your minister to marry so as to be as much unlike me as possible; to please you he did so. I shall not sympathise with you." This is his own account of what he told them. Several of the Dissenters, I believe, came to church after this.

Another story he tells is, that he found that when some of his school children, in reading the Bible, came to a long name that they did not know how to pronounce, they would substitute the word "Jerusalem," and when found fault with for so doing, declared it was done in their chapel. This he found was the case. One Sunday, coming from his afternoon service at Alciston, he stood outside the chapel to listen and heard the reader do so. Two other stories I must give of him before I pass on to another man. Bishop Durnford made him Chancellor of the Cathedral. One day he was at work in the library attached to Chichester Cathedral, and was much disturbed by the organ, which he imagined was being tuned. He called one of the vergers and requested him to go at once to the organist, and to ask him to put off the tuning till he had finished some writing he had to do. The verger was astonished and informed him that an organ recital was going on. Needless to remark, Parish was not musical.

When Curate of Firle, he asked a farmer for a subscription to some object. The farmer refused, saying he already subscribed thirty pounds to charity. Mr. Parish said he would like to know how he made out that amount, producing as he spoke pencil and paper out of his pocket to make a list. Amongst the items given was a guinea to the Lewes Fat Stock Show, another guinea to the Hailsham Show, and the list ended up with ten pounds to the foxhounds!

For many years we had two Rev. Robert Suttons in the Diocese, one in East Sussex, one in West, no relation to each other. One, Robert Sutton, Vicar of Slinfold, was in 1875 made the Vicar of Pevensey, and afterwards Archdeacon of Lewes. Some years ago both men happened to take a holiday at the same time and strangely enough fixed on the same house or hotel (I forget which) in Hastings. A visitor called and asked for "Mr. Sutton." "Which Mr. Sutton, sir? There are two staying here." "Mr. Robert Sutton." "Both are Mr. Robert Suttons." "The clergyman." "Both are clergymen." The visitor then tried to describe. Both were Prebendaries, both married men, both had their families staying with them.

BLIND HARRY BOYS

My blind cousin, Henry Boys, commonly called by us all "Blind Harry," was of a most happy and cheerful disposition, and a very pleasant companion. When his father and mother returned to St. Helena in 1819, he, with his sister Mary, was left with his uncle, Dr. Sankey, at Wingham, for education. Harry was educated to be a doctor. Whilst at a hospital studying to be a surgeon, he, one day, in using a penknife to cut some stick, let it slip, and it went into an eye, the sight of which was destroyed, and through sympathy the sight of the other eye soon followed.

In his blindness he wanted to "see" everything. He visited Oxford whilst I was in residence, and he was delighted at my taking him round to the various colleges.

When we went into a chapel or a hall, he would pace it for its size; with his voice he would make a very good calculation as to the height; and I described to him the portraits and carvings. He took interest in every detail that I mentioned.

Once, when staying at Glynde, he went with me to Plummer Verrall's the auctioneer's, and as usual I described what was before us. On my describing a large painting of Blenheim, he took a great fancy to it, and after some bidding it was knocked down to him. He afterwards presented it to my father, and for many years it hung on the staircase at Landport.

He was very musical and played very sweetly on the flute. Once while staying with me at Berwick he tuned an old piano that I had.

At one time he took up phrenology and wanted to feel people's bumps. On one of his frequent visits to Glynde, there was another visitor staying at the same time, a Captain Bird, son of the Dean of Battle, whose head he desired to feel. Just as Captain Bird had consented and was going to seat himself to have his bumps examined, my father slipped into the chair in Captain Bird's stead. it was a shame to deceive Harry, but he took it in very good part, and joined in the laugh which followed his declaring that my father's bumps proved him to be "a deuce of a fellow for fighting." Afterwards, without any loss of temper, he proceeded to feel Captain Bird's head.

After Harry's visit came to an end, he, to be near us, took lodgings in Lewes at Jeffrey's, the tailor's, just opposite Mr. John Smith's house, whose daughter Sarah took pity upon the blind man, and would read his letters to him. When he wanted her assistance he would pull his blind half-way down, which, when she perceived, Miss Smith would go over to him.

On one of these occasions it was to read a letter which had just arrived, in which, unfortunately, the writer joked Harry about his friendship with Miss Sarah, but both were too sensible to be really disconcerted thereby, though both were annoyed at the writer's bad taste.

On one occasion, shortly before an election, I took my Cousin Harry to an agricultural dinner to hear the speeches. On the toast of "The Bishop and Clergy" being given, there was much cheering, whereupon my cousin remarked, "It is clear that there are no Dissenters here." Whereupon my neighbour of Tilton, who was sitting close to him, said, "I am a Dissenter." Harry cleverly got out of his difficulty by saying, "I mean no dissenters to the toast."

Harry Boys was a charming companion. In spite of his affliction he was always cheerful, and delighted in meeting people. He took the greatest interest in politics and in hearing about any new discovery in the scientific world. He used to hire a man to come in and read to him, and was always most grateful when anyone looked in upon him who would read debates, etc., without paining his ears, as his reader did, by mispronunciation.

Harry afterwards married a wife who had some little property of her own, and their united means enabled him to have a home. His wife would never reveal her age to him. He imagined her to be young and good-looking, whereas she was older than he was by some years and remarkably plain, but no one was cruel enough to undeceive him.

They resided at Harbledown, just out of Canterbury. On one of my visits to him there, he took me round his grounds, describing to me the different trees, etc. On my mentioning a small mountain-ash, which he did not know he possessed, he was highly delighted, and evidently made mental notes of exact size, shape, and distance behind other trees.

My Grandfather Boys, though strict, had a temper which was not easily disturbed. Once, through the carelessness of a groom, one of the pair of coach-horses was strangled in the stable. The groom came in and confessed his carelessness to his master, who heard him to the end; then, instead of showing the anger the groom expected, remarked that it was Sandwich Fair Day, so the groom must ride the other horse to Sandwich Fair and see whether there was one at the Fair that would match it.

To show my Grandfather Boys' discipline of his children, I would mention that very early one morning his son Richard (who afterwards joined the Royal Engineers and finally took Holy Orders) appeared at Betshanger, having in the night escaped from his school (King's School, Canterbury). He immediately, without allowing him to wait for any breakfast, sent him back to school under charge of the groom.

While Uncle Richard was in the Royal Engineers he was stationed for a time in the Channel Islands, and was employed in the construction of some of the works at Fort George, Guernsey. Soon afterwards he left the Army and went to Cambridge, and there became the intimate friend of Kirke White, in whose published works appears a letter addressed to him under the signature of R. B.

Afterwards he was Chaplain at St. Helena, and whilst there was presented by Napoleon with a snuff-box, but on it being represented to Sir Hudson Lowe, he was compelled to return it to the disgusted Emperor, it being contrary to the regulations that any official should accept a present from the ex-Emperor.

My uncle and godfather, Captain Edward Boys, was as a mid-shipman taken prisoner during the French War, and endured many hardships in French prisons. Eventually, he and three other fellow officers managed to escape (by burrowing under walls, and scaling others, out of what the French considered an impregnable fortress), leaving word for their jailers that the only thing that could keep an Englishman prisoner would be to put him on his parole d'honneur. For months he and his companions hid in woods and ditches until they could get a boat. He returned home to find his family in mourning for him, as they believed him dead.

He wrote an account of his adventures, and Captain Marryatt, who was a friend of his in after life, made him figure in his novels.

My grandparents did not wish to have more than one son at sea, so when my youngest uncle, Robert, had a great desire to join the Royal Navy, my grandfather persuaded a friend of his to let Uncle Robert join his ship in the Thames, with the private understanding that he was to be thoroughly sickened of it, which was effected in a few days, and he was quite willing to return home.

In after years Uncle Robert was once staying with us at Southover, when he heard a man calling "Ducks." On looking out of the window he recognised the ducks which had been stolen early that morning at Stanton. The man was convicted of the theft. Once he was reproving a workman for neglecting him family, and, pointing to a sow with a large litter of pigs, said, "That sow, in looking after her young, ought to shame you." The man replied as an excuse for himself, "The boar don't."

ANECDOTES

Lord Chichester, who was an abstainer, once called on one of his tenants at Laughton on a bitterly cold day, when he was thoroughly chilled. He refused wine or spirits, whereupon the tenant's wife produced a bottle of her home-made cordial and urged him to take a glass of it, saying she was sure it would do him good. He smelt it, and asked whether it was not cherry brandy. She said it was not, but refused to tell him what she had made it of, and in the end prevailed upon him to take a glass. He acknowledged he felt the better for it, but renewed his application to know what the wonderful cordial could be. She then told him it was cherry gin.

Miss Anna Maria Gage, second daughter of Lord Gage, was once travelling with her father by train, soon after the South Coast line was opened. On alighting at Glynde Station an occupant of the same first-class carriage showed especial attention to them by helping to hand out their parcels, for which Lord Gage thanked him. As the train left the station his daughter informed him that he would not have done so had he known what had happened in the train. In passing through a tunnel she had felt the stranger's hand in her pocket. She said not a word, but taking out her large shawl-pin, with all her force thrust it into his hand, which was immediately withdrawn.

This was the same Miss Gage from whose body seventeen or eighteen needles were from time to time extracted. My sister Catharine – afterwards Mrs. Scutt – was a great favourite of Lord and Lady Gage's, and often stayed at Firle Place as a child. During one visit, as the children were playing together, Anna Maria took from my sister's work-box a small round ivory needle case and somehow let it slip down her throat. Years passed on and the incident was almost forgotten when, strangely enough, my sister and her husband were dining at the Gage's London house, when during dinner Miss Anna Maria felt a peculiar pricking in her hand, and it was found that a needle-point was protruding from the flesh. The needle-case had evidently taken years to dissolve, and until then Miss Gage had felt no inconvenience from it. All the needles were of one size, with the exception of one darner. All were more or less rusty; some came out whole, others in pieces. They came out in various parts of her body, but strangely enough caused no pain in their travels, only when they came to the surface.

A century ago no qualification was required for a medical man. Hence in the country districts men often acted as doctors who certainly possessed no medical degree. Mr. Skinner was the regular practitioner at Alfriston.

At that time William Stace, of this parish – father of the farmer in my time – usually kept a couple of fowls cooped up till they were wanted for the table. It was noticed that frequently after the doctor's visit a fowl was missing, and the groom who had to look after them grew suspicious. Consequently one day, when he found the doctor was in the house, he went to the stable and there found the doctor's horse tied up, with the doctor's great coat thrown over him. The groom examined the pockets, discovering in one a fowl which was alive in the coop a short time before.

Mr. Stace submitted the case to my grandfather for his advice as to how he ought to act. My grandfather's decision was that he should tell Skinner that he would not prosecute, but that if he ever denied the theft, the full particulars should be published in the newspaper. The fact of the theft and of my grandfather's decision soon became widely known, and (as may be imagined) the doctor was frequently twitted on the subject.

Skinner's son succeeded his father as medical man, and shortly before I came to Berwick sold the practice to his assistant, Mr. Sanger, he himself retiring to Sherrington, which he had purchased. Dr. Skinner once told me that when he was in practice he was frequently called to a governess in a farmhouse, who had hysterics. He knew that there was nothing really the matter with her; so at last one day he dragged her to the pump and held her there whilst the servant, in compliance with his directions, pumped water upon her head. It had the desired effect, for he was never sent for again. Doctors in those days did not give in to nerves.

Writing of Dr. Skinner reminds me of Mr. James Watts, the doctor at Battle, who, on being asked what was good for a cold, said: "Take a tumbler, put in it two glasses of sherry and one of brandy; fill up the tumbler with water. Take this mixture the last thing before going to bed." I should be sorry for the person who tried this remedy!

I never came across the small-pox but once. It was whilst I was at Wartling Vicarage. My servants, Henry Elphick and his wife, who lived in the house, first had it slightly, but so lightly that neither they nor myself had any suspicion what it was, and no doctor was called in. The servant-girl I had to help Mrs. Elphick then had it. I got her mother, who resided about half a mile off, to come and see her, and then called in the doctor, Mr. Hackney, who at once pronounced it to be small-pox. In the course of some days her face was a mass of sores, from which the stench was most sickening. The girl, even when at the worst, only seemed afraid that she should lose her good looks and be marked by the small pox. I told her not to pick at her face, but to let the scabs come off naturally. Her great desire that her good looks should not be marred, led her to obey my advice, notwithstanding the intense irritation; and she had no marks when she recovered. Her mother, who nursed her, caught the disease, and was very severely marked. Fortunately I had been re-vaccinated the previous year, and so escaped entirely. There was, however, a general fear of me. For some weeks I avoided the schools, both Sunday and Day, and all unnecessary visiting. When taking the services on Sundays, my congregations fell off for the time being.

Dr. Hackney had had experience of small-pox, as he had himself had it three times, and was very much marked.

My brother-in-law Scutt also had it three times; the third time when in Canada. He was left for a time alone being thought by the

Indians, with whom he was travelling, to be past recovery.

Amongst my parishioners at Wartling was an old man of the name of Marchant, who was gardener at Herstmonceux Castle at the time of its dismantlement, in 1777.

About that time, or soon after, there was much small-pox in the neighbourhood. It was the custom when a death from small-pox took place for a man with a bell to precede the corpse on its way to the churchyard, so that everyone might hear the bell and get out of the way.

On one occasion Marchant was employed under the superintendence of his mistress, in planting trees in the grounds attached to Herstmonceux Place. He was digging close to the fence on the roadside when his mistress suddenly covered up her face and rushed away. As she did so, Marchant heard the bell which preceded a corpse on its way to burial. Not being in the road, but the other side of a high fence, the man did not run away but continued digging. On his mistress's return, she told him that he was sure to have the small-pox. And so it happened, for that night he sat up brewing, and the small-pox came out on that side of him that was nearest to the fence. This account was given me by the old man himself.

When the cholera visited England many years ago, Sussex almost escaped. The only case I heard of was of a poor tramp-woman at Bognor, who was found in some hovel very ill, in fact, she was supposed to be dead. The doctor said he should like to see the state of her tongue. To the astonishment of all present, including the doctor himself, the woman they thought dead put out her tongue. It appeared that she was perfectly conscious, but so prostrate that she was unable to move even a feature; but on hearing the doctor's words she made a great effort and so saved herself from being buried alive.

LOCAL MATTERS

My grandfather and father were both Commissioners of Taxes, and I have been one for more than forty years. As I write, I remember one amusing scene that we had at an appeal meeting at Firle.

At that time there was, as a Surveyor of Taxes, an official who was very much disliked, and we had, in consequence, many appeals, most of which were successful.

The licenses on vehicles with more than two wheels had recently been much lowered, on condition that the owner's name and place of residence were painted in Roman letters of an inch long at the back of the cart. Among others, Mr. Charles Ade, of Milton Court, who prided himself upon his antiquarian knowledge, came, as an appellant, about his cart. The surveyor, finding that he had brought the cart with him, went down with us to see if it was properly marked. On seeing the inscription he declared that it did not comply with the Act of Parliament. He complained that it could not be read, and that the down strokes of the letters were no thicker than the upstrokes, that there was no division between the words, and lastly, that Sussex was spelt with a V instead of a U.

On each point Mr. Ade declared that he was only strictly following the Act, which especially mentioned Roman letters; that he could produce various Roman inscriptions on coins or otherwise, which would show that the Romans made no distinction between the upward and downward strokes of the letters; that in their MSS. the words were always run together, and that V was always used and not U.

We, of course, supported the appellant, and the surveyor was very angry, and threatened to bring the case before the judge, but afterwards thought he had better not. I have never had a decision of mine appealed against, and experience has taught me that nothing is gained by bluster in an official.

When by the new Poor Law (1835) out-door relief to able-bodied men was made illegal, benefit societies were started throughout the land to give relief in cases of illness. One of the principal attractions to join a benefit club apparently seemed to be in many instances the fact of having an annual club day, when the members paraded the streets with banners and a band of music, each member wearing a rosette of the colours of his club; in the end attending church and dining together.

In the sameness of their lives, a day's holiday once a year, when members could meet friends whom they could meet at no other time, and enjoy a chat, all helped to make benefit clubs popular. The steady, respectable working-man was glad to feel that by paying a small weekly sum he insured his family against want in case of illness, without the necessity of falling back on the "parish."

At the end of the year, as a rule, the members shared out any money left over of their monthly payment after the sick relief had been paid. Most of the employers subscribed to the fund of the various clubs to encourage the men in self-help. Unfortunately it frequently happened, that as the club dinner was usually held at a public-house, most of the sharing-out money would be spent in beer before the party broke up.

Whilst Curate of Berwick, in 1839, I was asked to preach on the club day for the Alfriston Club, and was shocked at the irreverence displayed.

The principal flag was carried within the Communion rails, and having a pole at each end, was set up against the east wall, over the Communion table. Several of the members, who evidently had had too much to drink, retired from church for several minutes, and I saw a good deal going on of which I could but disapprove.

These clubs were usually attached to some public house, and in an advertisement for the sale of a public house, I once saw it stated that the house had three clubs attached to it. I should mention that when a club had its meetings at a public, and monthly payments were made there, it was the usual rule that threepence extra should be paid on each occasion for the benefit of the landlord, which threepence members might each take out in beer.

Of course, there was a limit to the age at admission, and a doctor's certificate of health was required. But when, in the course of years, some of the members became permanently laid aside by illness, the young and healthy members, finding the sharing-out dwindling, would often strive to break up the club; and often, if an illness lasted for weeks some of the other members would do all they could to get the sick member turned out of the club, thus defeating the object for which the club was formed.

Steady, straightforward men were often cheated by fellow-members, who were lazy or dishonest. I came across the case of a lazy man who, when in work, earned twelve shillings a week. Whenever he got a chance he would declare he was ill, and go on the Alfriston Club; he was also a member of two other clubs, so when he was ill he drew thirty shillings a week. When members moved to a distance it was very easy to cheat the club, and I have heard of instances where a member has drawn several weeks' pay, without being ill at all, he having forged a doctor's certificate. The Alfriston Club at last came to grief, and was broken up. The young and healthy members immediately started it afresh, whereupon some of the older members, who had failed to get elected, consulted together and agreed to form a separate club for themselves. They asked why it was that the old club had been broken up. The answer was because there had been so much sickness. So the first of their new rules was, "that nothing should be paid out in case of illness." At the end of the year they spent their monthly payments in a supper, with an unusual amount of beer. Some of the rules of these early clubs were, in time, amended.

I started our little Berwick Club in 1860, and am thankful to say it is still prospering. I was told again and again that it would soon break down – that it was impossible to have a club for one small village, unless outsiders were admitted. I hope it will not be broken up after my death.

In drawing out the club rules I have been very careful to avoid the evils that have ruined various clubs. * Amongst the rules of our club are that no man is to belong to any other benefit club, that a man must be residing or working in the parish, so that all have the

* Note. – My father was always very particular with regard to tho Berwick Provident Club. The very fact of membership in the club was regarded as a proof
o   f
respectability and the men were on very friendly terms with one another. The monthly meeting alwaya took place at the Rectory. Only four days before his death, he saw the Steward, talked over club business and expressed to him the

same doctor, that no meeting should be allowed to take place in any public-house, that nothing is to be spent on dinner, beer, or band, and that honorary subscriptions should go to the reserve fund in case of need. Each year they have had the club dinner at the Rectory, and as long as I am spared they will be invited.

WADHAM

By the original statutes of Wadham College the Warden was to be an unmarried man. Dr. Tournay, who was Warden before my time, got the law altered, but from a high sense of honour he would not avail himself of the alteration. He had been made Warden before the statute was altered, therefore he thought he ought not to take advantage of what he had got done for the sake of those who came after him. This was most honourable of him, as he had for long been deeply enamoured of his second cousin, my great aunt, Anne Maude Harvey, who for his sake spent her long life of upwards of eighty years in single blessedness.

Before he became Warden he was Rector of St. James', Dover, where he continually had his female relations staying with him as his guests. My mother had, in her girlhood days, there stayed with him at the house at the top of St. James' Street, which was after-wards pulled down to widen the upper end of the road. The money for which the house was sold (£200) was for many years laid aside till it was employed by my brother in-law, the Rev. W. E. Light, in building the new Rectory.

My two aunts, Anne Maude and Emily, used to stay with him at Wadham, the former being a special favourite, as being the name-sake, niece and godchild of his beloved and beautiful Anne Maude.

Large families can very seldom all meet together, but I recollect my father and mother going to a family gathering at Each, at the house of a brother; all the twelve brothers and sisters, with their wives and husbands, being present, not having met before for twenty two years.

In my time Symons was the Warden of Wadham. He had

succeeded Dr. Tournay, and was the first married Warden. Mrs. Symons was the daughter of Masterman, the banker, and very earnest in her missionary zeal. She instituted at Wadham missionary meetings, and it was these meetings that aroused, or at any rate strengthened, the ardour of the missionary, Fox. Amongst my contemporaries at Wadham were Bishop Tufnell and Dean Church.

One of the Chaplains at Wadham was an old man of the name of Rogers, an old bachelor. He was almost as deaf as a post in my time. He had been presented to a college living more than twenty years previously, but he was so miserable away from Oxford that he returned to Wadham, and was made Chaplain. Rogers used to hurry through the daily service, and, if neither the Warden or the Tutors were present, he would frequently after the First Lesson go on to the *Jubilate*, thus omitting the *Te Deum* and Second Lesson, making his deafness an excuse for forgetting which Lesson had just been read.

He always wore black knee-breeches, and my Uncle Barrow told me an anecdote of him in his earlier days. In the common room one day, one of the Fellows said to him, "Do you know, Rogers, that you have a hole in your breeches?" He answered that it was impossible, as he had only put them on new that day. He then discovered that in the morning he had made a mistake. He had met a beggar in very dilapidated garments, and had told the man that if he would come to his rooms he would give him a pair of breeches. When the man came he presented him with a pair, and by mistake gave him the new pair, just come from the tailor's, instead of the old pair that he meant to reject.

Rogers was afterwards buried at Wadham. I happened to be in Oxford the same day, but could not wait to attend the funeral, as I wished to come home the same night.

I have been told of two of my Wadham contemporaries being reduced to beggary.

One great cause of contracting expensive habits at the University was (certainly in my time) the strong dislike of the Oxford tradesmen to take ready money. I had two accounts with bookseller (Vincent) and grocer, which I regularly settled every term, but otherwise I paid ready money. If I went into a shop for an article, and pulled out my purse to pay, I was invariably asked to allow it to be put down to my account, and on my refusing to do so and putting down the money, requesting the article to be sent to my rooms, I do not recollect a single instance of its being so sent without my calling at least once again about it.

Tradesmen are better now at Oxford, but it is a very bad practice to allow young men to run up debts, which it will often be years before they can save money to pay.

Whilst I was at Wadham, Joy, the tailor, lived opposite. He had a clever son, whom he sent in to try for a scholarship at Wadham, which he won. Dr. Symons advised Joy to send the lad to Cambridge instead, which I believe he did.

I always liked walking; it was my one form of exercise at Oxford. Rushbridger and I daily walked together each afternoon for two hours. Once T. C. Whitehead joined Rushbridger and myself in our walk, and boasted of his walking powers. So I proposed to walk with him nine miles in two hours, starting from the next mile post we came to. Rushbridger would not try, so he left us, but we two walked on to the sixth milestone at Nuneham and back to the second at Iffley, and then, finding that we had nearly a quarter of an hour to spare, I proposed to add another mile, but Whitehead declined, and put on an Aeger the next morning.

I have walked from Deal to Dover – nine miles – in an hour and three-quarters, fair toe-and-heel walking. That was during the Long Vacation, when I was reading with Walker at Dover in 1835. About the same time, on July 10th, I crossed over to Calais for the day as I had never been abroad. We left the Calais harbour to return at 9 p.m. I always preferred remaining on deck, however rough it might be. I happened to be whistling as I clung on to a rail, watching the waves, when one of the sailors came up to me, saying angrily, "Stop that horrid noise; I'm sure we have wind enough!" The sailor's superstition was that by whistling a storm becomes worse.

The roughest weather I recollect being out in was on the night of September 17th, 1837, in crossing from Liverpool to Kingstown. I pitied the suffering of some poor Irish labourers, who were returning from harvesting. They were dashed from one side of the vessel and then back again with the roll, and were thoroughly soaked, each wave breaking over the vessel. Soon after midnight the mate came round with some whiskey, and gave each man a small glass of it, which wonderfully revived their spirits.

Speaking of storms, my cousin, William Boys, when in command of a ship in the Indian Ocean, received some personal damage in a tornado, and his false teeth were knocked out of his mouth. Presenting himself at the Admiralty on his return, to his surprise he received compensation for the loss of the false teeth as well as for other things.

Windmills in rough weather are liable to be set on fire by the friction of the sweeps breaking loose. One night the mill on Wind'ore was burnt down, and at the time it was supposed to have been done by the Alfriston gang of sheep stealers. Shortly before the fire a large quantity of corn had been deposited in the mill, and after the fire – among the debris – nothing like burnt corn was discovered. It was a very rough night, and it was thought that the corn was first carried away, and then the sweeps were set going and the mill set on fire to hide the robbery. The mill was rebuilt, and it is a curious fact that it has since again been burnt down, through the sweeps breaking loose on a stormy night. The same fate has since overtaken Berwick mill – burnt down by the sweeps breaking loose in a storm.

In former times it was the custom to build mills in high and exposed situations for the sake of getting all the wind possible. About 1830 I remember the mill on the top of Beddingham Hill being moved off the Downs without being taken to pieces.

Windmills are not now nearly as numerous as formerly. Upwards of sixty years since (written 1888) from the summit of the hill I have counted as many as thirty windmills in sight. A windmill could do but a limited quantity of grinding, and even then occasionally, owing to calm weather continuing for a long period, could not keep up the supply for the regular customers.

For very many years the Tide Mill as Bishopstone carried on a very extensive business, often grinding for the various windmill customers when the weather was calm.

Steam now appears to be the principal motive power, and with the improvement of communication seems likely in the course of a few years to take the place of the old windmills.

BERWICK

I have frequently been asked as to the origin of the mound in Berwick churchyard. It is probably partly composed of soil removed from where the south aisle now is, but solid chalk comes within a foot of the surface, showing it to be a spur of the Downs. In rebuilding the south aisle in 1856, a skeleton was discovered under the original foundation, which shows that the churchyard was used for burials before the south aisle was built. From the rough flint work then exposed at the foot of the pillar of the arcade, it was clear that the aisle, when first added to the church, was at a higher level than it is now, and the ground of that part of the churchyard being so much higher than the church floor, that a considerable quantity of earth must have been removed at some time or other. The mound was increased in height during the last century. John Potter, who died in 1838, at the age of eight-four, declared that when a lad he was employed by the Rev. William Hawes to wheel earth from the lower part of the churchyard to the mound, and that Mr. Hawes pitched a tent on top of the mound, in which he used to sit and drink. I may mention that in 1783 Mr. Hawes married Miss Bean, of Clapham House, which even in my time has been visible from the mound, but is now shut out from view by the trees that have since been planted. Tradition says that Mr. Hawes had a flagstaff on the mound, and used to signal to Clapham.

He died in the following year, being at that time in possession of the sunken garden to the west of the Rectory, which he used as a yard for cattle, and at his death two fat oxen were seized as heriots thereon. The cottage in the garden was left by Mr. Hawes

Drusilla's Tea Cottage, Berwick. c1900

to his old housekeeper for her life. She died in 1813 at the age of eighty-seven. This cottage was rendered uninhabitable by the storm in November, 1836, which did so much damage in Sussex. My father refused to purchase it with the advowson of the living, but it was purchased by Mr. Fuller, who sold it with his other property to Lord Gage, lord of the manor, and subsequently, in the exchange of glebe, became attached to the living free of all heriots.

As I mentioned before, the roof of Berwick Church before its restoration in 1856, was a regular rabbit warren, access thereto being by a buttress on the south side, where the ground is so much higher, and at that time had not been trenched away from the south wall.

William Jenner, an old parishioner, who was born in 1800, told me he well remembered the wooden remains of the water-mill, mentioned in Domesday, immediately to the north of Berwick Court garden; to which mill the course of the stream to supply it can be still easily traced from where it leaves the river a little way above Sherman's Bridge.

Before the Commutation of Tithes, there were with some Incumbents, frequent disturbances. It was usual for the Rector's man to go through the corn-fields and stick a bough in every tenth shock; these shocks were afterwards left, when the farmer carried off the rest. Tithe barns were accordingly necessary, for corn was never thrashed except in a barn.

When horse thrashing machines were first used there were great disturbances, and gangs of men went about the country destroying them, as the labourers supposed that they would lose their usual winter's employment of thrashing out with a flail. At that time Mr. Stace, who was at the Church Farm, had procured a machine, and he buried it under the hedge in the field near the Rectory for safety.

At Berwick Rectory there used to be two large barns, one to the north of the yard on the site of the kitchen garden, which was pulled down in 1812 when the present stable, cowshed, etc., were built. The other barn was still standing in 1844, but in a very dilapidated state, much of its thatch having been stripped off in the gale of 1836. Mr. West always refused to repair the barn, saying that with the Commutation of Tithes, a barn was no longer necessary. While I was away in Wartling the barn was pulled down, but as it was taken down without the proper authority, I was allowed for it in the dilapidations. Since, by the exchange of glebe, the only arable land remaining to the rectory of Berwick is four and a half acres at Winton, a barn is no longer necessary.

When I broke up the ground to the west of the kitchen garden wall, which was formerly a brickyard, my first crop there was potatoes. On digging one up I found one enormous potato which weighed $11^{1}/_{4}$ pounds, besides nearly a gallon of smaller potatoes on the same root. The large potato had upwards of one hundred eyes, and I cut from it thirty-five sets, which I planted, but they never yielded anything particular. The inside of the potato, over five pounds, I had boiled, and when mashed it filled the vegetable dish.

Writing of growing potatoes leads me to think of tools. New tools are, I think, generally devised by the workmen themselves. As instances, I may mention the following which were not known when I came to Berwick: the four or five pronged garden spade, the swop instead of the reap-hook (I have never seen a sickle which is distinguished from a reap-hook by being notched), and the stone shovel is now made with open prongs. When I first went to Berwick I found that a man used constantly to visit the kitchen garden to get what he could. The culprit proved to be a man named Goldsmith, who had a large family whom he brought up very badly. One of his daughters, Mary Goldsmith, once lived as servant at the blacksmith's, who frequently had his windows smashed of an evening. He thought the sitting-room window was smashed by stone throwing, and would rush out to try and find the boy who threw the stone, but never could. At last one evening he got some-one to watch outside, and then it appeared that when Mary had put the children to bed, she would lean out of the bed room window and with a broom smash the window beneath, then hastily shut the window and watch her master run out. This same girl afterwards was a servant to a Mrs. Peter Pagden, at Dean's Place, Alfriston.

Mrs. Pagden was very fond of smart attire. One day, at a dinner party at Dean's Place, Mary waited at table wearing one of her mistress's smart caps. Before her company, of course, the mistress could say nothing, but on speaking to Mary afterwards, the girl declared that she did not mean to steal the cap, but only borrowed it as she had no nice cap of her own for the occasion, and she knew her mistress liked her to appear nice when there was company.

Mr. Stace, the farmer at Upper Berwick, was continually losing old posts and rails, so he bored a hole in one, and, after filling the hole up with gunpowder, plugged it up. Of course, there was an explosion when the post was put on the fire. The culprit proved to be Goldsmith, the gardener.

Mrs. Seale, my first servant, before she came to live with me, lived at a Mr. Saxby's, at Ringmer. She told me that there was a man living in the house whose work it was to look after the stock. One morning, after a rough night with much snow, the man did not come in for his breakfast till after 9 o'clock, and explained to his master how he had been detained. About 11 the master came into the kitchen and found the man still sitting over his breakfast, so suggested that is it was so near dinner-time (12 o'clock, he had better take his dinner now that he was in, to which he immediately agreed. Whereupon Mr. Saxby said to Mrs. Seale, "Bring John his dinner," and John immediately made as hearty a dinner as usual.

My next servant, after Mrs. Seale married again, was a very old woman, who had been a very good cook in her younger days. She soon left me, finding even my easy place too much for her infirmities. Shortly after she left I went to see her at Lewes, and found her keeping school, though she could neither read nor write. She had fourteen children around her of from two to six years of age, and one of the elder children was teaching another its letters.

I have known several instances of men unable to read or write, who yet could keep complicated accounts in their heads. Amongst them was Thomas Blaber, foreman at the Church Farm, who at intervals rendered his accounts to his master.

Drowley, a drunken horse-dealer at Lewes, once sent for my

father, as he thought he was going to die. My father found him with the Bible open before him upside down. On my father remarking about it, Drowley said, "If he liked to read it so it was nothing to nobody else." He could neither read nor write.

ANECDOTES

Before the establishment of the Penny Postage in 1840, the postage of a letter from the West Indies was two and sixpence, and from South America three and six. The postage from London to Lewes was eightpence, and for every letter delivered at Berwick I had to pay an extra penny, which came especially hard for some time after the Penny Post was established, by reason of the many circulars which then began to be sent by post. Our letters were seldom delivered till after 10, and our outgoing letters called for about half-past 3, the postman walking to and fro from Lewes. But even then we could not be sure of his arriving in Lewes in time for our letters to go by the same day's mail.

At that time Southeram Farm (one mile from Lewes) was occupied by Stunt, a powerful man. Day after day he lost from a field near the road some turnips, so, one evening, he hid himself and watched. By-and-by the postman came along, and Stunt saw him filling his basket with turnips. Stunt did not show himself at once, but suffered the postman to proceed on his way, and followed at a short distance. At the entrance of Lewes he stopped the man, and made him carry the turnips back to the field after he had extracted two of them. As the postman returned with his load, Stunt walked behind him carrying a turnip in each hand, with which he belaboured each side of the man's head, frequently observing, "Turmits, you rascal! I'll teach you to steal my turmits," all the way to the field. Of course, the letters were extra late, and so the matter came to the knowledge of the Post Office.

I may mention here that on another day Stunt caught three soldiers stealing his "turmits." He seized two of them by their arms, told the third that if he did not walk quietly in front, he would break every bone in his skin, and marched all three into the police-station at Lewes, and thus without help gave three soldiers into custody.

In mentioning coaching anecdotes I forgot the following. Once my father was travelling by a fast coach, and he noticed a Quaker driving a donkey, which he kept ahead of the coach for more than a mile. My father observed to the coachman that if he was driving he would not like a donkey to keep ahead of them in that way. So the coachman whipped up his horses; the Quaker, on hearing the coach closer behind him, merely looked round, put his whip down behind him and gave the donkey his head, and was soon out of sight.

A good donkey, well groomed and well fed, can go a fine pace. My sister Emily had a pair of donkeys which she used to drive long distances. On one occasion, on spending the day with some friends, the groom, in harnessing the animals, put the donkey that was driven on the off side to the near side and vice versa, much to the animals' disgust, and they refused to proceed until they were put in their accustomed places.

In passing toll-gates, donkeys had to be paid for at the same rate as horses. Two-storied houses as toll-bar gates I have only seen in the West of England and in Wiltshire. I used to say from the look of the toll houses, and from the stiles in crossing a field, I could tell in what part of England I was.

Once in the West of England I read this inscription over the window of a small village shop:– "Sold here, Morisons' pills, warranted to cure any medical or surgical disease whatever."

It is very remarkable how certain inn signs are common in particular districts, such as the "Red Lion," or the "Black Bear," and "The Barley Mow."

The pictorial representation of some signs are very misleading as to the original name. For instance, "The Tumble-down-Dick," near Farnborough, or "Labour in Vain," at Guernsey, and else-where.

I look upon "The Five Alls" at Dover, and other places as retaining its original meaning; "The Parson," "I Pray for All," "The

Doctor," "I Physick All," "The Lawyer," "I Cheat All," "The Farmer," "I Pay for All." The subject of the fifth "all" I forget.

The late Mr. H. B. Curtis, of Windmill Hill, told me that he had in his library a book (I am not sure that he did not say an MS.), in which it was stated that in the eighth or ninth century, what is now Pevensey Marsh was sea. It is a well-known fact that in digging fresh ditches in the marsh, large trunks of trees are found, which shows that there was a time when there was land there before the sea broke in.

Another fact that is not generally known, is what I was told by the Expenditor of the Lewes Levels, that in the middle of the last century, the Dutch offered a large sum for Cuckmere Haven, that they might make it a harbour of refuge for the shipping passing up and down the Channel.

When the chalk-pit was first opened on this side of Lewes (about 1823), the idea was gradually to cut a way through the hill to join the new piece of road made in 1819. The undertaking was found to be too great, so instead of going ahead as they did for some years, they widened the cutting and went deeper for the chalk. Of course after the railroad was made no more thought was given to such an improvement of the turnpike road.

There have been many instances of people losing their way on the Downs, however well they know the country. In fogs or after dark, shepherds have missed their way and fallen down the chalk-pits.

When I was a boy, about 1828, I lost myself on the Downs in a thick fog, and though I thought I knew the contour of the different hills, I became thoroughly bewildered as to the points of the compass, but at last, after wandering for some hours, I found my position by coming to Beddingham Mill, which then stood on the top of the Downs.

Many years after, on the same Downs, Mr. Farmer, Curate of Beddingham, lost his way in returning from Toy Farm Cottages. Fortunately it was known where he had gone, and as the hours passed and he did not return, though night was coming on, a search party was organised. He was discovered about midnight, having found a lodge with some straw in it, where he had made up his mind to ensconce himself till daylight.

In the beginning of the century, William Hider, a Lower Berwick boy of seven, went up the Downs to fly his kite. When evening came on his parents were naturally alarmed about his non-appearance. Hearing that he had been seen going up the hill, his father, with several neighbours, took lanterns and went up and searched, but without finding any trace of the lad. At daylight he reappeared, having, when darkness came on, crept under a thick patch of furze and there spent the night.

On yet another occasion, Mr. Bedford, of Denton, was coming to me to breakfast, as I was going to drive him over to the Chapter meeting at Ripe. He did not make his appearance for some hours, and then sank on the sofa utterly exhausted. He had lost his way and been wandering on top of the Downs, until he had fortunately met a shepherd.

When my mother was a bride in 1811, she was riding with my father on top of Mount Caburn, the highest point of the Glynde range. Her horse took fright and galloped off down the steepest side, across where the railway is now, right into the river. Of course, once he began to descend he could not stop himself, but how he kept his feet is a mystery, as Mount Caburn is excessively steep on the south side.

It was proposed once that there should be a county memorial to my grandfather Ellman erected on the summit of Mount Caburn, but in the end the idea was given up.

Sound carries a long distance. At Glynde, de St. Croix told me, on the occasion of the destruction of the "Alabama," of Cherbourg, the firing was distinctly heard. I myself, at Berwick, have distinctly heard St. Michael's (Lewes) clock strike the midnight hour, nine miles off. I have also heard guns fired at Portsmouth, a distance of about sixty miles; and I once heard three successive explosions at the Hounslow Powder Mills, a still further distance.

The firing at the Battle of Waterloo was heard at Deal, I believe.

MISCELLANEOUS STORIES

In 1851 a return was required of the attendance at each place of worship on the Sunday on which the census was taken, so that returns as to various religions should be made. As a curiosity, the return was shown me which had been made by Moore, the Dissenting preacher at Alciston, of the numbers attending his service in his cottage kitchen that Sunday.

The numbers were given as morning 119 and afternoon 165. The cottage was small, and the remark was made that they must have been packed like herrings in a barrel!

An old woman at Wartling was once speaking to me about the dread of Bonaparte's invasion at the beginning of the century, and asked me if I recollected something in connection with it. Whereupon I said, "How old do you take me to be?" She looked at me and said, "Seventy." Whereupon I laughed. She then said, "I know you are, because you laugh." I left Wartling in 1846, and I think at that time I looked rather young for my age.

One morning in London, when my father was walking down a street, a woman who was cleaning a doorstep stood up just as he passed and said, "Am I not an active old woman, sir, I am on my four score?" Whereupon my father stopped and looking at her said, "You cannot possibly be that?" "Yes I am, sir. I was sixty yesterday."

This reminds me of an old man whose cottage my grandfather Boys used to pass in riding from Betshanger to London. On one occasion my grandfather said to him, "How old are you now?" His answer was, "In my two hundred." He had just completed his first hundred years. I believe he died at 103.

My father was supposed to be very like Liston, and was often mistaken for him in the streets of London. There was something in his very countenance that often strangers would familiarly address him, and he seemed a general favourite with all classes.

When young I was very fond of whistling. A groom, named William Mainwaring, who lived with us at Southover, was a first-rate whistler, and hearing him first made me as a small child fond of it.

My blind cousin, Harry Boys, would whistle a good second to his own accompaniment on the piano. William Jenner, of this parish, could take two parts at the same time, whistling one and humming the other.

Previous to the year 1830 I never saw a scarlet uniform, the usual colour being a dull red. At that time it was not unusual for an extremely dark shade of green to be used for black. Soon afterwards some people tried to introduce red trimmings on black as mourning, but it collapsed almost immediately.

I once went to see some falconry by the Duke of St. Albans, His Majesty's Falconer. It was on the hill above Falmer. Herons and pigeons were turned out. The herons fell an easier prey to the hawks than the pigeons, of which one sought shelter amongst the carriages of the visitors.

When in Brighton in 1832-1834, there was an archery ground close by, so I subscribed to it and became tolerably efficient. Edward Turner, house surgeon at the Hospital, was the one I used to shoot with.

In writing about Guernsey and our life there, I might have mentioned that the schoolboys frequently used to write on the walls, "Only so many weeks to the holidays." At Guernsey we only came home for the summer holidays – once a year – and I remember seeing written up "Only forty-eight weeks to the holidays."

In my Oxford days I used to purchase eggs from an elderly woman, who was allowed to come into college to sell eggs to the men. Regularly every week she came to my rooms with a basket on each arm, and I bought my eggs from her. She used to assert that her eggs were always quite fresh, and as proof of this statement would mention that "Mr. — —, of Trinity, had told her that when he went away for the Long, he left some of her eggs in his cupboard, and when he came back after seventeen weeks' absence, they were just as fresh as the day they were laid!" On one occasion my cousin, Edward Boys, who was also at Wadham, on looking at her eggs suggested that they were not fresh. Whereupon the poor old woman assured him that she knew they were fresh, for she had laid them herself! meaning, of course, that her own hens had laid them; as she used to collect from neighbours to fill up her baskets.

People don't always consider the damaging statements they make. A Litlington woman, whose boy had been had up for repeatedly stealing hen's eggs, had frequently asserted her boy's perfect innocence in the matter, but ended up by saying "She was sure that master need not have made such a fuss about it, as the last lot were every one bad." It then came out that the boy often took home two or three eggs at a time, but on the last occasion, on finding a nest full of eggs, thought he had secured a prize, and took all – not think ing that they had been spoilt by the hen sitting upon them.

Another Litlington woman was heard to say to her boy, "Don't you go and tumble in the water and get drowned, and then come back and say that Mrs. Scutt's big dog has eaten me up."

One poor woman said that she knew all men were wicked, and that they were much worse than women, for the Bible said, "All men are sinners," but never once said that all women were sinners.

One of Mr. Parish's anecdotes was that his school children in singing the Christmas hymn would say, "Wild shepherds watched their flocks by night," in spite of frequent correction. At last he said to them, "What were the shepherds doing?" The answer he got was, "Drinking," which was the only reason the children could imagine men sitting up to do, and thought them to be rough men.

I remember years ago hearing of a man on the Dicker, who exchanged a very ancient goose for some beef. The next Hailsham market day he waylaid the butcher as he passed, to complain of the beef. But the butcher was equal to the occasion, for on seeing the cobbler standing in front of his house, waiting to waylay him, he pulled up, and before the cobbler could get a word in, began complaining about the goose. As soon as the butcher paused, the other complained about the beef, that he could not get his teeth through it; whereupon the butcher expressed his surprise that the man had attempted to eat the beef, and said he sold it to him thinking he wanted to make a new leather apron. Both men had been trying to cheat each other.

My great grandfather, Richard Ellman, as a young man went to live at Framfield in a farmhouse, which was afterwards purchased by Mr. Alexander Donovan, an Irishman, who had a very excitable temper. On one occasion at a shooting party at my great grandfather's he was very angry with a boy for putting up a covey of birds, and shouted out, "I will give you a good bating." His Irishism produced a laugh from those who were present. He immediately said, "That there was nothing like it in the English language; that that was *Paulo-post futurum*, and would have a far greater effect on the boy, knowing that the punishment would not be long delayed.

I may mention that my great grandfather, grandfather, and my father, all possessed property in Framfield. My grandfather owned High Cross, and enlarged the house; my father owning Wharton's – a delightful old residence.

When I was a boy, I took a spade to the Priory ruins; and began clearing out some steps which I thought must lead to something, but after clearing out the three or four bottom ones, I was stopped by the lessee, who caught me at it. At that time there were goats in the Priory grounds, which frequently climbed up the ivy-covered ruins, and gazed down upon one from the top.

I consider it is most foolish to tell one's dreams, but still I will recount this remarkable one. I dreamt that I was conducting my own funeral service, and that I had a strong desire to do so, feeling it was the last service that I could take. I distinctly remember seeing my coffin in church, placed not on the bier, but on the tops of the seats, and that it was a very narrow one, as if I were much wasted away. I was considering what to do about signing the Burial register, and whether it would not confuse future generations to have my signature as taking my own funeral.

One morning a boy brought back to my uncle, Dr. Sankey, some medicine he had sent the evening before, with the following message, "Master's compliments, and please he don't want any more medicine, because he is dead." The poor boy was trying to obey his late master's orders, which were always to give his compliments when taking a message to the doctor.

My cousin, George Boys, was full of fun. On one occasion he was just home after an absence of some years and went to an evening party. Sailor-like he thoroughly enjoyed meeting English women again. He was talking to three girls of a sailor's loneliness, and someone suggested that he should marry. He laughed, said it was a good idea, and instantly proposed to one of the three girls. She declined him; he proposed to the next, and then to the third, but none of the three accepted the merry sailor on that occasion.

When I was a boy, pound bank notes were in common circulation, and (I believe) the Bank of England had no special privilege, and accordingly their notes were not valued more than country bank notes. I do not profess to know the monetary laws, but I know that up to 1825 all banks were bound to pay in gold if called upon; but since then in gold or Bank of England notes. At that time lotteries were in full swing. The shop at Lewes for the sale of lottery tickets was English's, the cutler's.

INDEX OF SURNAMES

INDEX OF PLACE-NAMES